T0418771

Disgraced

Disgraced

How Sex Scandals Transformed American Protestantism

SUZANNA KRIVULSKAYA

OXFORD
UNIVERSITY PRESS

OXFORD
UNIVERSITY PRESS

Oxford University Press is a department of the University of Oxford.
It furthers the University's objective of excellence in research, scholarship,
and education by publishing worldwide. Oxford is a registered trade mark of
Oxford University Press in the UK and in certain other countries.

Published in the United States of America by Oxford University Press
198 Madison Avenue, New York, NY 10016, United States of America.

Library of Congress Cataloging-in-Publication Data
Names: Krivulskaya, Suzanna, author.
Title: Disgraced : how sex scandals transformed American Protestantism /
Suzanna Krivulskaya.
Description: New York, NY : Oxford University Press, [2025] | Includes
bibliographical references and index.
Identifiers: LCCN 2024037180 (print) | LCCN 2024037181 (ebook) |
ISBN 9780197599686 (hardback) | ISBN 9780197599709 (epub)
Subjects: LCSH: Sex scandals—United States—History—19th century. | Sex
scandals—United States—History—20th century. | Protestantism—United
States—History. | Protestants—United States.
Classification: LCC HQ18.U5 K75 2025 (print) | LCC HQ18.U5 (ebook) |
DDC 280/.40973—dc23/eng/20240911
LC record available at https://lccn.loc.gov/2024037180
LC ebook record available at https://lccn.loc.gov/2024037181

DOI: 10.1093/oso/9780197599686.001.0001

Integrated Books International, United States of America

The manufacturer's authorised representative in the EU for product safety is
Oxford University Press España S.A. of el Parque Empresarial San Fernando
de Henares, Avenida de Castilla, 2 - 28830 Madrid (www.oup.es/en)

For Larisa Shekunova and Tatsiana Sablina

Contents

Acknowledgments

I always read the acknowledgments first. If authors cannot articulate how the people in their life have shaped and sustained them, I become a little less excited about the rest of the book. While it is impossible to fully express the extent of my gratitude in a few pages, what follows is an abbreviated testament to some enviable human kindness, generosity, and grace.

This book began as a dissertation, and I could not have asked for a better mentor than Darren Dochuk. In a profession not immune to the affliction of self-importance, Darren stands out as both one of the sharpest minds in the field and one of the kindest, most approachable, and most generous. Thanks, too, to my dissertation committee: Gail Bederman, Jon Coleman, Erika Doss, and Thomas Tweed. Their encouragement, careful reading of my work, and generative suggestions for revision greatly improved this manuscript.

Scholars from across academic fields, institutions, and vocations have inspired and encouraged my growth as a historian. At Yale University, Kathryn Lofton brilliantly modeled how to formulate and answer the kinds of scholarly questions that I wanted to pursue. Her intellectual curiosity, moral clarity, excellent humor, and unending kindness are well documented in others' acknowledgments. I will just add that she has been there for me, with advice and enthusiasm, whenever I've needed it most.

I will never stop being impressed with historians who not only go out of their way to encourage junior scholars but also share actual archival findings and key historiographical insights. Timothy Gloege modeled scholarly generosity back when this book was just an idea. Without his guidance and encyclopedic knowledge of American fundamentalism, my archival trips to Moody Bible Institute would have been far less productive, and I may not have ever come across the two big sex scandals that MBI had worked so hard to hide in the early twentieth century. I thank Heather R. White for her mentorship, collegiality, and generosity over the past decade. Heather shared her archival materials on Bernard Crocker, whose story is central to what became Chapter 6 of this book. Thanks also to Heath Carter, Rebecca Davis, Kristen Kobes DuMez, Audrey Clare Farley, Megan Goodwin, Luke

Harlow, Katie Hemphill, Sara Moslener, Bob Orsi, and Daniel Silliman for their, good humor, collegial spirit, and interest in my work.

For my time at Yale, thank you to Jan Holton, Kristen Leslie, Carolyn Sharp, Diana Swancutt, Emilie Townes, Tisa Wenger, and Laura Wexler. Between my graduate degrees, I was part of Elena Grigorenko's lab at the Yale Child Study Center. Thanks to Elena and the members of her team, especially Baptiste Barbot, Sascha Hein, Leslie Hart, Natalia Rakhlin, Jodi Reich, Mei Tan, and Cheri Stahl.

During my two years at Washington University in St. Louis, the Department of History and the John C. Danforth Center on Religion and Politics helped me navigate my first steps as a would-be academic. Thanks especially to Jean Allman, Elizabeth Borgwardt, Andrea Friedman, Peter Kastor, and Nancy Reynolds. Fellow graduate students Philip Byers, Adwoa Opong, and Sarah Siegel made our little cohort friendly and fun. The Danforth Center quickly became my second intellectual home. Thanks to Marie Griffith, Rachel Gross, Emily Johnson, Mark Jordan, Debra Kennard, Rachel Lindsey, Laurie Maffly-Kipp, Lerone Martin, Sheri Peña, Leigh Schmidt, Ronit Stahl, Lauren Turek, and Mark Valeri for their warmth and expertise.

At Notre Dame, a friendly and cheerful cohort of faculty and graduate students made my time there intellectually productive and socially rewarding. Thanks especially to James Breen, Philip Byers, Peter Cajka, Annie Gilbert Coleman, Kathleen Sprows Cummings, Maggie Elmore, Christopher Flanagan, Karen Graubart, Erica Hastings, Anna Holdorf, Danae Jacobson, Lauren Jean, Sejoo Kim, Alexa McCall, John McGreevy, Mark Noll, Johnny Nelson, Catherine Perl, Jonathan Riddle, Emily Smith, Ian Van Dyke, and Carla Villanueva.

As historians know, archivists and librarians are angels in disguise. We could not produce scholarship without them, and the way they think about their labor and the archives entrusted to them has direct implications for the quality and ease of our work. Debra Dochuk, previously of Special Collections at Notre Dame, is a superb specialist and dear friend. The Hesburgh Library Interlibrary Loan department procured volumes of obscure materials and stacks of microfilm reels. Julie Vecchio at the Navari Family Center for Digital Scholarship is a dedicated professional whose people skills and libraries know-how are exemplary. Thanks also to Rachel Bohlmann, Daniel Johnson, Jean McManus, and Matthew Sisk.

Historical research demands that one leave the confines of the home institution and travel to other archival repositories scattered across the country. Thanks to Liesl Olson, Mary Hale, Alison Hinderliter, and Catherine Grandgeorge at the Newberry Library; Kären Mason and Janet Weaver at the Iowa Women's Archives; Corie Zylstra at the Moody Bible Institute; Steve Zeleny at the Foursquare Heritage Archives; Joanna Lamaida at the Brooklyn Historical Society; and Aaron Michael Lisec at the Southern Illinois University Special Collections Research Center. Thanks also to the archivists, librarians, and staff members at the American Antiquarian Society, the Beinecke Library, the Fall River Historical Society, the Manuscripts and Archives Division at the New York Public Library, the New-York Historical Society, the Portsmouth Athenaeum Research Library, the Special Collections at Wheaton College's Buswell Library, and the Manuscripts and Archives at Yale University Library.

The following groups, centers, organizations, foundations, and agencies made my work possible through grants, fellowships, and awards. At Washington University in St. Louis, thanks to the Evan Frankel Fellowship, the R. W. Davis Travel Grant, and the Danforth Center on Religion and Politics. At Notre Dame, thanks to the Professionalization Fund Award from the Union of Graduate Historians and the Conference Presentation Grant from the Graduate Student Union. Thanks to Sharon Groves, the Human Rights Campaign, and the E. Rhodes and Leona B. Carpenter Foundation for the HRC summer institute for religious and theological study at Vanderbilt University. Thanks to the Collegeville Institute for Ecumenical and Cultural Research for the summer workshop in writing for the broader public with the brilliant Lisa Webster and Evan Derkacz. Thank you, Iowa Women's Archives and Linda Kerber, for the Linda and Richard Kerber Fund award for research in women's history. Thanks to the Society for Historians of the Gilded Age and Progressive Era for helping graduate students attend the annual meetings of the Organization of American Historians through the Conference Travel Award for PhD Students. Thank you to the American Historical Association Council for its Annual Meeting Travel Grant. Thank you to the Mellon Foundation for funding a remarkably important Newberry Library seminar in archival theory, form, and practice. Thank you to the Roy Rosenzweig Center for History and New Media at George Mason University for the Current Research in Digital History conference travel grant. Thanks to the Sarah Pettit Doctoral

Fellowship in LGBT Studies at Yale University, masterfully led by Katie Lofton and Linn Tonstad. The Sacred Writes Public Scholarship Training was made possible through the generosity of the Henry Luce Foundation and the significant effort of two excellent public scholars and wonderful people: Liz Bucar and Megan Goodwin. Thanks also to Mark Bowman and everyone at the LGBTQ Religious Archives Network for the Virginia Ramey Mollenkott Award (formerly the LGBTQ Religious History Award).

The best writing is produced in conversation. I'm grateful for the hours my trusted readers have dedicated to working through obscure references and half-formed ideas. Lisa Webster and Evan Derkacz first convinced me that writing was a duty. I have kept their kind words of encouragement in mind as I worked through my sentences in this project and beyond. Thanks also to the participants in the Collegeville workshop. At Notre Dame, the weekly Colloquium on Religion and History was a gentle and instructive intellectual home for workshopping ideas. The monthly women's writing group was a warm and welcoming place to solicit helpful and honest feedback. Thank you, Ashley Foster, Danae Jacobson, and Carla Villanueva for your kind and thoughtful critiques. Twice during my time at Notre Dame, I participated in a workshop with Bielefeld University in Germany. I thank the participants and organizers for their insights and advice. Thanks also to the Sarah Pettit LGBT Studies Fellowship workshop at Yale for helping me think through questions of religion and sexuality in new ways. The participants of the Rocky Mountain American Religion Seminar asked questions and made suggestions that made one of the manuscript chapters much stronger. The multitalented Joseph Stuart, who convened the seminar, also helped me with the book index, and I thank him for his dedication, patience, and care. Finally, thank you to the manuscript reviewers, Oxford University Press, Zara Cannon-Mohammed, and my editor Nancy Toff for her enthusiasm, wisdom, and guidance.

I also thank the editors and anonymous reviewers of the *Journal of the Gilded Age and Progressive Era* and *Religion and Culture: A Journal of Interpretation* for helping shape my thinking for this book. Chapter 3 contains material previously published in my article "The Itinerant Passions of Protestant Pastors: Ministerial Elopement Scandals in the Gilded Age and Progressive Era Press," *Journal of the Gilded Age and Progressive Era* 19, no. 1 (January 2020): 77–95. © 2020 Society for Historians of the Gilded Age and Progressive Era; reprinted with permission. Chapters 6 and 7 contain material previously published in my article "Queer Rumors: Protestant

Ministers, Unnatural Deeds, and Church Censure in the Twentieth-Century United States," *Religion and American Culture* 31, no. 1 (Winter 2021): 1–32. © 2020 The Center for the Study of Religion and American Culture; reprinted with permission.

My friends have been fundamental in forming my thinking about the ideas found in this book and beyond. I owe them much of who I am. I am also indebted to them for more tangible things: hosting me, feeding me, making me laugh, and convincing me that the small joys of life are worth the interruption from academic pursuits. Beginning in Belarus, I thank Andrea Huff, Jennifer Jeanneret, Tanya Kolesnikova, Igor Kopylov, Yulia Kopylova, Evgeniya Kudianova, Irina Marhun, Victoria Schnose, Galina Sidarenka, and Ulyana Sparks for their support at various stages of the first half of my life. At LCC International University, thanks to Stephanie Chase Bradbury, Geri Henderson, Maija Kozlova, Sarah Schoolcraft, Jen Stewart, and Janneke Van Hofwegen for their friendship and mentorship. Feruza Aripova has been a trusted friend since our first days in Klaipėda, and while neither of us is anywhere close to the people we were back then, I'm lucky to still have her in my life.

In New Haven, thanks to Sachin Ramabhadran, whom I met on the first day of orientation at Yale Divinity School and who still always makes sure I'm doing okay. Kat Jetson was first an internet friend and then—quickly and still to this day—someone to cry and laugh with while feeling cared for and safe. Thanks to Kat's wife Krystal Beisick for being a delight. Abby Ferjak, Rebecca Floyd Marshall, Becca Seely, and Rachel Sommer invited me into their lives as family. Thanks, too, to their families: Linda and Ken Ferjak, Barb and Kip Seely, Rick and Martha Floyd, Lynn Sommer and Scott Weaver, Alex Floyd Marshall, Matthew Sware, and all the little ones. Michelle Morgan: I don't know where I would be without you. Thanks for bringing the hilarious and wonderful Kate Donato into my life. Thanks to Carrie Beaulieu Morgan, Jaime Myers-McPhail, Jan Waldron, and David McPhail for their hospitality and good humor. Thanks to Rebekah Cannon, Briallen Hopper, Emily Johnson, Alana Massey, and Rachel Schiff for their friendship. Thanks also to Sarah Stone and Pam McFarlane for their instrumental role at a crucially important time in my life.

My Twitter friend Kristen Mohn Dellaporta and I first met in New York City on a warm fall day in 2009, and I knew Kristen would always be a part of my life then and there. I'd also been talking to another Twitter friend, Michael Dellaporta, and—since their last names have already mercilessly given away the plot—I'll just say that Kristen and Michael were married in 2013. I was lucky enough to score the entirely age-inappropriate ring-bearer gig in their wedding. It was a lovely day. Kristen died after a relentless battle with cancer in 2015. I miss her terribly.

I'm grateful for the people who helped me thrive during my time in Indiana. Mark Lackowski and Laura Donnelly arrived around the same time and quickly became my closest friends in town. Our adventures in South Bend and Chicago were always a bright spot in the occasionally grim Midwestern landscape. Carl and Carolyn Friesen: thank you for your warmth and hospitality. Thanks also to Vanesa Bijol, James Breen, Philip Byers, Sarah Davies, Anna Holdorf, Jisoo Hong, Andrea Howard, Danae Jacobson, Beth Jarvis, Sejoo Kim, Johnny Nelson, Luke Schleif, Daniel Silliman, Emily Smith, and Ian Van Dyke for their friendship and patient affection. Thanks to Maggie Elmore and Natalie Mendoza for modeling kindness to friends and strangers at what would turn out to be a turning point in my career.

In California, thanks to my colleagues in the Department of History and beyond at California State University San Marcos. My job has been enriched tremendously through their mentorship and support. I'm also grateful to CSUSM students for always asking the right questions. Thanks to Julia Lewandoski and Kim Quinney for their friendship, laughter, and a shared committeemen to finding the best food in San Diego County.

When I moved to Carlsbad, I could not have guessed that the small suburb would introduce me to someone as delightful, lovely, and kind as Elizabeth Speck. Thank you for your optimism and grace. Thanks, too, to the soothing snoozing noises occasionally coming from my dog Phoebe Waller-Bridge-Krivulskaya, who faithfully sleeps by my desk when I write.

Finally, although we have been divided by an ocean for years, my mother Tatsiana Sablina and grandmother Larisa Shekunova have been constant sources of inspiration and support. Grandma Larisa was an orphaned infant who survived World War II, so she takes nothing for granted. A hardworking single mother of two, she attended night school to finish her secondary education. In total, it took Larisa thirty-five years to finish just nine grades—which puts the whole PhD thing into perspective. My mother Tatsiana has been my greatest cheerleader despite the pessimism inherent in our shared Eastern European outlook. She has worked hard, suffered greatly, and persevered regardless. I remain in awe of her humor and grace. Tatsiana and Larisa may not be able to read this book in the original English, but they are found on every page.

Introduction

Before pastor Ted Haggard was exposed for visiting a male sex worker from whom he occasionally purchased crystal methamphetamine, the minister had a thriving career in Christian morality. When his scandal broke in 2006, Haggard was one of the most powerful evangelicals in the United States. The founder of the New Life megachurch in Colorado Springs, he was also president of the National Association of Evangelicals (NAE) and held frequent phone conferences with the White House.[1] In 2004, as President George W. Bush endorsed a constitutional amendment that would ban same-sex marriage, President Haggard's NAE formally adopted the position that homosexuality was a choice and, therefore, not entitled to equal protection under the law.[2] When escort Mike Jones saw Haggard on television two years later, he realized that his regular client who went by "Art from Kansas City" was actually Ted from the most influential evangelical organization in the country. To expose the contradictions between Haggard's public persona and private proclivities, Jones went to the press with the explosive details of their encounters.

Before long, Jones's revelation assumed the familiar contours of scandal. Sensational reporting, initial denials, emotional press conferences, tearful confessions, an inevitable interview with Oprah Winfrey—Haggard and his long-suffering wife Gayle went through all the stages of the scandal's unfolding.[3] The American public, fluent in the tropes of scandal, was only marginally surprised to discover another instance of hypocrisy among the divines. The memory of televangelists' sex scandals from the 1980s and 1990s was still alive and well. Just two years earlier, Paul Crouch, the founder of the Trinity Broadcasting Network, was implicated in a homosexual scandal by a former employee.[4] In many ways, by the start of the new millennium, Protestant sex scandals had become par for the course. Yet Haggard's scandal attracted so much public attention because it powerfully spoke to the hypocrisy at the heart of the most pious denunciations of queerness. For some, Haggard's standing as a national evangelical leader inspired new confidence that antigay rhetoric among conservative Christians would finally

Disgraced: How Sex Scandals Transformed American Protestantism. Suzanna Krivulskaya, Oxford University Press.

be undermined by the evidence of their leaders' queer indiscretions. Secular observers giddily suggested that clerical sex scandals were on the brink of discrediting all Christian morality systems and ushering in a new age of better sexual ethics, free of the hypocrisy that conservative religion purportedly begot.[5]

Defenders of Christianity, on their end, mounted a swift response. Leith Anderson, the man who succeeded Haggard as president of the NAE, addressed the media with a positive spin on the scandal. "There are more than 400,000 pastors in America," Anderson would later recall saying, "and 399,999 of them were not in the news for unethical behavior that weekend.... The reason the Haggard story was national news was because it was so very unusual."[6] Just how unusual scandals like Haggard's have been in the history of Protestantism is a question at the heart of this book. Protestantism has laid claims on the morality of the nation from its inception.[7] What happens when the best and brightest teachers of Christian morality are exposed for doing the opposite of what they preach? How does religion survive when scandal persists?

Far from being occasional aberrations, sex scandals have plagued pastors' reputations since the birth of the modern press in the 1830s. Yet Protestants have been remarkably successful at rehabilitating their public image in the aftermath of scandal. It helped that through much of this history, the press was determined to protect the reputation of Protestantism. At the dawn of the new nation, it was the religion of the majority. Ministers were supposed to safeguard the public from the excesses of the age of independence, so the press initially hesitated to publicize clerical scandals. During the Gilded Age, the partnership between the pulpit and the press—two institutions built to nourish and protect the fledgling democracy—dissolved.[8] The press, having fully embraced the charge of exposing corruption in high places, now also began to target mainstream religion. Publicizing sex scandals was an easy, effective, and profitable way of exposing clerical vices.

These splinters between religion and the press grew exponentially by the turn of the twentieth century. As newspapers devoted greater column space to all manner of sensation, denominational bodies developed strategies for restoring the image of innocence that had been compromised as a result of their ministers' sexual misbehavior. Protestant institutions attempted to get into the good graces of local news editors, formed church publicity departments, and conspired to keep embarrassing episodes of pastors' sex lives secret. When attempts at getting the secular press on their side failed, the most entrepreneurial Protestants launched their own media empires—which, by the end of the century, no longer needed to rely on denominational support. Charisma, it turned out, covered a multitude of sins. By the end of the millennium, the average American had become desensitized to scandal.[9] Protestant adherents were more willing than ever to forgive their leaders and restore them to power, as long as the fallen ministers' confessions seemed appropriately sincere.[10] Throughout this history, Americans have given their disgraced pastors a million second chances. That, in part, is how the unofficial faith of the nation has retained its grip on the culture writ large—scandal and all.

Colloquially, "I know it when I see it" logic has applied to scandal as often as it has to pornography or, for that matter, religion.[11] Scholars have tried to remedy this problem. Sociologists and media theorists date the rise of modern scandals to the mid-nineteenth century.[12] Their studies conceptualize scandals as publicized private acts that denote some kind of transgression and generate significant public interest.[13] The broader definition of scandal predates the notion of the public sphere. The root of the word has its origins in ancient Greek: *skandalon* means "stumbling block" or "cause of moral stumbling." In the Christian Bible, *skandalon* has to do with sin—erroneously walking away from the path of righteousness.

In contemporary usage, definitions of scandal involve audiences as much as protagonists.[14] When it comes to religion, public disapproval often concerns the seemingly hypocritical incongruity between professed belief and actual behavior. For example, Haggard's secular critics did not primarily condemn his same-sex attraction (or, in some cases, even his infidelity) but rather the fact that he was paying a gay man for sex while working to undermine the civil rights of LGBTQ+ people. So in the realm of religious sex scandals, instead of imagining a singular, unified public whose shared sensibilities get offended by scandal, it is more productive to think of a multiplicity of publics and a range of reasons for such offense.

Scandals occur when a publicized private transgression of a public figure either breaks a shared moral code or contradicts the espoused beliefs of that individual. Serial coverage differentiates scandal from the more singular phenomenon of sensation. The other, related feature is the cultural significance of the person or people involved. Sensations can be one-off, human-interest stories about transgressions that are varied in nature and do not necessarily warrant a follow-up or a broader cultural conversation. For example, a married man being caught in an affair with an office intern might make a headline and constitute a sensation. A sitting US president acting in the same manner rises to the level of scandal. Coverage begets commentary. Often scandal may provoke a broader cultural negotiation regarding issues on which the transgression hinges in a way that was not formally sanctioned before the offense was revealed. These are frequently questions about authority, power, gender relations, and sexual norms—especially when the protagonist of the scandal is a religious leader.

It is these breaches of silence in the realm of the sexual, which scandals sometimes occasion, that make this subject a productive form of historical inquiry. To be sure, scandal often reinscribes normalcy by compelling its subjects to confess and repent of that which is deemed transgressive, but the rare moments of rupture, of renegotiation—or even of simply open public discussion—with regard to previously taboo subjects are what make scandal an exciting entry point into the study of religion and sexuality.[15] As philosopher and theologian Mark D. Jordan writes on the subject of Catholic sex abuse scandals, "Pursuing the silences produced around priestly sex requires that we look at other effects of silence around sex, and it leads us to expand any picture we might have of telling truths in church."[16] Whatever accusations of triviality the genre might justifiably invite, scandal has been a vehicle for shaking large groups of people out of quotidian complacency.

Disgraced highlights some of the most consequential instances of Protestant sex scandals from the birth of the modern press to the rise of internet culture. The book shows how scandal coverage transformed American Protestantism in three ways: it allowed the press to compete with the pulpit as a source of moral authority, forced religious communities to adapt in light of scandals' revelations, and emboldened sustained public scrutiny of religious piety. Rather than being episodic aberrations in the history of Protestantism, sex scandals have, in fact, been integral to its development.[17] Through their encounters with the inconvenient truths that scandal revealed, Protestants were forced to publicly navigate the forbidden topics of sex and sexuality. In the process, scandal coverage ushered in opportunities for public engagement with previously unprintable and unspeakable matters.

1

Deplorable Subjects

The story begins with a murder. The body, frozen and hanging from a haystack pole on a Rhode Island farm, was found in the early morning of December 21, 1832, by an unsuspecting farmer out on his morning errands. It belonged to Sarah Maria Cornell, an unmarried factory worker in her late twenties. She was a "virtuous girl," at least according to Ira Bidwell, the Methodist minister who was summoned to identify the deceased, though the virtue of the young woman would soon become the subject of rumor and speculation.[1] The scene was staged to look like a suicide. Upon further inspection, however, the coroner began to suspect that the death had involved foul play.

The farmer who discovered the body traveled to Cornell's rented room in the neighboring town of Fall River, Massachusetts, to find out more about the victim. Cornell's trunk contained three letters, each more mysterious than the previous one. The first was an anonymous half-page missive addressed to "Miss Sarah M. Connell"—a misspelling, perhaps intentional. It was dated "Nov. 13, 1832" and signed with only the words "Yours in haste" and no other identification. "Keep your secret," the author urged, and "say nothing to no one." The second letter, this one signed with a pseudonym, asked for a meeting on December 18—or the twentieth, in case of a winter storm. The third, a sealed letter that was never sent, was written by Cornell herself. It was addressed to her pastor, Reverend Bidwell, the man who would identify her body. Cornell wanted to inform Bidwell of her decision to abandon the Methodist faith. "I once knew what it was to love God with all my heart," she wrote, "and felt that God was my father Jesus my friend and Heaven my home, but I have awfully departed—and sometimes fear I shall lose my soul forever."[2]

The reason Cornell felt that she had strayed from God was her out-of-wedlock pregnancy. That was the secret to which the mysterious anonymous letters found in her trunk referred. Indeed, after a hasty burial for what was originally ruled a suicide, Cornell's body was exhumed and examined to reveal that she had been pregnant at the time of death. New

Disgraced: How Sex Scandals Transformed American Protestantism. Suzanna Krivulskaya, Oxford University Press.
© Oxford University Press 2025. DOI: 10.1093/oso/9780197599686.003.0002

evidence surfaced as well. Local women, who decided to search Cornell's room again for good measure, found the proverbial smoking gun. In Cornell's bandbox (a circular cardboard box for storing hats), they found a note that pointed to the potential father of the child and the likely culprit in the murder: "If I am missing," Cornell had written just before she died, "inquire of the Rev. Mr. Avery of Bristol he will know where I am gone. S M Cornell. Dec 20th."[3]

The minister in question, Ephraim Kingsbury Avery, was a local Methodist pastor. Tall and handsome, the preacher had an air of authority about him despite having little formal education or ministerial training. Cornell had met Avery through her Methodist connections in 1830. When she moved to Lowell, Massachusetts, where Avery lived with his wife and three children, Cornell sought employment in their home.[4] She did not get the job, but her relationship with the minister continued—culminating two years later in a pregnancy that Avery decided to conceal by taking Cornell's life.

Cornell's murder may have remained a local curiosity had it not coincided with the dawn of the newspaper revolution. Unlike Europeans, who had been reading crime reporting for decades, it was not until the early 1830s that US Americans embraced human-interest journalism.[5] Before then, newspapers were mostly tools of commercial advertising and political persuasion.[6] Reporting on local curiosities was simply not the purview of the fledgling press in the new republic. In 1820, there were only 512 newspapers in the entire country. A meager 42 of those were printed daily, with an average circulation of just eight hundred copies per issue. The rest were weeklies. Dependent on subscription fees, these papers did not report on others' questionable practices, let alone on the behavior of Christian ministers—the self-proclaimed moral guardians of the nation. When news of clerical improprieties reached the public, as in the case of civil trials, newspapers provided minimal detail and used language intentionally designed to obscure the crime, especially if it happened to be of sexual nature.

Prior to the rise of human-interest journalism, some crimes were simply unprintable. In 1820, forty-nine-year-old Episcopal minister Ammi Rogers stood trial for performing an abortion after seducing and impregnating a much younger woman. The victim, Asenath Caroline Smith, resided in Griswold, Connecticut, with her family. Rogers, an itinerant preacher, had become friendly with the Smiths. In 1817, Smith got pregnant. Sometime in the second trimester, Rogers, promising marriage, convinced her to have an abortion. The couple then absconded to Massachusetts. When Smith decided to come back to Griswold, Rogers was arrested but escaped while out on bail. Recaptured in 1820, Rogers was tried, convicted, and sentenced to two years in prison.[7]

Only a handful of local newspapers appear to have covered the case. Most articles described the crime as "seduction" and provided only the vaguest details.[8] While a reader versed in innuendo could have deciphered what Rogers's crime entailed, the meager and veiled reporting did not make its scandalous content immediately transparent. The 1820s press did not, as a rule, deal in such unsavory matters.

A local attorney, scandalized by the crime and troubled by the fact that it was perpetrated by a Christian minister, published an anonymous pamphlet about Rogers's trial.[9] But even he confessed hesitation about releasing the details in print: "The propriety of giving publicity to a series of facts, like those developed in the following trial, may, I am aware, be questioned."[10] Concerned with the possible disintegration of public morals when presented with the details of others' depravity in print, Christians like the anonymous pamphleteer advocated erring on the side of silence. Rogers's case, however, warranted more publicity precisely because it had already become public. What outraged the author most was the fact that Rogers was supposed to represent a higher moral standard. Instead of delivering on the promise of his vocation, Rogers used his position to take advantage of innocent souls. As the presiding judge reportedly exclaimed in his address to the jury at Rogers's trial, "How lamentable that an influence so salutary, should be so deplorably scandalized and sold to infamy."[11] By "salutary influence" the judge meant the clerical profession and the presumed high moral standing of the men who occupied it. He may not have realized that Rogers was far from an anomaly. Within a decade, many more ministers would be subject to public scrutiny, publishing scandal would become a lucrative enterprise, and newspaper editors would embrace "deplorable" subjects as a legitimate domain of journalistic expertise.

This was a significant departure from how Christians had conceived of the future influence and purpose of the press. Early nineteenth-century Protestants treated the written word—and the press in particular—with a peculiar kind of devotion. "The pulpit and the press are inseparably connected," proclaimed the *Christian Herald* in 1823. "The press, then, is to be regarded with a sacred veneration and supported with religious care. The press must be supported or the pulpit falls."[12] By the 1830s, the mutual support would dwindle. In many cases, the press worked to undermine the church. Scandal sold, and stories of impropriety in high places proved to be a marketable venture. The democratization of journalism did not, in the end, advance the cause of religion. Now, with more papers, voices, and readers who loved the sensational, religion would become vulnerable to public critique.

This fundamental change in scandal coverage was propelled by a handful of enterprising men who began publishing human-interest stories in major cities. They sold their "penny papers" for a cent or two apiece, eschewed flat subscription costs, and relied on sensationalism's grip to push their product. It turned out that Americans wanted to read about more than just politics and shipping news. Already by 1830, the nation's 13 million inhabitants had access to more newspapers than all of Europe—a continent of 190 million (Table 1.1).[13] And with the arrival of cheap newspapers, more Americans than ever before could partake in the ever-expanding press market.

By 1833, though American journalism was still in its infancy, scandal had become a profitable enterprise. No one was safe from unwanted publicity. Religion was an especially easy target: the increasingly democratizing religious landscape of the 1830s provided both opportunities for experimentation and reasons for concern.[14] Were new religious movements safe for the

Table 1.1 The growth of the newspaper industry in the United States, 1800–1880

Year	Newspapers	Population
1800	235	5,308,483
1810	359	7,239,881
1820	512	9,638,453
1830	1,200	12,866,020
1840	1,631	17,069,453
1850	2,526	23,191,876
1860	3,000	31,443,321
1870	5,464	38,558,371
1880	10,761	50,189,209

The American Almanac and Repository of Useful Knowledge for the Year 1835 (Boston: Charles Bowen, 1835); Frederic Hudson, Journalism in the United States, from 1690 to 1872 (New York: Harper & Brothers, 1873); Alfred M. Lee, The Daily Newspaper in America (New York: Macmillan, 1937)

young democratic nation, concerned with cultivating republican virtue among the citizenry? Or were they loaded with potential for false teaching, cult of personality, and misguided emotionalism? Ministerial scandals and denominational responses to scandal would provide one metric for establishing what counted as legitimate, good religion and what constituted a dangerous and promiscuous kind of faith.

When the Avery-Cornell story broke, Methodism—the rapidly growing movement of British origin—was considered suspect in the United States. The emphasis on religious enthusiasm, bodily manifestations of divine presence, and intense feeling as spiritual awakening rendered Methodists radical revolutionaries in the eyes of religious traditionalists. Congregationalism was the default religion of white settlers in New England. Descendants of the once radical Puritans, Congregationalists had grown complacent by the 1830s. They lacked the spirit of revivalism that newer denominations appeared to flaunt. So when more energetic, egalitarian movements like Methodism threatened Congregationalism's authority, traditionalists turned to sermons and religious newspapers to warn the public about the dangers of new religious movements.[15]

Despite this opposition, Methodism appeared unstoppable in claiming the attention and souls of Americans. In 1771, Methodists in the American colonies numbered exactly four ministers and approximately three hundred adherents.[16] By 1776, Methodism claimed sixty-five congregations and seven thousand members. An export of the Old World, Methodism's very survival was threatened by the events of the American Revolution. Yet the movement not only persevered but also quickly overshadowed other Protestant denominations. By 1830, there were almost half a million Methodists in the young republic. Two decades later, Methodists comprised more than 34 percent of total church membership.[17] Organized through a network of itinerant preachers, Methodism appealed to people looking to escape the confines of stuffy traditionalism.

Like many New Englanders of her generation, Sarah Maria Cornell had been raised a Congregationalist. And like many of her peers, the single, independent young woman found Methodism more appealing. Methodist ministers emphasized individual faith and unmediated access to the divine. They offered the kind of egalitarianism that the Congregational elites derided. The emotional revival meetings encouraged the expression of individual spiritual feeling that would have been scoffed at in more conservative environments. Being around young, charismatic preachers only

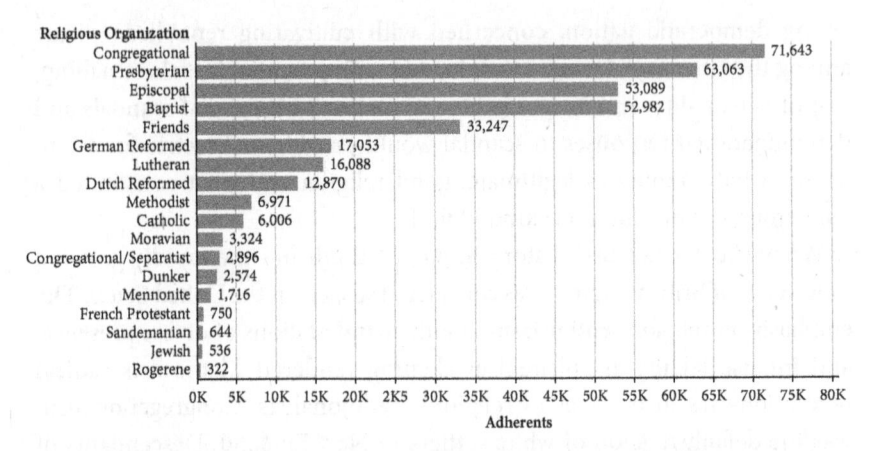

In 1776, most religious colonists belonged to Congregational, Presbyterian, Episcopal, and Baptist churches. The young Methodist movement claimed just under seven thousand adherents, which represented about 2 percent of total church membership.

William M. Newman and Peter L. Halvorson, *Atlas of American Religion: The Denominational Era, 1776–1990* (New York: Rowman & Littlefield, 2000), 18

enhanced the appeal of the new movement. Women like Cornell were captivated by the preachers' message and by their charm.[18]

Indeed, one of the charges against Methodism was the purportedly permissive climate of religious ecstasy at camp meetings. Contemporary critics claimed that the gatherings "produced more souls than they saved."[19] The confluence of unmarried young women, enigmatic preachers, and around-the-clock meetings filled with bodies undergoing emotional spiritual awakenings made Methodism subject to speculation and rumor.[20] The Cornell-Avery scandal did little to help the reputation of Methodist meetings as sites of licentiousness. In August 1832, Cornell attended a camp meeting during which, she later alleged, Avery coerced her into having sex with him.[21] When he found out about the pregnancy, the minister decided to get rid of the evidence of one crime by committing another.

Cornell's death, first reported as a tragic suicide, instantly became a local sensation. It contained all ingredients of a titillating story: an independent young woman, a suspect religious movement, and a seduction. The mysterious correspondence discovered at Cornell's residence along with the "inquire of the Rev. Mr. Avery" note in her bandbox led to a more thorough investigation. Her body, exhumed two days after a hasty funeral, bore evidence of the pregnancy. Avery was arrested on December 23, 1832, four days after the murder.

Public interest in the story kept growing, and newspaper editors continued to excite it with headlines like "Fall River Outrage" and "Outrage and Murder."[22] Readers would have understood the word "outrage" to be synonymous with some form of sexual crime.[23] Local newspapers spelled out every detail in their coverage of the complicated tale. Even with increased attention, their tone was initially measured. As the *Rhode Island American* put it, "We are unwilling to lend our aid to prejudice the public mind, or to avert the course of justice. But people demand to be informed on subjects of so much interest, and we deem it our duty to lay before them such facts as we may obtain, without comment."[24] Soon newspapers would eschew such restraint. The story was too astonishing to offer without commentary, especially when after two weeks of preliminary hearings, the court ruled that there was not enough evidence to convict Avery and set the prisoner free.

One of the presiding judges consoled himself and the public by opining that "though the guilty may escape an earthly judgment, there is a Judge whom he cannot escape."[25] Despite promises of eventual divine retribution, the public wanted the accused to receive a more corporeal castigation. Once the transcript of Avery's hearing came out in print two days after the verdict, public indignation intensified. It was inspired, in no small part, by the many newspaper editorials that proclaimed their unshaken belief in the culpability of the "Rev. Criminal."[26]

Newspapers were not the only ones to sound the alarm. Printmakers joined the public protest against the ruling. Henry R. Robinson, a New York lithographer who generally avoided the subject of religion, used his art to discredit Avery.[27] Robinson produced two prints: one depicting the scene of Cornell's murder and the other portraying Avery being taken to hell in a boat full of demons. In both prints, Cornell is portrayed as a tragic figure, Avery a conniving villain. In the first print, the demons are worried about the court of public opinion, while in the second, they execute Avery's punishment for the callous murder. With moral clarity and a sense of duty, the demons in Robinson's lithographs deliver the judgment that the court would not.

Public outrage eventually escalated into concrete action. Harvey Harnden, Bristol County's deputy sheriff, led the community's efforts to

Ephraim Avery strangles Sarah Maria Cornell, as demons in the background warn about the judgment of a criminal jury and the court of public opinion. Like newspapers, commercially sold lithographs provided commentary on the Avery murder trial and attempted to persuade viewers of the minister's guilt.
Library of Congress Prints and Photographs Division, LC-USZ62-50464

bring Avery to justice. A zealous guardian of social order, Harnden held public meetings in local Congregational churches, gathered witness testimony, and even procured a new warrant for Avery's arrest. (Avery had been examined in Bristol, Rhode Island, where he lived, while the crime had occurred just outside of Fall River, Massachusetts, where Cornell rented a room, and the citizens of Fall River wanted to re-examine Avery on their turf.) The only problem was that by the time Harnden reached Bristol with the new warrant, Avery was nowhere to be found. The governor of Rhode Island was now offering a $300 reward for the minister's arrest. In the end, the fugitive was not hard to locate. Avery's attempt at a disguise consisted of "allowing his whiskers to grow, which previously had been shaved" and hiding at a friend's house in New Hampshire.[28] It took Harnden only a few days to find Avery in late January 1833, one month after Cornell's murder.

A MINISTER EXTRAORDINARY TAKING PASSAGE & BOUND ON A FOREIGN MISSION TO THE COURT OF HIS SATANIC MAJESTY!

Ephraim Avery rows to hell after committing the murder of Sarah Maria Cornell, whose lifeless body hangs on a haystack frame. Avery is surrounded by demons who are taking him "to the court of his Satanic Majesty," while evidence of the murder—including a note—is scattered on the shore not far from Cornell's body.

Library of Congress Prints and Photographs Division, LC-USZ62-1567

For much of the public, the minister's attempted escape served as further evidence of his guilt.

Avery's second examination unleashed greater scrutiny of Methodism via its association with the fugitive. Competing religious groups joined secular newspapers in their quest of bringing Methodism to task. The Universalists accused the Methodists of blatantly covering up the crime to protect the preacher.[29] According to one report, local Methodists had pressured a Providence newspaper that was critical of the denomination so much that the publication folded.[30] Whether the report was accurate remains unclear. There were hundreds of short-lived newspapers in the early 1830s, as editors tried to gauge what kinds of stories sold well enough to sustain business. Still, the press was growing increasingly more critical of Methodism by the day.

Meanwhile, Avery was charged with assault and murder. His trial was scheduled for May. By then, the story had become so well known that the court had trouble filling the jury with impartial peers.[31] Avery's defense strategy was to paint Cornell as a promiscuous woman of questionable reputation, a capricious manipulator whose accusations could not be trusted. Cornell, Avery's lawyers argued, held a grudge against the minister because he had recommended that she be excommunicated from the Methodist Church on account of her loose behavior. In response, she decided to set Avery up by leaving a note implicating the minister in her pregnancy. (That the setup came at the price of Cornell's own life somehow did not figure into the lawyers' theory of Cornell's machinations.)

Methodists unequivocally supported Avery. The denomination raised funds for the defense, while several ministers defamed the victim's character from the stand. Denominational leaders recognized that the trial would become a symbolic test case of Methodism's legitimacy.[32] The church could not afford to be associated with the scandal.

Attempting to avoid scandal inspired more negative coverage. Some publications used the Methodists' support of Avery as evidence of the denomination's antidemocratic nature—a rhetorical move usually reserved for Catholics in this era. "The Methodist is the most arbitrary and dangerous sect in the United States," complained William Mercein, editor of New York's *Christian Intelligencer*. "Their church is an absolute monarchy. With them there is nothing republican." The *Intelligencer*, published by the Dutch Reformed Church, accused Methodism of being incompatible with the democratic values of the young nation. "There is no spice of liberty or equality in their system—a system not only hostile, but really dangerous to every republican principle under our government," the editorial continued. The case "of their favorite Ephraim K. Avery" proved to the *Intelligencer* just how corrupt the denomination was due to "its influence even over our Courts of Justice." Boston Universalists' *Trumpet and Universalist Magazine* reprinted the piece, presumably joining the *Intelligencer* in its anti-Methodist sentiments.[33]

Despite widespread criticism, the Methodists' strategy of questioning Cornell's moral character and accusing her of framing Avery paid off. The jury found the idea of female independence and sexual agency distasteful. Theirs was the first generation that witnessed rapid industrialization and, with it, newly emerging female independence: women who left their fathers' farms not for the comforts of their husbands' homes but rather for the urban labor markets. Cornell's sad fate became a lesson in the inherent dangers of women stepping out of the roles prescribed to them by tradition. Under the gender ideologies of republican motherhood and true womanhood, women were supposed to be responsible for men's chastity, so Cornell's seduction and pregnancy were automatically assumed to be her fault.[34] Avery's defenders also blamed Cornell's ambition. Had she not traded the safety of her father's home for the dangers of factory work, she might well have survived. As one newspaper argued, the whole affair was "an awful warning to the youthful and inexperienced of [her] sex."[35] Girls were not supposed to venture out into the world in search of religious experimentation and sexual independence. And so, six months after the murder, Avery was once again a free man.

If the dismissal of the minister after the hearing in January 1833 had caused a stir, the acquittal in June created an uproar. With the trial adjourned, the court of public opinion was now in session. For Avery's supporters, the acquittal meant that Christianity was also exonerated. In a letter to a Methodist journal, one man argued that if Avery "had been proved guilty of the horrid crimes of seduction and murder, a deep wound would have been inflicted not upon the Methodist Episcopal Church only, but upon our common Christianity; and the enemies of the cross of Christ might have triumphed in having this additional excuse, however flimsy it would be, for their unbelief."[36] The writer recognized that the case had direct bearing on religion's legitimacy. Methodists, on their end, stood by Avery until the end—acquitting him in an internal hearing not only of the murder but also of "illicit intercourse with the deceased."[37] He was fully restored as a minister in good standing within weeks of the trial's conclusion.

Outside of Methodist circles, Avery became a pariah. A play, written in the aftermath of the trial, lamented the injustice of the verdict, as one of the characters prayed that until "Heaven will, in its own time avenge the murder, . . . may the execration of ten times ten thousand virtuous hearts pursue the assassin of poor Sarah Maria Cornell."[38] And they did. In Boston, a mob assaulted Avery with "opprobrious epithets" until the sheriff put a stop to the unrest.[39] In Rhode Island, another group carved Avery's name into an empty coffin and sent it down the Providence River.[40] Other angry New Englanders shot at, hung, and burned Avery effigies.[41] The public did not buy the verdict, but they were buying newspapers, which provided ample commentary on the case for months after its legal resolution.

By the end of summer, the essence of the scandal, for many, lay not in the facts of the case but rather in the Methodists' unconditional defense of Avery. One minister's presumed innocence ironically turned into an indictment of his entire denomination. Newspapers asked, "Are not the friends and defenders of E. K. Avery aware that the charity of the public for their motives, is well nigh exhausted, and that a longer continuance in the course they have pursued, will, in the public estimation, make them partakers of his guilt?"[42] One Methodist journal lamented the role of "a portion of the public press" in pursuing "a course of systematic and unparalleled injustice throughout every period of the public agitation on this subject."[43] These papers, the article ascertained, used the trial "not only to attack the sacred office of the ministry with scurrilous insinuations and base innuendoes, but an attempt has been made to identify [Avery] and all the imputed guilt of seduction and murder, with the denomination of which he is a minister, and with Christianity itself." The Methodists were right to be afraid: criticisms of Christianity vis-à-vis Avery abounded.

Perhaps the most outspoken critic was Thomas Wilson Dorr, a Rhode Island lawyer and politician who would eventually lead the 1841 Dorr Rebellion in protest of the state's outdated electoral rules. In 1833, Dorr was still writing under the pseudonym "Aristides" for Providence's *Republican Herald*.[44] He had published multiple articles on the Avery affair, disparaging the Methodists and pointing out inconsistencies in the minister's defense. In September, after the Methodists acquitted Avery, Dorr published an entire pamphlet on the case.[45] Explaining his motivations, Dorr wrote:

> The public feels itself injured, common justice and common decorum, religion and morality, feel themselves outraged, not so much by the acquittal of Avery in a legal point of view, as by the bold and daring manifesto of the Methodist Conference, which acquits Avery even of suspicion, which all know to be incorrect, thrusts him into the pulpit as a public teacher of religion, who should be free from the very appearance of evil, and virtually recommends him as a man of unimpeachable integrity and purity of character, when it is well known that he has been guilty of ... the utterance of falsehood respecting his visit to Rhode-Island, on the 20th of December last.[46]

Dorr argued that the post of a Christian minister entailed a presumed degree of respectability that Avery lacked. The public, according to the lawyer, was unhappy not simply because people disagreed with the jury's verdict, but because continuing to endow Avery with the same kind of spiritual authority as before Cornell's murder compromised their trust in religion writ large.

The last section of the pamphlet appealed directly to the Methodists and asked, "Gentlemen, do you owe nothing to the cause of religion? . . . What influence but a most pernicious one can it produce in point of religion and morals; of what other effect can it be productive, in regard to either, than to lessen its value in the minds of youth, to see a man offered them as a guide to follow, as an example to copy, whom they hear and believe to be, and who there is good reason to suspect, is guilty of the foulest crime?"[47] Dorr recognized that Christian denominations did religion no favors by protecting clergy accused of immorality. Decades ahead of his time on questions of marketing and public opinion, Dorr urged the Methodists to sacrifice Avery so that religion might be saved in the eyes of the public.

Avery, in the meantime, was trying to redeem his reputation. In 1834, the minister and a few of his allies published a pamphlet titled *Vindication of the Result of the Trial of the Rev. Ephraim K. Avery*, which included a statement from the accused.[48] In the piece, Avery attempted to account for the mysterious circumstances that connected him to Cornell's death, produced a few alibis, and commended fellow Methodists for their confidence and support. The epistolary attempt at redemption failed. Avery's damaged reputation caused him to leave ministry in 1836.[49] To make ends meet for his family, he took up carpentry and farming, eventually moving to Ohio, where he remained until his death in 1869. There, as one obituary put it, "where less was known about him," he lived "as a farmer for thirty years, making many friends, it is said."[50]

In the end, the Avery drama turned out to be about much more than sex and murder. It was also a referendum on religion.[51] The scandal prompted Avery's defenders to plead with the press to stop publishing anti-Methodist editorials, and it inspired his critics to appeal to the Methodists to abandon Avery's defense. Both sides recognized that religion's reputation hung in the balance. Both turned to newspapers to argue their case. As they did so, they continued to incite public excitement. The rapidly democratizing press, in the meantime, began to cover ministerial scandals with less self-censorship. Denominational bodies faced difficult decisions: the unprecedented amount of publicity that clerical scandals attracted forced religious institutions to take a public stance on their ministers' alleged crimes. Religion's reputation would now depend on newspaper coverage and denominational response.

By 1835, newspapers that dealt in scandal had established themselves as a staple, if not universally admired, part of journalism. Human-interest and crime stories brought in great profits, which is why it is especially curious that some ministers were still able to get away with their alleged crimes with minimal press scrutiny. What set them apart from men like Ephraim Avery, at least in the case of the Reverend Eleazer Sherman, was the nature of the crime. If adultery and seduction were whispered about in the 1820s and openly discussed by the early 1830s, same-sex acts were still a taboo subject, even after the newspaper revolution took hold. When it came to deviant sexuality, there were conventions that even the most sensationalist newspapers were unwilling to violate.

The fact that Sherman's story survived at all is surprising, given the lengths to which his contemporaries went to avoid naming his queer proclivities. Ironically, historians may have to thank a handful of Christian sexual purity advocates for preserving the story of this divine's deviance.[52] Moral reformers publicized the case in order to warn the public of the dangers of breaking established sexual codes. Yet through the very act of recording the details of the case, these crusaders unwittingly helped preserve an archive of early nineteenth-century queerness.

This was not the first time Christian reformers clumsily inspired public discussion of sexual behaviors they worked hard to eradicate. New York City's anti-vice crusader J. R. McDowell, for example, produced material that was itself later adjudged obscene in an ecclesiastical hearing.[53] In pursuit of moral reform, he published descriptions of seedy neighborhoods, accused fellow New Yorkers of frequenting houses of ill repute, and reprinted testimonies of reformed sex workers. His Christian brethren found his work "notorious and indecent."[54] Reformers' attempts to dissuade the public from veering off the proverbial straight-and-narrow path of sexual morality thus sometimes involved tactics that were themselves scandalous. Still, they were not afraid to shock fellow Christians into sexual conformity. To preserve the purity of religion and the chastity of the nation, moral crusaders dove into the dirty and the obscene with zeal and determination.

An especially eager adopter of such tactics, the young anti-vice crusader Joseph A. Whitmarsh, published the short-lived newspaper *Light! or, the Two-Edged Sword* in 1835. Most of the material in the publication dealt with the sin of "self-pollution" (masturbation) and was otherwise concerned with men's sex lives. The sensational subject matter caused conservative critics to castigate the paper as distasteful.[55] While the public was getting well acquainted with reading about certain kinds of scandal, *Light* covered topics that were still not palatable for the average citizen. The editors of the *Long-Island Farmer*, for example, reported being "shocked by the gross vulgarity and coarse obscenity of [*Light*'s] contents, by which we were made acquainted with many secret arts and practices of the most loathsome description, of which we before never had any idea, and never wish to have; and were still more shocked to find that this polluted periodical was under the sanction of the Society for Moral Reform!!"[56] Feigning ignorance of sexual subjects, newspapers accused Whitmarsh's publication of crudeness and vulgarity. Only two issues of *Light* survive, and the one that began the Eleazer Sherman debacle is not among them. Other contemporary sources confirm, however, that in an early 1835 issue, Whitmarsh accused Sherman of having made sexual advances toward men. The accusation's impact was significant enough to warrant an ecclesiastical trial.

Sherman was a member of the Christian Connection, a small Protestant denomination that emphasized unity among different strands of Christianity and freedom from "the bondage of creed."[57] By the mid-1830s, Sherman had established himself as a prominent leader—preaching the gospel, engaging in interdenominational dialogue, and even printing four different editions of his popular memoir, which he had published at the age of thirty-three.[58] By all accounts, Sherman was a charming and magnetic figure. He preached thousands of sermons, visited hundreds of meeting-houses, and enjoyed the hospitality of countless friends, who provided him with good company and a warm place to stay.

In July 1835, Sherman was called by the ecclesiastical council in Providence, Rhode Island, to answer for his extracurricular activities. According to his accusers, Sherman got a little too close to some of his male friends. While it was not uncommon for itinerant men to share a bed, it was less common to engage in sexual activities with one's bedfellow. Sherman was in trouble.

The only reason any details of Sherman's trial survive is because of a heavily redacted pamphlet published in late 1835. Prefatory notes by the anonymous author make it clear that the main motivation for publishing the story was to expose Sherman as a deviant lest he attempt to corrupt others and to warn the "many young men and boys who indulge in some of the ruinous vices exposed in this pamphlet."[59] This preoccupation with male sexual habits sounds not unlike the focus of Whitmarsh's *Light* or any number of other moral reformers' publications. Whoever authored the pamphlet wanted to ensure not only that Sherman's career was ruined but also that the testimony of the case would survive in print—thus protecting other young men from preachers like Sherman.

Nine men testified against Sherman. Five claimed that he had made sexual advances toward them. Two accused the minister of attempting the crime "described in the first chapter of Romans"—a reference to verse 27, which bemoans the fact that "men, leaving the natural use of the woman, burned in their lust one toward another."[60] Hiram Brooks was the first to take the stand. He described sharing a bed with Sherman and being "suddenly awakened by some unknown cause" and then kissed. Brooks also accused Sherman of taking "other improper liberties with [Brooks's] person." After Brooks objected to unwanted touching, Sherman relented, laughed it off, and then proceeded to teach Brooks about sex and human anatomy. Brooks testified that everything published about Sherman in *Light* was true.[61]

Other witnesses offered similar testimonies. A Reverend White, who met Sherman in 1833, recalled one night when Sherman's hand passed "over different parts of [White's] person." Next came the testimony of James Allen, whose story was more explosive since it involved accusations of attempted sodomy. While the pamphlet dared not print the word (substituting a dash to disguise the expletive), it did describe Sherman's encounter with Allen as one in which the former "attempted the accomplishment of his most diabolical purposes." The pamphlet's author had prepared the readers for the vagueness of his report in the preface by explaining that although he could not bring himself to publish the account of the trial verbatim, he "put much of the testimony in another dress of language, thereby disguising many of its disgusting features, and leaving out many facts which could not be hinted at with any degree of delicacy."[62]

So unspeakable were Sherman's alleged crimes that when another witness rose to testify about attempted sodomy, the members of the ecclesiastical council asked him to refrain from recounting the story in order to avoid self-incrimination.[63] Should the reader have any hesitations about the exact nature of the accusations, the pamphlet's appendix provided an excerpt from the penal code of Rhode Island, spelling out the punishment for the crime of sodomy. The first offense could result in the convict being carried to the gallows, spending a few hours there as a warning to onlookers, and then being imprisoned for up to three years. The second offense would result in capital punishment. Of course, the ecclesiastical council was not seeking civil punishment for Sherman; they simply wanted him to cease religious work. They understood, as the author of the pamphlet put it, that if "a minister of the gospel should be guilty of the vices recorded in the following pages, is a consideration sufficient, in the minds of some persons, to make every good man tremble for the fate of the Christian cause."[64] Sodomy could ruin religion.

For his part, Sherman attempted to mount a defense using the very men who accused him of the unprintable crimes. With naive confidence, he tried to plead with the former friends who had now turned against him. Why, Sherman asked, would Hiram Brooks not have come to him "as a Christian brother" and confront him about whatever conduct he found disagreeable? Why would the other men be friendly with Sherman even after his allegedly unwanted advances? Why would they still come to hear him preach? Sherman did not know who wrote the article accusing him of improper conduct, but he believed that he was unjustly persecuted.

The council did not find Sherman's defense convincing. They pronounced him guilty "of gross immoral conduct" and removed him from ministerial ranks. They prayed, too, that Sherman would repent and receive forgiveness from God. As far as the council was concerned, no earthly forgiveness would be granted. Sherman was advised to find employment in the secular realm.

Only two contemporary periodicals appear to have covered the case. Although the *Light* article clearly made enough of an impression on its readers to warrant an investigation and an ecclesiastical trial, the coverage of the case was absent from the pages of most other newspapers. The August 6, 1835 issue of the New Hampshire *Christian Journal* announced Sherman's defrocking but provided no details of his crime. The article explained that "the best interests of the cause are subserved more fully" when "such public censure embraces as few specifications as possible."[65] The less the public knew, the better it was for all involved.

Despite Christian publishers' best efforts to keep the details of the case obscure, by November, the *Boston Investigator*, a freethought periodical that normally reveled in reporting on ministers' sins, had heard of Sherman's troubles. Freethinkers were a beleaguered minority of unbelievers in a de facto Protestant nation. Like their religious counterparts, they had entered the publishing business in the 1820s. They, too, competed for the eyes, ears, and souls of readers in the burgeoning marketplace of early nineteenth-century religion.[66]

Atheists like *Boston Investigator*'s editor Abner Kneeland sought to persuade fellow citizens of the follies of institutional religion and church hierarchy. In an article facetiously titled "Clerical Morality," the newspaper presented Sherman's case as a sign of trouble for religion: "If the accused be guilty, it only adds one more to the long list of black-coated *reverends* who have been a disgrace to their order, if not to the human race." If Sherman was innocent, then his accusers were "guilty of persecution most foul." In either case, "Let it be remembered that both the accused and accusers are not only christians, but mostly christian ministers." As Christians battled it out in ecclesiastical courts, the *Investigator* argued, they cast doubt on their collective morality. All that freethinkers had to do was observe and report on religion's demise. Remarkably, even the anti-religious *Investigator* would not reveal the details of Sherman's crime. Instead, the editors wrote, "If our readers wish to know the nature of the charges brought against 'Elder Sherman,' they will find one of them alluded to in Rom. i.27" (the same verse about men's lust for each other that had been mentioned in the trial pamphlet). The readers, assumed fluent in their biblical references, would have understood that Sherman had been accused of same-sex intimacy of some kind, but no further details were supplied.[67]

Why were Avery's and Sherman's cases treated differently in the press? Both men were locally well-known, popular ministers who represented emerging denominations. Both preached morality, temperance, and moderation. The testimony against both was sufficient to convince the public that they were guilty of the crimes with which they were charged. Yet Avery's trial inspired plays, novels, illustrations, and hundreds of newspaper articles, while almost nothing is preserved in the historical record regarding Sherman's troubles. His crime was unspeakable. Whereas the crime of "seduction" had become palatable, perhaps even titillating by the mid-1830s, sodomy was still an unprintable offense.

Curiously, what stood out to the author of the Sherman pamphlet as his greatest crime was not, in fact, the realized or attempted carnal acts. As much as the pamphleteer was outraged by the acts he opaquely described, he appeared more concerned with the corrupting influence of Sherman's teaching and uncensored speaking about sexual matters on the minds of young men. The author warned his readers most pressingly about ideas, not acts. It is remarkable, for example, that half of the printed account of Hiram Brooks's testimony against Sherman recounted their conversation after Sherman's alleged sexual advances:

Sherman affected a laugh, and said he meant no harm; but as he (witness) was a young man, he would in confidence, learn him many things which it was very necessary for him to know. He (witness) said to Sherman, that he had ever avoided all knowledge, as far as practicable, of such subjects, and thought his ignorance of them, one effectual safeguard to virtue; therefore he did not wish to be better informed. Sherman replied to him, he was glad to see him so scrupulously modest, and assured him that man was formed for society, and he must acquaint himself with all its social, domestic and connubial relations, if he would be happy and useful. He said it had been the business of priests and prophets to regulate the inter-course of the sexes, and he (witness) must necessarily acquaint himself with all of these connections. (From this he proceeded to converse on the subject of *anatomy*, and made some remarks clearly showing the bent of his mind and inclinations.)[68]

Sherman may have indeed believed that carnal knowledge was essential to spiritual instruction. Since pastors were supposed to be ethical guides for their church flock, they had to be familiar with all manner of sexual expres-sions—or at least that was how Sherman reportedly justified whatever he was doing with Brooks that night. The pamphlet's author thus argued that Sherman was to be removed from ministerial ranks as much for teaching young men about sexuality as for unwanted touch. What scandalized the author even more than Sherman's sexual preferences were Sherman's ideas.

The press did not make such distinctions when talking about ministerial misconduct. For the first generation of the modern press, it was sexual acts—not theological reflections or anatomical conjectures—that served as evidence of religious hypocrisy. But since sodomy was still an unprintable offense, men like Sherman all but disappeared from the historical record. Their peculiarities did not become scandalous because even the cheap newspapers still upheld some taboos. Crimes of seduction would be sensa-tionalized; sodomy could, for now, go mostly unnoticed.[69]

Ministers who indulged their opposite-sex extramarital desires were less fortunate. In the quarter century between 1835 and 1860, at least thirty-five Christian ministers were accused of sex crimes, including adultery, seduc-tion, sexual assault, and rape.[70] In comparison, there were only four cases of clerical sexual misconduct publicized in the quarter century between 1810 and 1835. To be sure, whether four, forty, or four hundred, ministers who got caught engaging in inappropriate sexual behavior represented a minority of the profession. There were tens of thousands Protestant clergy in any given decade of the century. Nonetheless, the publicity their crimes garnered indicated a sizable rise in both public interest and press attention to whether the nation's moral guardians were living up to their espoused ethical standards.

In 1850, Nathaniel Hawthorne published his bestselling novel *The Scarlett Letter*. The plot concerned a hypocritical minister and a young woman who bore the brunt of the community's anger for bearing his out-of-wedlock child. Hawthorne would have been familiar with Avery's case, and his novel was likely inspired by Cornell's murder.[71] Between fictional representations and sensational reports, ministerial scandal had become a familiar genre by the midcentury. Scandal sold, and scandal-ridden newspapers became some of the most successful ventures in popular publishing. James Gordon Bennett's sensationalist *New York Herald*, for example, would become the most popular national newspaper by 1860—with seventy-seven thousand daily readers (compared to twenty thousand in 1836).[72] As the news became a lucrative business, publications went to great lengths to secure the attention of audiences constantly presented with a multiplicity of options. As the sales of Hawthorne's novel showed (the first printing of twenty-five hundred copies sold out in ten days), few things attracted more attention than stories about the country's ministers falling from grace.[73] The higher the status, the more scandalous the fall. And savvy newspaper editors were not afraid to exaggerate, embellish, or publish unverified reports to attract the readers' attention.

In just a quarter century, the press firmly established itself as the fourth estate. As the editors of the *Washington Union* declared in 1858, "The newspaper press controls the state and the church; it directs the family, the legislator, the magistrate and the minister. None rise above its influence, none sink below its authority."[74] As newspapers ascended to this new level of authority, religious bodies began to grow concerned with the explosive potential of scandal. No church, creed, or denomination could avoid the scrutinizing gaze of the press. Early nineteenth-century predictions of harmony and coöperation between the pulpit and the press proved to be far too optimistic. Newspapers' growing influence jeopardized Christianity's authority by threatening to disclose uncomfortable truths about its pastors. One minister's scandal could undermine an entire denomination.

Religious leaders had begun to speak out against the dangerous influence of newspapers at the midcentury. Henry Ward Beecher, a young Congregational minister from an accomplished East Coast family, criticized newspapers for their "vulgar drollery" and derided "the black mail papers; their very hope is to make you wince and dance to their lash." Christian newspapers were not spared either. Beecher complained about denominational newspapers' insularity, claiming that they "refuse to let anything go past without a snap or a growl, which does not belong to their door." For Beecher, newspapers had gotten out of hand. False reports, partisan editorials, and vulgar sensationalism rendered them both mean-spirited and untrustworthy. He did not know then that, twenty years later, he would find himself at the center of the biggest ministerial sex scandal of the century.[75]

2

Alienated Affections

The eve of Independence Day in 1870 found the Tilton household in Brooklyn, New York, in disarray. Theodore Tilton had finally confirmed his worst suspicions: his wife Elizabeth was having an affair with the man who had officiated at the couple's wedding fifteen years earlier. The Reverend Henry Ward Beecher had been the family's pastor, Theodore's employer, and Elizabeth's confidant. He would also become the man ultimately responsible for the dissolution of their marriage.

According to women's rights activist Victoria Woodhull, who would later publicize the affair, when Theodore first questioned his wife, she offered no explanation. He then turned to an unlikely witness: his young daughter. Did Beecher come by the house when Theodore was gone? Did the pastor and Elizabeth spend time alone, secluding themselves in the parlor? The child answered both questions in the affirmative. Elizabeth, confronted with her daughter's testimony, confessed to the affair. The usually serene house descended into chaos. Theodore rushed to his recently commissioned portrait of Beecher and ripped it off the wall. How could he—the most respected pastor in the nation—have defiled Theodore's marital bed? It soon dawned on Theodore that the child Elizabeth was carrying might not be his.[1]

After several months of trying to process what happened to his family, Theodore confided in his friend Frank Moulton, who confronted the minister. For years to come, Moulton would maintain that Beecher confessed to the affair and begged for forgiveness. Moulton also approached Elizabeth but employed harsher strategies with her. With his gun drawn, Moulton demanded that Elizabeth produce an immediate written confession, "under penalty of instant death."[2] Elizabeth complied. Soon all of Brooklyn—and, eventually, the nation—would come to learn of the affair. The Beecher-Tilton scandal would become the biggest religious sensation of the nineteenth century.

This Gilded Age drama unfolded during an unprecedented time of expansion for the press. The publishing industry had grown exponentially

Disgraced: How Sex Scandals Transformed American Protestantism. Suzanna Krivulskaya, Oxford University Press.
© Oxford University Press 2025. DOI: 10.1093/oso/9780197599686.003.0003

in the four decades since the penny press revolution changed the course of media history. As newspapers multiplied in volume and circulation, the subjects they covered and the language they employed transformed as well. What had been unspeakable (or, at least, unprintable) in the 1830s was now discussed with newfound candor. By the 1870s, scandal had become common newspaper parlance.[3]

It began with politics. In 1871, the *New York Times* ran a series of stories that implicated the head of New York's Tammany Hall, William "Boss" Tweed, in cronyism, political corruption, and financial fraud. Tweed himself recognized the political and social power of newspapers as he complained about Thomas Nast, the preeminent illustrator for *Harper's Weekly*, who had been printing cartoons that were critical of the Tweed administration.[4] "Stop them damned pictures," Tweed reportedly pleaded. "I don't care so much what the papers say about me. My constituents can't read. But, damn it, they can see pictures!"[5] Tweed even attempted to bribe Nast— offering the artist an all-expenses-paid European vacation in exchange for a halt to the cartoons.[6] Nast declined the desperate bid and remained in the business of pithy, biting commentary on the realities of the new age of excess.

The following year, the *New York Sun* would break another story of political corruption—this one reaching all the way to the executive branch of the federal government. In 1867, Oakes Ames, a congressman from Massachusetts, had bribed fellow lawmakers, including Vice President Schuyler Colfax, with cash and discounted shares in Crédit Mobilier—a scam construction company set up by the executives at Union Pacific Railroad to build the transcontinental railroad and line their pockets in the process. Following an investigation, Ames was censured by the House of Representatives. The Republican Party took Schuyler Colfax's name off the ticket in the quickly approaching presidential election, as the press cemented its newly harnessed power to hold politicians accountable.

If lawmakers were being exposed as dangerously corrupt, could religious leaders be any more trustworthy? Probing this query became one of the goals of Gilded Age newspapers—even ones that had previously been skeptical of dealing in sensation. The leap from politics to religion was an obvious one: the two domains were intimately connected in the nation's history. In the antebellum era, Anglo-Americans were profoundly concerned with the potentially harmful influence of all forms of non-Protestant religion as they worried about sustaining their young democracy.

Nativism—the distrust, fear, and hatred of groups deemed not authentically "American"—first emerged as a coherent ideology in the first half of the nineteenth century. Disestablishment and freedom of religion notwithstanding, Anglo-Americans were wary of religious diversity. Increasing rates of Catholic immigration and the rapid rise of new religious movements only added to white Protestants' fears that they might lose their claims to cultural supremacy. In the late 1840s, new political groups, such as the Know-Nothing Party, formed with the explicit goal to amplify anti-immigrant sentiments and enact anti-immigrant laws.

Nativists were no kinder to homegrown movements that deviated from the Protestant ideal. Soon after Joseph Smith rose to prominence as the founder of the Church of Jesus Christ of Latter-day Saints, the prophet and his followers were met with polemical denunciations and physical violence.[7] In 1862, the federal government introduced legislation specifically designed to curb the rise of polygamous marriages sanctioned by the Mormon church.[8] Whatever threatened Protestant hegemony—newcomers, new theologies, or new family arrangements—was met with determined assault from the majority. Clergy lectured against Catholic devotion.[9] Lay alarmists denounced Mormon doctrines.[10] Newspapers provided no shortage of sensationalism in their grim tales of Catholic dens and Mormon depravity.[11] And while coverage of Protestant ministers' misdeeds was certainly not unheard of prior to the Gilded Age, it was hardly ubiquitous. This changed when the news of Henry Ward Beecher's affair became public.

It is difficult to overstate the level of celebrity Beecher enjoyed in the 1870s. The minister seemed to have an almost genetic predisposition for fame. He was the son of Lyman Beecher, prominent revivalist and president of a theological seminary, nine of whose thirteen children would become writers. Two of the daughters, women's education advocate Catharine Beecher and bestselling novelist Harriet Beecher Stowe, achieved significant renown at a time when public recognition was largely reserved for men. Their brother Henry first rose to prominence as a fiery lecture circuit orator in the 1850s. An important voice on social issues of his day, he had rubbed shoulders with abolitionist William Lloyd Garrison, President Abraham Lincoln, and women's rights advocates Susan B. Anthony and Elizabeth Cady Stanton. Men admired him. Women loved him. By 1870, Beecher had become, in the words of one biographer, "the most famous man in America."[12]

REV. HENRY WARD BEECHER.

Reverend Henry Ward Beecher was the most famous American preacher of the nineteenth century. As fellow minister Lyman Abbott wrote about Beecher, "His wit and humor, his imagination, his emotional power, dazzle and sway men. While they are under the charm of his personality they do not stop to consider whither he is carrying them; when they look back they do not know who has carried them, and so unconscious has been the transference that often they are unaware that it has even taken place." Library of Congress Prints and Photographs Division, LC-DIG-pga-02132

Within the first decade of leading Brooklyn's Plymouth Church, Beecher became America's favorite pastor. With him in charge, membership skyrocketed. The average Sunday attendance rose to three thousand, though the building was designed to accommodate only twenty-five hundred parishioners. Plymouth soon became the center of Brooklyn's social life. Connections forged at church bound the neighborhood together in ways both metaphysical and practical. As one contemporary observer remarked, "It is possible to live in Brooklyn without owning a pew in Beecher's Church, but it is not respectable. Your butcher will not trust you unless you do, and you will find it impossible to run up a bill at the baker's."[13] Tourists made visiting Plymouth Church a priority for their itineraries. Luckily, the church was not difficult to find. As one anecdote went, when prospective visitors from Manhattan asked for directions, they were told to "cross Fulton Ferry and follow the crowd."[14] All Sunday crowds in New York led to Beecher.

When the allegations of an affair with Elizabeth Tilton surfaced, Beecher's admirers were shaken. For Beecher to fall due to infidelity meant that the nation would be forced to weather a kind of spiritual crisis. People trusted Beecher and his moral guidance on issues as significant as abolitionism and civil war. They believed his theology. Just as importantly, they enjoyed and needed Beecher. In a nation divided by theological, ideological, and social differences, Beecher provided a platform for the kind of inoffensive gospel that had the potential to unite the faithful. The "Gospel of Love," they called it. As the *New York Times* explained, Beecher's message could "be summed up in this formula—that there is nothing in the Christian religion but love."[15] The characterization was not entirely accurate: the Calvinism of Beecher's youth and religious training still informed his theology of divine judgment and punishment, but Beecher's emphasis on love was, indeed, revolutionary.[16] Unlike his Puritan predecessors' deity, Beecher's God was forgiving, loving, and profoundly unconcerned with dogma.[17] Through several national crises, Beecher's theology managed to speak across regional and ideological divides. This was a softer, gentler, more leisurely kind of gospel: mild enough to appeal to the majority. Now, in the midst of Beecher's personal crisis, the majority needed the pastor to defend his reputation so their own faith might emerge vindicated.

Despite the almost universal approval, Beecher had his critics, too. Conservatives begrudged him his liberal theology, while freethinkers faulted him for not being progressive enough. One freethinker would be single-handedly responsible for publicizing Beecher's domestic woes. Victoria Woodhull was a prominent spiritualist and free love advocate. She was famous and ambitious. A champion of women's rights, she was the first woman to run for president, with the African American abolitionist Frederick Douglass as her vice presidential running mate, in 1872. To no one's surprise, the Woodhull-Douglass ticket lost, but Woodhull still managed to stay in the public eye. Three days before Americans voted to re-elect President Ulysses S. Grant, Woodhull published "The Beecher-Tilton Scandal Case" in her newspaper, *Woodhull & Claflin's Weekly*. In the article,

WASHINGTON, D. C.—THE JUDICIARY COMMITTEE OF THE HOUSE OF REPRESENTATIVES RECEIVING A DEPUTATION OF FEMALE SUFFRAGISTS, JANUARY 11TH—A LADY DELEGATE READING HER ARGUMENT IN FAVOR OF WOMAN'S VOTING, ON THE BASIS OF THE FOURTEENTH AND FIFTEENTH CONSTITUTIONAL AMENDMENTS.—See Page 317.

Victoria Woodhull testifies in favor of women's suffrage before the House Judiciary Committee in 1871. She is surrounded by fellow women's rights advocates, many of whom would turn against her after she published her exposé of Henry Ward Beecher the following year.
Library of Congress Prints and Photographs Division, LC-DIG-ppmsca-58145

Woodhull publicized Theodore Tilton's discovery of the "criminal intimacy" that had taken place between his pastor and his wife.[18] The story became an instant sensation. The newspaper, which Woodhull ran with her sister Tennessee Claflin, had a modest circulation of three thousand copies and cost readers two dollars with an annual subscription or ten cents per issue if purchased individually.[19] At the end of 1872, after the Beecher story ran, the sisters claimed that the circulation rose to 27,500.[20]

Woodhull's motivations for exposing Beecher were more sophisticated than the sensational nature of her exposé would suggest. She was an ardent defender of women's rights, including the right of women to control their bodies and to choose their sexual partners. Like other radical freethinkers, Woodhull believed that marriage was a corrupt institution that took away women's fundamental freedoms. Under the legal system of coverture inherited from British common law, as soon as a woman married, she lost most individual rights. Wives were subsumed by the legal personas of their husbands. As a feme covert, a married woman could not make contracts, draft wills, or trade property without her husband's authority and consent.[21]

In most states, divorce could be obtained only by presenting evidence of abuse or adultery. Few women dared to bring such lawsuits, and fewer still were believed by the courts when they did.[22] Marriage thus bound men and women together for life. Woodhull reasoned that if two citizens—born free and endowed with inalienable rights—got married but later decided to break that union, they ought to be free to do so without interference from the state. "To love," Woodhull argued, was "a right higher than the Constitution or the laws."[23] What was adulterous, she said, was not leaving a previous partner in a consensual manner, but rather staying in a marriage out of convenience or, worse, legal obligation. What Woodhull wanted was, in short, free love: the ability to enter and end relationships without government interference.

This stance, reasonable as it may have seemed to Woodhull, was controversial in the 1870s. Woodhull's unconventional positions ostracized her from the more conservative women's rights activists, including one Beecher sister, Isabella Beecher Hooker. Shortly before Woodhull published her exposé, Hooker tried to disparage Woodhull's radical views at a public gathering. Hooker's critical comments were quickly silenced, however, when another attendee pointed out that "it would ill become these women and especially a Beecher, to talk of antecedents or to cast any smirch on Mrs. Woodhull, for I am reliably assured that Henry Ward Beecher preaches to at least twenty of his mistresses every Sunday."[24] Woodhull knew that this comment was more than a clever retort. She had just heard that Elizabeth Tilton had confessed to her affair with the pastor. Like her defender at that meeting, Woodhull believed that the Beechers were hypocritical in their views on sexual morality. Perhaps exposing the Reverend Beecher—the beloved symbol of Christian innocence—as a free lover would finally get her point across.

Woodhull searched the archives of other reform movements for strategies. From abolitionist William Lloyd Garrison, who started the nation's first anti-slavery newspaper, Woodhull learned that sometimes, in order to change things, "reputations had to suffer." Garrison had taught her the merits of not only attacking slavery in the abstract but also "dragging to the light" the individual perpetuators of the system, thereby shocking the public out of its complicity. Woodhull decided that Beecher's reputation was both a worthy sacrifice for her cause and a good strategic target. He was charismatic, well liked, and, as far as Woodhull was concerned, ostensibly a free lover. For Woodhull, Beecher's crime lay not in his rumored affairs but in his hypocrisy. She saw nothing wrong with a more open kind of sexuality, as long as one's theology could also be liberal enough to allow for more flexible familial arrangements. Unlike most Americans who would come to see infidelity as Beecher's most egregious crime, Woodhull intended to condemn his theology, not his adultery per se. "The fault I find with Mr. Beecher," she explained, was "the exact opposite to that for which the world will condemn him."[25]

Woodhull's revelation immediately became a local sensation, and the struggling enterprise that was *Woodhull and Claflin's Weekly* was suddenly revived. Copies of the November 2 issue sold secondhand for as much as $40 apiece—the equivalent of over $800 today.[26] The sensation became costly in another sense too: Woodhull and her sister were arrested on federal obscenity charges and taken to Ludlow Street jail the day after publishing the exposé.[27]

The architect of Woodhull's arrest was the young and ambitious Presbyterian moral reformer Anthony Comstock. At twenty-eight, he was at the start of what would turn out to be an illustrious career in anti-vice activism, and Woodhull became his perfect target. She was, in Comstock's view, a rabble-rouser whose dangerous, un-Christian ideas could corrupt the nation. Prosecuting Woodhull for obscenity would eliminate the most outspoken critic of Victorian sexual mores and bring much-needed attention to Comstock himself.[28] Although Woodhull got off on a technicality (the federal obscenity law on the books in 1872 did not yet apply to newspapers), the arrest, the negative publicity, and the drawn-out court battle put a damper on her crusade for free love. Comstock, on the other hand, would use the arrest to bolster his résumé in anti-vice work. The 1873 federal legislation colloquially known as the Comstock Act criminalized the dissemination of "obscene" materials through the mail. Publishing scandal was now perilous business.

For a while after Woodhull's arrest, the Beecher-Tilton case was discussed only in whispers. Few dared repeat the allegations in print, but curiosity lingered. Leon Oliver, a Woodhull sympathizer, published the first of many books about the scandal in 1873. He opened with a note of caution: "In presenting this book to the reading public, neither the author, or publishers, have any desire, or intention, to pander to prurient or depraved tastes, or to violate the sanctity of private lives." But, the prefatory note continued, Beecher and Tilton were hardly private citizens: they were public figures who had used "the press, the pulpit and the platform" to broadcast their "peculiar doctrines and theories." Besides, since they had made their domestic affairs public, it was only fair for outside observers "to canvass their actions, and inquire how far *their own lives* conform to the rules they so zealously prescribe for the guidance of others." As far as Oliver was concerned, being a public person was an inherent impediment to privacy. In a short passage, Oliver articulated what would ultimately become the creed of gossip columns: celebrity came at the cost of constant public scrutiny.[29]

Journalists, who were constrained by libel and obscenity laws, grew frustrated by Beecher's silence on the matter. His parishioners reported that the pastor dismissed the allegations by equating Woodhull's revelations to metaphorical garbage. "If I am walking down the street," Beecher said, "and a chambermaid empties a slop bucket on my head, what else can I do than go home, take a bath, and put on clean clothes?"[30] Dismissing rumors of infidelity with a joke, Beecher tried to avoid further speculation. Privately, he had labored to keep the story from becoming public for several years—offering Theodore Tilton prestigious editorial positions and urging Frank Moulton to keep their secret.[31]

For a while, silence behooved Beecher. Much of the public and most of his colleagues stood behind the minister. Letters of unconditional confidence in his upstanding character began pouring in the day of the exposé's unveiling. Richard Storrs, the second most popular pastor in New York City, offered to help defend Beecher from slander. The Plymouth Church congregation recommended that the pastor's salary, which was already at a record high of $20,000, be increased by 25 percent. Beecher declined the offer but relished the sentiment.[32] Brooklyn newspapers such as the *Daily Eagle* refused to reprint the accusations and assumed the scandal would go away, since neither they nor their respectable readers took Woodhull seriously. As the *New York Evening Telegram* put it, "Mr. Beecher is too strong, too self-centered, too well anchored on moral ground; he has too secure a lodgment in the public heart; not to rise superior over all this mountain of nastiness."[33] Letters to newspaper editors echoed this sentiment. "As far as I am concerned," wrote one reader of the *Eagle*, "and I may say as far as the true friends of Mr. Beecher are concerned, the matter is already fully and justly disposed of by his contempt and silence."[34]

Still, the "mountain of nastiness" continued to grow. Silence could prevail only for a moment. The credibility of Beecher's entire denomination—not just his personal reputation—was at stake in the scandal. As one Chicago Congregational weekly opined, "The Christian public are anxious that Mr. Beecher should be vindicated from these ruthless assaults, which they believe to have originated in malice and attempts to collect blackmail."[35] Other denominations' publications were beginning to feel less charitable toward the minister. To them, Beecher's "ominous and protracted" silence was no longer a sign of innocence but of culpability. "Why is it," asked the Methodist *Vermont Christian Messenger*, "that, through some duly qualified representatives, Mr. Beecher does not give his friends throughout the country, and the general public, the benefit of an authorized and unqualified denial of the Woodhull charges?"[36] The gravity of the accusation demanded a response.

In their search for answers, some newspapermen established entire new enterprises. The New York editor Edward H. G. Clark grew so frustrated with Beecher's silence that he took to the printing press himself. The *Thunderbolt*, a four-page leaflet Clark produced, was dedicated exclusively to Beecher's scandal. The editor was far from a freethinker, let alone an advocate of free love, but he argued that the "orthodox pulpit" that tried to shield Beecher from allegations of adultery was as much "a menace" to the public as were Woodhull's radical ideas about marriage. "If Beecher himself," Clark wrote, "*would only be honest, and not try to garrote the prospects of his race to cover his own frailties*, I could hug him in ten minutes. But he prefers the 'orthodox' embraces of 'twenty mistresses' and a few millions of fools." Although Clark had little patience for Woodhull (he believed that she "ought to be hanged" for exposing the scandal), he was even less charitable toward those who, he thought, worked to cover up the affair. "The American press," he argued, "has been the mere skunk of the church, bribed by subscription-list to save Beecher in a universal stench of black-mail!" Tasteless as he found Woodhull's tactics, Clark recognized the importance of the exposé's meaning for the nation. He believed that Beecher had to be disgraced so that honest religion could flourish.[37]

In the summer of 1873, the story got more complicated. Henry C. Bowen was the editor of the abolitionist Congregational weekly *The Independent*, for which both Beecher and Tilton had worked. Bowen was also a prominent member of Beecher's congregation. In fact, it was Bowen who had convinced Beecher to change pastorates and leave Indianapolis for Brooklyn in 1847. Bowen had stood by the minister at the start of the saga, but in June 1873, he made several statements that appeared to incriminate Beecher. (Rumor had it that Bowen's late wife had confessed to an affair with the pastor on her deathbed.) As Bowen joined the chorus of Beecher's accusers, the *Chicago Times* challenged Beecher to respond to the new charges, no matter the consequences: "Come to the front and center, Henry Ward Beecher, you are but human—let us have the truth though the heavens fall!"[38] Given the gravity of the accusations, newspapers began to demand the truth—or, at the very least, sensation. Silence did not sell.

Beecher responded by writing a letter to the editor of his hometown newspaper, the *Brooklyn Daily Eagle*. The minister dismissed the idea that credible evidence against his moral soundness existed. He provided no new evidence, concluding instead, "I will only add that the stories and rumors which have for some time past been circulated about me, are grossly untrue, and I stamp them in general and in particular as utterly false."[39]

By 1874, the media seemed united in urging Beecher to respond to the allegations fully. The *Chicago Daily Tribune* voiced the demand: "The country calls on Mr. Beecher to come forward and in express terms make affidavit of his innocence, or confess his guilt.... If while he preaches purity he practices the arts of the seducer, and attempts the ruin of other men's wives; if, in other words, his preaching and practice do not agree, he is a hypocrite."[40] Congregationalists, the *Tribune* advised, would be wise to thoroughly examine all accusations and dismiss Beecher if necessary in order to save the purity of their religion from the corrupting influence of hypocrisy. Other newspapers echoed the *Tribune*'s challenge: Beecher had to either prove the allegations false or step down from his position and succumb to the consequences of his immorality. From the *New York Times* to the *Memphis Appeal*, newspapers around the country pleaded with Beecher and the Congregationalists to address the rumors of adultery.[41] Even some newspapers that had defended Beecher prior to 1874 joined the campaign to get the minister to speak on the matter. San Francisco's Black newspaper *The Elevator* reprinted a *New York Tribune* appeal for Beecher to make "some reply" to the serious attack against him.[42]

Although most Christian newspapers bemoaned the persistent perpetuation of the drama, some began to question Beecher's innocence. "No tenderness for any individual, man or woman, should delay for a single day that full explanation that should scatter forever this cloud of suspicion," wrote the editors of the *New York Evangelist*. Beecher owed it to the nation and to the cause of Christianity to come clean with the truth—which, the paper hoped, would be enough to stop any future rumors. After all, this larger-than-life figure stood for larger-than-life things: "The Name which is above every name suffers by being dragged into the dust in the person of its representatives." Through Beecher, God was slandered by scandal.[43]

Although exaggerated, such analyses were not entirely ungrounded. For some observers, Beecher's troubles became personal hurdles in their spiritual journeys. If Beecher fell, their worlds would collapse with him. A man from Babylon, New York, who had never met Beecher in person, expressed as much in his letter to the minister.

> Dear Sir,
> Please do excuse the forwardness of one who almost worships you. Although I have never seen your face and never heard you speak your sermons and Friday eve talks is [sic] ever present with me. I have confidence in you and have gained or made many enemies by my plain expressions with relation to you. I have always been confident of your innocence of the charges laid to you. I have said and say now if you fall, *no more of humanity for me.* I told a clergyman today in my own place if you should plead guilty of the charges made against you, I should never place confidence in any mortal being and *I would not.* I have perfect confidence in your innocence, and all I wish is a chance to take your hand and expect my good feeling and confidence in you as a Leader of all men and a pattern for us all to follow. If you will give me your address and the day and hour that I can see you in Brooklyn or NY City, I should be satisfied and consider it an inestimable priveldge [sic].
>
> Yours,
> J. O. Smith[44]

In addition to potentially harming religion's reputation, the scandal was also dangerous for American morality writ large. "The corrupting influence of the scandal upon public morals," argued the editors of one southern newspaper, "can scarcely be over-estimated. Here is a subject that under ordinary circumstances would be tabooed in decent society. But because a great clergyman is involved it necessarily fills the thoughts of everybody."[45] Public morality was especially compromised when it came to women, who existed in the impossible position of being imagined as both the guardians of Victorian mores and also, simultaneously, porously impressionable blank slates. *Frank Leslie's Illustrated Newspaper* charged that the scandal was "calculated to injure religion and to debase the morals of young girls who read newspapers."[46]

Girls who read newspapers (and even girls who did not) had always been a particular concern for the Beecher clan. The oldest of the Beecher siblings, Catharine, published her celebrated *Treatise on Domestic Economy for the Use of Young Ladies at Home and at School* in 1841. The book portrayed women as the nation's moral guardians, whose sensibilities had to be cultivated through domesticity, piety, and moral instruction. If Henry Ward Beecher was now leading women astray from the domestic ideal, the Beecher brand would suffer. The siblings may have disagreed on whether their brother was innocent (Isabella Beecher Hooker believed that Woodhull's charges were true), but they all wished that the scandal would go away. The sooner Beecher addressed the rumors, the sooner public morality would be restored to its proper equilibrium.

In July 1874, Beecher reluctantly appointed six men—all prominent Brooklynites in good standing with Plymouth Church—to an internal committee tasked with investigating Woodhull's charges. Theodore Tilton and Frank Moulton, the primary accusers, were invited to testify. Newspapers rushed to cover the affair. Several dozen reporters attended the hearings and described the developments in daily columns.

Elizabeth Tilton, who had confessed to the affair four years earlier, had since retracted her confession. She also moved out of the house that she shared with Theodore and was now defending Beecher. But Theodore Tilton and Frank Moulton had damning evidence on hand: Elizabeth's letter of confession, penned under duress in 1870, and Beecher's letter of apology, written the following year, in which the pastor sorrowfully acknowledged an unspecified wrongdoing against the Tiltons.

To get ahead of the new evidence, Beecher took to the press. The minister understood that the press controlled public sentiment; he had once referred to the newspaper as "the most efficacious secular book that ever was published in America."[47] A few days before the investigation was set to commence, Beecher wrote to the editor of the *Brooklyn Argus* and gave "the most explicit, comprehensive and solemn denial" of any dishonorable connection between himself and Elizabeth Tilton.[48]

Beecher's adamant denial came a little too late. Wealthy nineteenth-century men wrote a lot of letters, and many of the letters Beecher, Tilton, and Moulton exchanged had already been leaked to the press. Newspapers like New York's *Daily Graphic* trusted the evidence of the letters more than any abstract denunciation of adultery rumors. "No one can read [Moulton's] statement," read one opinion piece, "without being convinced that the first preacher in America has been guilty of a foul and dastardly wrong, and has doubled the original crime by his efforts to hide it." The *Graphic* proclaimed that the newspaper's purpose was "to expose all shams and smite down all hypocrisies," without regard for "persons, positions, or respectabilities." Beecher was guilty, and the *Graphic* would not rest until everyone knew it.[49]

Why was the *Graphic* so harsh on Beecher and so certain of his guilt? The answer lies, in part, in its roster of contributors. Among them was prominent women's rights leader Elizabeth Cady Stanton, who worried about how the negative publicity generated by the scandal might affect her cause. Stanton and her colleague Susan B. Anthony were themselves implicated in the drama: the women were friendly with the Tiltons, who had shared the story of adultery with them back in 1870. Theodore Tilton confided in Stanton; Elizabeth confessed to Anthony. Elizabeth would later deny this confession, but after multiple admissions and retractions, she was not a particularly reliable witness. Whatever the truth of the affair may have been, Stanton and Anthony were anxious about how their connection to the scandal would affect the fragile movement for women's rights.

One thing was clear: these early feminists did not care for America's favorite pastor. Anthony had a close friendship with Isabella Beecher Hooker—the only Beecher sibling who would openly question her brother's innocence (and who would later be ostracized by the family on account of her skepticism). In 1873, Anthony had advised Isabella, who was understandably shaken by the scandal, not to "allow your feelings to be so wrought upon because of another's falseness." The main actors in the scandal, Anthony believed, "seem to have put their heads together to lie through the whole with a perfect God and Truth defying spirit—and they must go their own way to destruction." Anthony encouraged Isabella to channel her energy into working for women's suffrage instead of getting any more involved in the controversy.[50]

Stanton echoed Anthony's sentiments. By 1874, she regretted having been involved in the saga—and especially repeating what she knew to Woodhull. "Of course I admit," Stanton wrote to Anthony, "that I have made an awful blunder in not keeping silent so far as you were concerned on this terrible Beecher-Tilton scandal." Stanton lamented the fact that the "whole odium of this *scandalum magnatum*" had reflected negatively on the suffrage movement and explained that she was "hence obliged" to work against being associated with Beecher's troubles. That the cause of women's rights had come under scrutiny made Stanton "feel like writing for every paper daily." She then admitted to having written several articles, incognito, for the *Daily Graphic*.[51]

So it was likely Stanton and perhaps other women's rights advocates who published anti-Beecher articles. Distancing themselves from the scandal, these activists attempted to condemn Beecher and defend women's rights, which was no easy task at a time when the very idea of women's equality was a radical proposition. "Whatever there was of respectability in this woman's rights movement," opined the *Detroit Free Press*, echoing other critics, "the Brooklyn scandal has killed it."[52] Understanding the importance of public perception—and the role of the press in cultivating good reputations—Stanton went on the offensive, even as she regretted being "too silent when I know I should be thundering against this wholesale slaughter of womanhood." Nonetheless, she remained optimistic. "When Beecher falls, as he must," she wrote to Anthony, "he will pull all he can down with him. But we must not let the cause of woman go down in the smash. It is innocent."[53]

In this publicity war, all parties were turning to newspapers, whose influence continued to expand. What began as a modest enterprise in 1830 with just 1,200 newspapers in the entire nation would increase almost tenfold by 1880, when the number reached 10,761. The daily newspaper industry grew at an even faster rate. Americans went from being able to read just 65 dailies in 1830 to having their choice of 971 by 1880.[54]

Beecher had the major Brooklyn newspapers in his corner. His critics did what they could on the pages of smaller New York and New England periodicals. The latest to join the newspaper war was Theodore Tilton—with one of the most influential midwestern newspapers on his side. Tilton befriended the *Chicago Daily Tribune*'s editor, George Alfred Townsend, who solicited private correspondence between the Tiltons. With Theodore's permission, Townsend reprinted the letters in his newspaper. In publicizing private missives, Tilton wanted to persuade the public that his relationship with Elizabeth was loving and pure—until it was corrupted by the lustful advances of their pastor.

The *Tribune* dedicated half of its August 13 issue to the letters. The correspondence dated back to the mid-1860s and revealed a warm relationship between the spouses. During long stretches of absence, the Tiltons wrote about their love, called each other by affectionate nicknames, and professed their commitment to the relationship. "My Delight," Elizabeth addressed one letter to Theodore, "Do all love as we do?" In another letter, she described intense feelings for Theodore: "I believe I love you as well as you wish me to; I should be wretched if I loved stronger....I have an irresistible desire to penetrate somewhere that I may once again look upon your dear face and kiss your sweet lips." Theodore reciprocated, closing one of his missives, "I re-read *all* your letters every day. My dear love, pet, wife, and guardian, you are more than half of my life." The picture that emerged from the letters was diametrically opposed to the story that Beecher's supporters were promoting in the press: that Theodore and Elizabeth had an unhappy marriage and that Beecher had nothing to do with its dissolution. The publication of the letters created a stir. The scandal had already produced hundreds of pages of articles and editorials, but none of the evidence presented to the public had been as detailed or as intimate as private correspondence between two spouses who trusted their pastor to nourish their union.[55]

The Christian home had long been revered in the Protestant imagination, and the Tilton letters exemplified the kind of intimacy that a godly marriage was supposed to cultivate. Beecher's alleged meddling in the marital union of his parishioners frightened those who idealized the Protestant family, as one reader of the *Tribune* explained in his letter to the editor. The question of Beecher's guilt or innocence had profound implications, the reader argued, because the investigation was supposed to reveal whether "the minister of the Gospel, welcomed in utmost confidence to our families and firesides, and to the sick-chambers of our wives and daughters, be a scoundrel and a hypocrite, or not."[56] The singularity of Beecher's crime did not matter. The danger lay in the proximity of pastors to families, which would need to be reconsidered if Beecher's guilt were to be proven.

Despite this newly articulated concern, the publication of the Tilton letters held little sway over the Plymouth Church committee, which presented its resolutions on August 27, 1874. Unsurprisingly, the group found Beecher not guilty and reaffirmed his "entire innocence and absolute personal purity." The congregation cheered with approval. When the vote to accept the committee's resolution came up, all but Frank Moulton rose from their seats to indicate their approval. When Moulton attempted to voice his protest, the congregation broke out in screams of dissent. To avoid violence, police officers were dispatched to the church. They escorted Moulton outside through the building's side door. Once Moulton made it to his carriage, the crowd followed. They chased him, yelling and hissing, for three city blocks. Unable to keep up with the carriage, the parishioners gave up, walked back to Plymouth, and stayed a while—discussing the scandal long after the church doors closed for the night. Beecher's support grew despite the opposition's best efforts.[57]

At the conclusion of the internal investigation, Beecher reported receiving sixty to seventy letters of support daily.[58] The minister proudly reprinted the letters in his own *Christian Union*—a weekly that, at the time, boasted the largest circulation among religious newspapers worldwide.[59] The support base was as wide as the newspaper's reach: Australian missionaries and Jewish rabbis alike wrote in with votes of confidence and words of encouragement for Beecher and his ministry. Public support undermined the evidence found in private revelations, no matter how hard Tilton and the anti-Beecher coalition worked to cast aspersions on the pastor.

Surviving archival evidence largely supports Beecher's *Christian Union* claims. His incoming correspondence from this period is filled with expressions of "the most heartfelt sympathy" and "the most absolute belief" in his "entire innocence." Some supporters even compared Beecher's troubles to Christ's suffering: here was a man whose closest friends (Tilton, Moulton, and Bowen) betrayed and abandoned him in his darkest hour. Like Christ, Beecher was expected to emerge victorious. A typical letter of support read, "I think you would rejoice did you know that the inmost heart of the Christian people of the country stands firmly by you....I beg the privilege of expressing the sympathy we feel for you and also the hope—most earnest and fond—that you will completely triumph over your enemies and that they may see their error and be led into the better way."[60]

The incessant coverage of the scandal may have ignited ordinary people's passionate defense of Beecher's innocence, but it also fueled the fire of his accusers. The investigative committee's verdict had virtually no impact on the amount of press coverage the case received. In the fall of 1874, months after the investigation concluded, the *New York Times* alone printed 105 stories and thirty-seven editorials about the scandal.[61] Publications that refused to discuss the case got called out by other newspapers for compromising public morality. Ignoring the scandal, those who publicized it argued, helped conceal corruption in high places.[62] In their defense, editors of newspapers that remained silent on the scandal claimed that they worried that publicizing it would result in free advertisement for Beecher's controversial liberal theological views and, as they called it, his "loose system of morality."[63] Even arguing about the merits of discussing the scandal fueled public excitement as the nation stood divided on the subject of Beecher's culpability. The only thing they could agree on was that Beecher's scandal and its coverage mattered a great deal.

In addition to newspapers, pamphlets, and books, the scandal was also making its way into popular culture through music. The 1870s saw a development of a new genre—political protest songs, often used by women's rights activists and temperance advocates. Political messages folded into rhymes and put to catchy melodies were disseminated across the country, capturing listeners' ears with hummable proselytizing. The music does not survive, but the lyrics to the popular song "The Beecher Scandal!" were printed on broadsides sometime in 1874. The first verse began,

> The Beecher scandal's all the rage,
> And full of jolly fun,
> It's the sensation of the age,
> A joke for every one;
> And every tongue is wagging fast,
> To keep it fresh and new,
> It's Tilton-Beecher first and last
> And Mrs. Tilton too.[64]

One African American newspaper in New Orleans printed a humorous report on the case from the perspective of "a Frenchman," in which intentional misspellings designed to replicate the French accent described the scandal in broad terms by misidentifying the main characters and mangling the details. In the piece, "Harriot Beechare Stowe" became "ze mozare of Onkle Tom, ze blind pianist" and Susan B. Anthony "ze sister of Mark Anthony, who was make love wiz Cleopatra." Adding levity to the otherwise serious matter for one of the nation's prominent abolitionists, the article concluded, "Ze greatest excitement prevails."[65]

The "sensation of the age" had become such an important part of popular culture by August 1874 that some observers bemoaned its omnipresence. "I am tired to death of the Beecher scandal," reported one young woman. "The whole story is revolting—and the letters in very bad taste, setting aside all idea of immorality."[66] Even abroad, casual observers were growing weary of the unending coverage. As the English novelist Anthony Trollope jokingly complained,

> It seems to me that all American news lately has centered in the horrible scandal of the Tiltons & Bechers [*sic*]. If a man is to take another mans [*sic*] wife, why cant [*sic*] he do it without such a fuss? Can it be that the frailties of any man or woman can be worth so much attention as have [*sic*] been given to this hero & heroine? As a writer of novels I feel jealous of the popularity of the story.[67]

Trollope must have felt even more envious of the attention the following year, when Theodore Tilton sued Beecher, and the already oversaturated coverage increased exponentially.

The civil trial unfolded over the course of six months, between January and July 1875. Tilton sued Beecher for "alienation of affections." The minister, Tilton alleged, "debauched and carnally knew" Elizabeth. In addition to compensation for legal fees, Tilton sought $100,000 (the equivalent of over $2 million today) in punitive damages.[68]

With money, reputations, and public morality at stake, the case was sure to continue selling newspapers. Fifty to sixty reporters attended the trial daily. A handful of journalists acted as stenographers—transcribing the proceedings and adding marginal notes that described the action in the courtroom.[69] Occasionally, the judge would ask the reporters to read recorded testimony back; the Beecher trial was a collaborative affair. Readers could not get enough. Tens of thousands of people read daily transcripts and examined sketches of court scenes in illustrated newspapers. "The Tilton case," editorialized one publication, "is more remarkable than any tale ever told in fiction."[70] So ubiquitous was the consumption of daily ratios of the story that some reported staying "up late to read the Beecher & Tilton scandal" in letters and diaries.[71]

This level of publicity was unprecedented. "It is astonishing," wrote one critic in 1875, "how much mankind and womankind have come to rely on the daily newspaper for time-killing. The actor, the poet, the orator, the pastry cook, the tapster, even the clergyman, is outdone by the journalist in the knack of gratifying society, with small trouble and cost." According to the article, some educators even proposed introducing newspapers into required school curricula in order to "cultivate among our boys and girls an early taste for newspaper reading." But the essay cautioned against such measures: "Suppose some morning, when our boys and girls shall have bought the papers, their chief attraction turns out to be, as it probably will, an enormous batch of the Beecher scandal, or some other savory dish of

Henry Ward Beecher is about to swear on the Bible before taking the stand in his defense in the 1875 *Tilton v. Beecher* civil trial. The satirical caption on the cover of Frank Leslie's newspaper reads, "The only thing he won't kiss." Library of Congress Prints and Photographs Division, LC-USZ62-114828 adultery such as first-class newspapers furnish—will that be nice for the school lesson and for the school recess?" The savory dish of adultery made newspapers both alluring and fraught with danger.[72]

New Yorkers who could afford to avoid daily menial labor flocked to the Brooklyn courthouse to hear the testimony. The building could comfortably hold three hundred spectators; the Beecher trial drew a daily crowd of five hundred, with hundreds more gathering outside and hoping to be admitted.[73] To solve the capacity problem, the court began issuing daily entry tickets, which inadvertently created a secondary market for scalpers, who resold them for five dollars apiece. With hundreds of hopeful spectators turned away, nearby saloons profited from the scandal by attracting daytime clientele.[74]

While the men drank, the women showered Beecher with flowers. A group of female supporters took to delivering elaborate daily bouquets to the courtroom. According to the *New York Times*, the flowers did not go unnoticed by the plaintiff, and soon both sides of the isle were covered with supporters' bouquets. If nothing else, the *Times* noted, the flowers helped to cover up the smell of the sweaty, overcrowded chamber.[75] Other commentators took a less favorable view of the flower competition and called the floral tributes "wreaths round the man-hole of a sewer."[76] Whatever the flowers' metaphorical significance was, when court adjourned for the day, the most eager spectators would collect the bouquets that were left behind and "carry them away as mementoes."[77] Everyone wanted a part of the case. As one contemporary observed, "No trial in modern times has so excited and so occupied the public mind as has this of Tilton *vs.* Beecher."[78]

Occasionally, the sensationalism of the trial cost people their sanity, and not just in the abstract. According to the *Chicago Tribune*, three people "went crazy over the great scandal" and were sent to the insane asylum in April 1875. "Two of them were women," who, the article explained with casual misogyny, "addled their weak brains with keeping track of the case."[79] Those who did not "go crazy" but still rigorously followed the developments in the case were decried by reporters as fanatical, especially if they happened to be women. Beecher's female parishioners, reported the *New York Sun*, "have been tempted into rather extravagant displays of zeal and devotion on his behalf" and reportedly got into the habit of "withdraw[ing] their patronage and society from those who doubt the innocence of their idol."[80] The pastor's trial was dividing the nation in tangible, physical ways.

Lay men were affected as well. Interest in the sensation transcended gender, even as men and women expressed their fascination in distinct ways. Men wrote strongly worded letters to newspaper editors. They chided their favorite publications' coverage of the trial. "Allow me to say that while I recognize the [New York] Tribune as a most excellent paper in many respects," wrote one disgruntled male reader, "I am thoroughly disgusted with your editorials on the Beecher trial." The letter writer accused the "daily synopses of the trial" of being "notoriously at variance with the evidence." Worse, he wrote, the twisting of facts "persistently labored to manufacture a public sentiment favorable to Mr. Beecher" was done "while professing a strict neutrality." Any other clergyman in Beecher's position, the letter concluded, "would have succumbed long ago."[81]

While it seemed that everyone in the nation had an opinion on the case, the power of the verdict lay with twelve Brooklyn men who, after 112 days of testimony and seven days of deliberation, still could not agree on a verdict. Nine of them believed in Beecher's innocence; three that he was guilty as charged. "We regret very much," the foreman told the judge, announcing a dull resolution to an otherwise dramatic trial, "that we find it impossible to agree."[82] To Beecher's supporters, the jury's indecision signified complete vindication. As the Minneapolis Daily Tribune put it, exaggerating the jury's confidence in Beecher's innocence, "The fact that eleven of the jury [the number was nine] hold Mr. Beecher innocent, seems to us very nearly equivalent to a verdict for the defendant."[83]

The trial had gone on for so long that even the newspapers that were certain of Beecher's guilt celebrated the unsatisfying conclusion of the proceedings. In an article titled "Let Us Have No More of It," the Memphis Public Ledger bemoaned the fact that the coverage had lasted as long as it did, indicted those who followed it closely, and predicted more moral corruption at the hands of ministers like Beecher. According to the Ledger, Beecher's heterodoxy rendered him dangerous for the morality of the average family. The "vain, pompous blasphemer" was to blame for the "many a household" that would "yet be disrupted."[84] While mourning the hung jury, the Ledger still celebrated the conclusion of the case.

The trial turned out to be a disaster for Tilton and a mere inconvenience, if a prolonged one, for Beecher. Tilton was excommunicated from Plymouth Church and became a pariah in the community. Having challenged the authority of New York's favorite pastor, he became utterly unemployable. Tilton lost his wife, his children, and any hope for a peaceful life or successful career in the United States. Broken and broke, he moved to Paris, where he would spend the rest of his life. Beecher, on the other hand, emerged victorious in the eyes of the adoring public. Another internal investigation by the Congregationalists found him, once again, not guilty. Beecher continued to enjoy broad popularity until his death in 1887.

For weeks after the trial, journalists continued to follow the story—interviewing jury members and reporting from Plymouth Church services. But the incessant, daily coverage subsided. Although the details of the alleged affair remained murky, the story was, for the most part, exhausted. There was not much more that the Tilton-Moulton camp could do to disparage Beecher. Those who believed in Beecher's innocence were content with the results of the trial. His critics remained confident of his guilt.

Despite the outcome, the lengthy trial, replete with messy disclosures, took away some of the nation's innocence. The fundamental question of whether depraved hypocrisy could reside in the holiest places was never fully resolved.[85] The lack of certainty embodied in a hung jury reinforced Americans' increasing skepticism about the inherent goodness of their religious leaders.

The clergy, meanwhile, appeared to back their own. The *New York Herald* summarized the gist of several dozen editorials in religious publications that came out after the verdict. The Baptists, the *Herald* reported, expressed unshaken confidence in Beecher's innocence. The Episcopalians commended the "goodness of Mr. Beecher, this universal benevolence in which he appears to love his enemies about as much as he loves his friends" and reaffirmed his innocence.[86] In addition to recapping the sentiments of the denominational press on the subject, the *Herald* also polled lawyers and clergymen from across the nation to arrive at "the country's verdict." After surveying 117 lawyers and fifty-four ministers from thirteen different states (Table 2.1), the *Herald* concluded that the majority of lawyers thought that Beecher was guilty, whereas the majority of ministers believed he was innocent of adultery, if indiscreet in his relationship with Elizabeth Tilton.

If the nation's clergy sided with the accused, many secular critics remained appalled at what they perceived to be the ongoing injustice of Beecher's vindication. The *New York Times* published a pamphlet reviewing the evidence in the trial and cast more doubt on the pastor's innocence. The publication opened with the assertion that there were "comparatively few who will not in their hearts be compelled to acknowledge that Mr. Beecher's management of his private friendships and affairs has been

Table 2.1 The *New York Herald* survey results regarding Henry Ward Beecher's culpability, representing 117 lawyers and 54 clergy from 13 states

Verdict	Lawyers	Clergy
Guilty	69	7
Innocent	32	26
Guilt of indiscretion only	8	10
In doubt	8	11
Total	**117**	**54**

"The Country's Verdict," *New York Herald*, July 3, 1875

entirely unworthy of his name, position and sacred calling." After reviewing the timeline of the saga and some of the most damning evidence against Beecher, the *Times* expressed hope that the scandal "may lead people in Brooklyn and elsewhere to distrust the new Gospel of Love, and to allow no priests or ministers to come between husband and wife, or to interfere with family ties or sully family honor."[87]

What troubled the *Times* about the trial's conclusion was not just Beecher's apparent guilt but the idea that religion might destroy the most sacred institution in American society: the family. This was a revolutionary assertion. Whereas Catholic priests and polygamous Mormon prophets had long been imagined in nativist literature as direct threats to the family, Protestant ministers had largely escaped such suspicions. In 1875, Protestant family values were the norm. The figure of the pastor was the de facto protector of the family. Beecher's trial changed that. Even Protestants now became suspected of the kind of immorality that threatened to undermine the family.

The *Daily Graphic*, characteristically critical of Beecher, agreed with this assessment. The pastor, the *Graphic* contended, came out of the trial "maimed for life, smitten through and through with a suspicion that to most minds has the moral force of a conviction." The public sentiment, "once so powerfully in his favor," the article claimed, "has completely changed." Beecher may have retained his post, "but his voice has lost its tone of authority and finds no resonance in the air."[88]

On the last point, the *Graphic* would be proven wrong: not only did Beecher manage to attain a new level of popularity, but his celebrity continued to swell long after the trial. The greatest orator in the United States was in no hurry to stop preaching, including on issues of morality. As one southern newspaper put it,

> Let a stranger go into Plymouth Church even one of these hot Sundays—if he is fortunate enough to squeeze his way in—and notice the devout throng of worshippers, hear the matchless sacred melody from thousands of voices, listen to the earnest pleading and preaching of the pastor, and take in the inspiring spirit of the whole surroundings, and it will be very hard for him to come away with the belief that Henry Ward Beecher is an adulterer, a perjurer, and a wanton violator of the sanctities of home.[89]

Persuasiveness, passion, and popularity aided Beecher's redemption.

Satire remained a last resort for Beecher's accusers. Long after the editorials ceased, cartoonists' depictions of the saga would remind onlookers of the great scandal of their age and of the dangers of unchecked power. In 1875, a lithograph titled *Testimony in the Great Beecher-Tilton Scandal Case Illustrated* presented all of the key actors as culpable in various kinds of immorality, from intemperance to adultery.

The central drawing portrays Elizabeth Tilton sitting in Beecher's lap as he caresses her breast. "How do you feel, Elizabeth?" Beecher asks in the picture. "Dear father, I feel so, so," she replies. In the background, her daughter watches. On either side of the couple are two open books: a Holy Bible and one titled *Free Love*. Other illustrations depict attendant depravities: gossip (Woodhull and Tilton taking a swim together), parlor romances (Frank Moulton's wife kissing Beecher), bribery (an African American servant being forced to be a go-between with a bribe in exchange for silence), and intimidation (Beecher's head on the body of a rat being cornered by two dogs with the heads of Moulton and Tilton). The lithograph makes the entire cast of characters morally suspect, with Beecher prominently positioned at the center of their downfall, in proportion to the power he wielded.

The scandal made waves one last time in 1878 when Elizabeth Tilton, once again reversing course, confessed to the affair. Without skipping a beat, Beecher turned to the newspapers to dismiss Elizabeth's latest confession. For the platform for his rebuttal, he chose one of his greatest critics, the *New York Times*.

> I confront Mrs. Tilton's confession with explicit and absolute denial. The testimony to her own innocence and to mine which, for four years, she has

In an ironic pose, Elizabeth Tilton sits on Henry Ward Beecher's lap with a Bible on her lap while her child watches in the background. Surrounding them are illustrations of the key actors in the Tilton-Beecher scandal, including Victoria Woodhull, Theodore Tilton, and Frank Moulton.
Library of Congress Prints and Photographs Division, LC-DIG-pga-03156

made to hundreds, in private and in public, before the court, in writing and orally, I declare to be true. And the allegations now made in contradiction of her uniform, solemn, and unvarying statements hitherto made I utterly deny. I declare her to be innocent of the great transgression.[90]

The Plymouth Church felt less charitable toward Elizabeth. As their pastor declared her innocence in the press, the congregation voted to remove Elizabeth from membership in retaliation. Bitter and resentful, Elizabeth stayed in Brooklyn but became a recluse. According to one obituary, toward the end of her life she refused to read the news and did not allow newspapers in her secluded home.[91] Sensationalism had done enough damage.

Beecher continued to pastor Plymouth Church until he retired in 1882. Few things changed for the minister, but the reputation of Protestantism suffered in his near downfall. After 1875, a shadow of suspicion followed fellow Protestants. The sexual panics at the heart of anti-Catholicism and anti-Mormonism finally extended to Protestant heterodoxy itself. Newspapers would continue to capitalize on the coverage of scandal-prone pastors.

At the height of the saga, when asked for his take on the scandal, a Methodist minister from Illinois remarked that while he was not certain about the verdict, he did not believe the incident would affect Beecher's legacy. "Five hundred years from now," he opined, "the world will read Beecher's sermons and take no notice of the sensation which is now agitating the world, any more than we now think of David's devilments with Uriah's wife."[92] Though sensible, that prediction has not come true. Among a handful of twentieth-century Beecher biographers, only one was hesitant to assign the minister guilt.[93] Whatever the historians' verdict, they seem to agree that the scandal was the most consequential episode in Beecher's life and legacy.

Back in February 1872, months before Victoria Woodhull published her exposé, Thomas Nast printed a *Harper's Weekly* cartoon disparaging her. The imagery would have reminded *Harper's* subscribers of scenes from John Bunyan's *The Pilgrim's Progress*, with Woodhull portrayed as the Gilded Age temptress of good Christian womanhood. In the cartoon, Woodhull is "Mrs. Satan"—complete with horns and wings. In the foreground, she is holding a poster that reads, "Be Saved by Free Love." She looks to the background, where a working-class mother is walking to the edge of a cliff. With her rags and staff, she is carrying two children and a drunken husband on her tired back. The heroic, if downtrodden, mother rejects Woodhull's promise of salvation. In the caption, she says: "I'd rather travel the hardest path of matrimony than follow your footsteps." Although the cartoon ultimately denounces Woodhull, Nast's portrayal of the disintegrating family also serves as a powerful critique of the status quo: the Victorian family ideal rarely worked in practice.

In 1875, it was not just drunken husbands and free love advocates who threatened the family. As both Beecher's defenders and detractors recognized, the scandal created a problem for Protestantism's posterity. The investigation, the trial, and the unending press coverage reversed the roles of temptress and tempter; lines between good religion and promiscuous heterodoxy were blurred. After Beecher, mainstream Protestantism joined the list of institutions whose reputations had been shaken by scandal. Beecher's guilt or innocence was irrelevant. Americans began to monitor

"GET THEE BEHIND ME, (MRS.) SATAN!"—[SEE PAGE 148.]
WIFE (*with heavy burden*). "I'D RATHER TRAVEL THE HARDEST PATH OF MATRIMONY THAN FOLLOW YOUR FOOTSTEPS."

This caricature in *Harper's Weekly* portrays Victoria Woodhull, who championed free love, as Lucifer, as she beckons a struggling wife and mother to abandon her drunken husband. The wife rejects Woodhull's offer and continues down "the hardest path of matrimony"—literally bearing the weight of her husband and two children.

Library of Congress Prints and Photographs Division, LC-USZ62-74994 their Protestant ministers with a posture of suspicion previously reserved for other religions. The moralistic gaze of the newly emboldened press ensured that, going forward, Protestant ministers would be scrutinized as closely as their Catholic and Mormon brethren. With popes, prophets, and preachers alike, universal suspicion now surrounded all manner of religious leaders.

3

Itinerant Passions

At his 1877 trial for adultery, seduction, robbery, and wife desertion, the Methodist minister Alfred Thompson did not appear remorseful. "We all do such things more or less," he told the court.[1] Though startlingly nonchalant, the minister's assessment was not entirely exaggerated. Between 1881 and 1914, one dedicated group of freethinkers documented the alleged crimes of thousands of North American ministers. The enterprising infidels found records of these misdeeds in newspapers across the United States and Canada and cataloged them in a small volume that underwent ten expanding editions in four decades of reissue. Scandal, the freethinkers hoped, could propel social change. The book *Crimes of Preachers in the United States and Canada* alerted believers to the predatory nature of the men (and the occasional woman) who wielded spiritual authority over them.[2] The exposure of scandal was one way through which critics of the existing religious order sought to undermine the establishment; the press, armed with sensation, was their best ally in this endeavor.[3] Each edition of the *Crimes of Preachers* opened with this poem:

> Ten little preachers preaching love divine,
> One kissed a servant girl, then there were nine.
> Nine little preachers preaching sinners' fate,
> One got drunk, then there were eight.
> Eight little preachers showing path to heaven,
> One seduced a brother's wife, then there were seven.
> Seven little preachers exposing Satan's tricks,
> One beat his patient wife, then there were six.
> Six little preachers preaching Christ alive,
> One debauched a little girl, then there were five.
> Five little preachers preaching "sin no more,"
> One raped a "sister," then there were four.
> Four little preachers, pure as they could be,
> One raped an eight-year-old, then there were three.

Disgraced: How Sex Scandals Transformed American Protestantism. Suzanna Krivulskaya, Oxford University Press.
© Oxford University Press 2025. DOI: 10.1093/oso/9780197599686.003.0004

Three little preachers, pity so few,
One murdered his paramour, then there were two.
Two little preachers following the son,
One whipped his child to death, then there was one.
One little preacher in the fold alone,
He committed suicide, then there were none.[4]

Among fraud, murder, swindling, and adultery, ministerial elopements emerged as a prominent thread in the book and in newspaper reporting. (Unlike contemporary elopements, which take the form of unannounced or secretive marriages, nineteenth-century elopements referred to the sudden absconding of two people—one or both of whom may have already been married.) Between 1870 and 1914, at least 266 Protestant ministers abandoned their posts, deserted their wives, and took off in search of better lives with other women.[5] Frequently, these women were their significantly younger parishioners, choir singers, and Sunday school teachers. In some cases, the ministers regretted their elopements and returned home repentant. Other pastors obtained divorces and married their runaway accomplices. Almost half managed to simply vanish and were never heard from again—at least not on the pages of the newspapers that covered their elopements. Practically unheard of before 1870 (*Crimes of Preachers* listed only six such cases from the 1850s and 1860s), stories of runaway preachers exploded in the press in the following decades. Elopement cases rose steadily between the 1870s and the 1890s and began to decline at the start of the twentieth century.

To be sure, elopers represented a minority of Protestant ministers—and an even smaller fraction of the American clerical profession as a whole. According to the US census, there were 43,874 clergy (67 of them were women) in 1870. By 1916, that number would reach 191,796. Considering the proportions, a few hundred runaway pastors hardly represent a trend. Yet on a smaller scale, the rise and fall of elopement scandals raises important questions about the relationship between sexuality and religion, publicity and anonymity, Victorian family ideals and emerging notions of romantic love. Proportionally distributed among all Protestant denominations, eloping pastors became a phenomenon serious enough to warrant significant attention from the press.[6] What motivated these ministers to abandon their careers and families? What exactly were they running from? And what were they running toward?

A priest sits behind prison bars on the cover of the ninth edition of *Crimes of Preachers in the United States and Canada* (1913). He is surrounded by illustrations of other preachers committing indecency, murder, drunkenness, assault, robbery, poisoning, suicide, profanity, and cruelty.

M. E. Billings, *Crimes of Preachers in the United States and Canada*, 9th ed. (New York: Truthseeker, 1913), courtesy New York Public Library

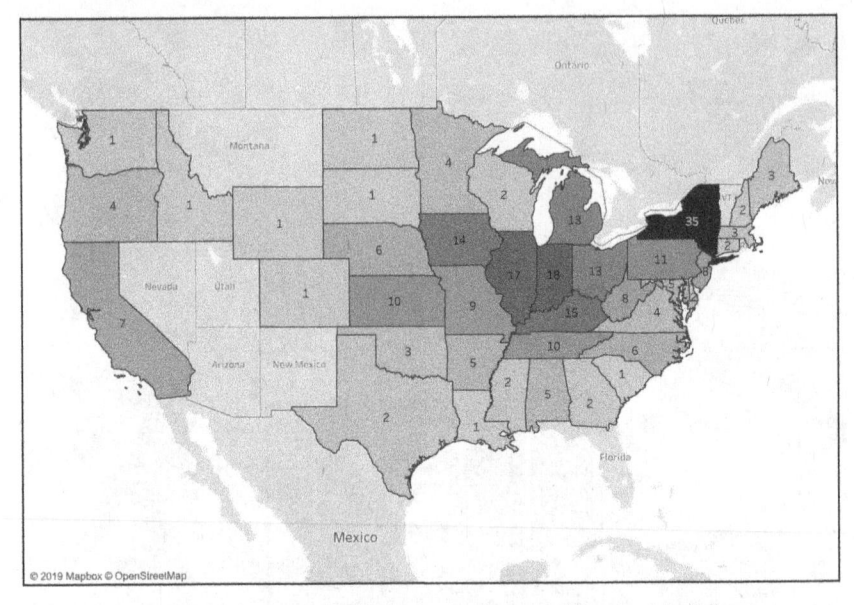

Between 1870 and 1914, at least 258 ministers eloped from within the contiguous United States. The number on each state indicates the total number of ministerial elopements reported in that state. The states with the darker shading represent higher numbers of elopements.

The late nineteenth century introduced unprecedented forms of mobility. The telegraph and the railroad revolutionized how information and bodies traveled through space.[7] This mobility extended to the seemingly unlimited opportunities for remaking oneself, which led some enterprising young men to exploit the very system that enabled such flexibility.[8] Confidence men engaged in all manner of counterfeiting—from faking currency to reinventing identity.[9] The press responded to these developments by exposing corruption and the potential for the abuse of power as serious impediments to the nation's continued success as a democracy.[10] Sensationalism did more than just propel newspaper sales; it also helped hold public figures accountable for their actions, which is perhaps why so many of them kept running away from negative coverage.[11]

Pastors were not exempt. Protestantism had long enjoyed the protections afforded to it by being the religion of the majority. Since the days of the early republic, the press had been called on to guarantee the success of the Protestant pulpit. By the 1870s, as more ministers got caught misbehaving, even Protestantism's journalistic allies were beginning to rethink their

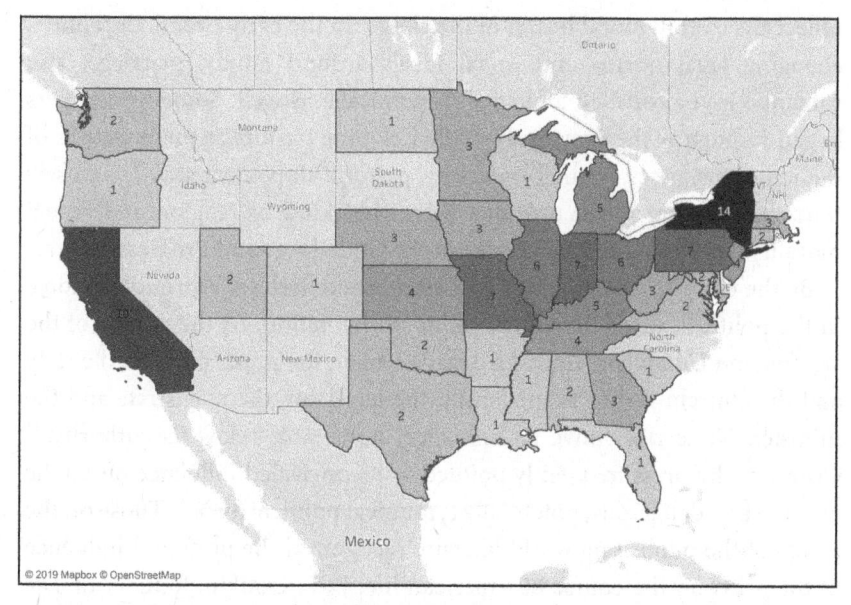

Of the 258 ministers who eloped between 1870 and 1914, 122 were found, arrested, or returned home voluntarily. The number on each state indicates the total number of ministers found in that state. The states with the darker shading represent higher numbers of cases.

allegiances. In an era that prized decorum, the very men who were supposed to guard American morality and embody Protestant respectability abandoned their careers and families in search of better lives with younger women. The press, attuned to the dangers of hypocrisy in the highest echelons of society, tracked their movements and used their scandals for their own purposes: ranging from publicizing sensational exposés aimed at undermining religion's credibility to making thoughtful demands that denominational bodies screen and discipline their erring pastors with more diligence.

In the course of ministerial elopement scandals' rise and fall, the press underwent three distinct stages in its coverage. In the 1870s, sex scandals prompted the press to debate the proper limits of what was morally acceptable to publicize when it came to the sins of Protestant pastors. Once scandal became a widely accepted mode of engagement with the controversial subjects of the day, the press divided into two camps. The first argued that Christian morality was fundamentally compromised. The second insisted that individual ministers' missteps were mere aberrations and did not reflect the overall moral health of the clergy. In the early twentieth century, changing legal norms and social ideals around family, marriage, and romantic love propelled a change in reportage as well. Some newspapers began to portray the previously vilified eloping pastors as mere victims of their circumstances. In their trajectory, pastoral elopement scandals closely mirrored cultural preoccupations with what kind of religion and sexual morality were going to rule the day in the Gilded Age and Progressive Era.

By the early 1870s, the press had established itself as a formidable force in the political, social, and cultural life of the nation. As the editors of the *Washington Union* had argued a decade earlier, the press "controls the state and the church; it directs the family, the legislator, the magistrate and the minister. None rise above its influence, none sink below its authority."[12] Critics of the press frequently pointed to its unrivaled influence on public opinion as a dangerous, potentially tyrannical political force.[13] Those on the inside of the publishing world likewise recognized the profound influence of the press on the course of American life. E. L. Godkin, founder of *The Nation* and editor of the *New York Evening Post*, argued that newspapers were "able, by their mode of reporting the events of the day, to mould public opinion completely."[14] Editors, according to Godkin, were thus tasked with the great responsibility of carefully scrutinizing what they chose to publish. The printed word could build or break reputations. Differentiating his own enterprise from sensational newspapers like the *New York Herald*, Godkin urged fellow newsmakers to reject the admittedly profitable sensationalism in favor of what was moral, good, and pure.[15]

It was not just pleas from editors like Godkin that put a damper on printing the sensational. The 1873 Comstock Act, passed by Congress shortly after Victoria Woodhull published her exposé of Henry Ward Beecher, significantly undermined the freedom of the press. The legislation prohibited the "trade in, and circulation of, obscene literature and articles of immoral use."[16] Designed to suppress the dissemination of "obscene, lewd, or lascivious" material through the mail, the act effectively criminalized not only the circulation of things like erotica, but also all discussion of contraceptives and any mention of sexual content in private correspondence or print. With government surveillance of citizens' morality legalized, those who dared criticize the religious and moral order found themselves vulnerable to censure and persecution.[17]

The concern with preserving the public's morality by censoring what subjects newspapers covered went back to at least the 1820s. For decades, the press and its critics had debated the limits of what was proper to commit to print in order to ensure that the sensitive reading public remained morally uncontaminated by avoiding the obscene. During Reconstruction, white Americans became especially preoccupied with sexual and racial purity. This concern revealed itself in, among other things, the uneven application of obscenity statutes to stories about people of color. Perpetuating racist stereotypes, illustrated newspapers like the *Police Gazette* eschewed reporting on white perpetrators and focused instead on exaggerated or entirely invented reports of sexual assault of white women by African American men.[18] The ostensible morality of white middle-class Americans was thus rhetorically protected through anti-Black discourses of criminality. This was the treacherous cultural moment in which the genre of elopement scandals entered the public imagination.

Like other delicate subjects, elopement coverage was a controversial matter. Sudden disappearances of married ministers were a relatively new development, and some journalists initially cautioned against sensationalizing such reports. In January 1870, the Methodist minister Horace Cooke disappeared from New York City, where he had recently moved with his wife and son. As far as he was concerned, Cooke ran out of love. All pastor Cooke left behind was a note: "I love Mattie; I will care for her tenderly, kindly, lovingly. Inconsistent as it may appear with my present conduct, I ask for no mercy, but am ready to part with my life for the possession of the woman I adore."[19] Mattie Johnson was a sixteen-year-old girl who attended Cooke's Seventh Avenue Methodist Church. Despite the age difference (Cooke was in his late thirties), Mattie had reportedly found Cooke's affections agreeable—having accepted his company on walks from school and written him romantic notes in the weeks prior to the disappearance.[20]

The age difference, a common element in these elopement stories, was not unusual for the time. Age-of-consent laws varied by state, and regional customs impacted what was considered "normal" with regard to age, marriage, and sexuality. Prior to 1880, the age of consent was, on average, ten.[21] Men tended to get married at an older age than women. There were, of course, critics of the practice. Women's rights activists, Christian ministers (of the non-eloping variety), and medical professionals began to mount critiques of early marriages already in the 1850s.[22] But adolescence as a concept did not emerge until the late nineteenth century, and it was not until the first decades of the 1900s that lawmakers began to raise the marriageable age in some states.[23] Even then, reformers were not necessarily inspired by a sophisticated understanding of psychological differences between children and adults.[24] It was not until the 1920s that the idea that marriage was bad for children took root.[25]

So it may not have disturbed contemporary observers when, on the afternoon of January 7, 1870, Cooke met Johnson after school and took her to a hotel in lower Manhattan. Concern arose only after newspapers reported that Johnson was apparently infatuated with her married pastor. "The girl is undoubtedly ruined," the *Pittsburgh Gazette* postulated.[26] It is unclear whether any ruinous activity took place in the five days after the elopement, but on January 12 Cooke sent a letter to Johnson's parents disclosing her location. The pastor had apparently come to the realization that he had made a mistake and decided to make things right by the girl, who still was, he insisted, "as pure as the snow."[27] He attributed his infatuation with Johnson to her inexplicable likeness to a girl he had loved in his youth. "Oh fool, fool that I was," Cooke exclaimed in an interview, reprimanding his former self for eloping.[28]

The pastor would soon learn that no amount of performative self-flagellation could stop the sensational coverage that rash decisions inspired. Dozens of city newspapers carried the story of his elopement in the days after the disappearance. One publication in particular dedicated extended column space to the tale. The front page of the January 11 edition of the *New York World* publicized the "priestly scandal." The *World* alleged that the elopement was just the newest instance in a long line of "irregular" behaviors at Cooke's pastoral posts. The minister's easy access to female congregants and the assumption of moral purity inherent in the position troubled the newspaper's editor. The *World* alleged undue intimacy between the pastor and several other female congregants and called Cooke "a faithless shepherd."[29]

To be fair, the *World* was known to publish the sensational and the occasionally untrue. During the Civil War, the newspaper, run by a Democratic editor, created a problem for President Abraham Lincoln. On May 18, 1864, the paper published a forged document that purported to be Lincoln's proclamation to add four hundred thousand troops to the Union army. Federal agents seized the newspaper offices and tried to halt the distribution of the issue that contained the offending document. They were too late. As a result, the newspaper was shut down by a presidential order but resumed business three days later—having established to Lincoln's satisfaction that it took no part in the conspiracy to forge the document that it reprinted.[30]

The day after the *World* returned to print, its editor, the outspoken (and now vengeful) Manton Marble, published a scathing pamphlet titled *Freedom of the Press Wantonly Violated*, in which he accused Lincoln of defying the Constitution by attempting to use the forgery mishap to silence the democratic press.[31]

In addition to promulgating his political stances through his paper, Marble was a habitual critic of Protestantism. A Baptist in his youth, he had jeopardized good standing with the church by 1864.[32] He tendered his request for withdrawal from membership soon after, explaining that he was leaving the church because he was not able "in conscience [to] continue to subscribe to some of the articles of faith which when I was baptized commanded my youthful assent."[33] Within a few years, scientific ideas and atheistic leanings of his age would persuade Marble to become an agnostic.[34] It is no wonder, then, that stories of Protestant preachers engaging in immoral behavior were at home in the *World*. Marble's agnosticism did not compel him to dismiss all religion per se; but, from presidents to pastors, Marble felt it was his duty to expose the men who abused their power.

Reading the *World*'s colorful version of his elopement and career, Cooke became enraged. He would later explain that he had decided to sail to Europe in search of a quieter life, but the *World*'s revelations put a damper on his plans. Flabbergasted, Cooke burst into the editorial offices of the paper and, waving a pistol, demanded to see the author of the article. Tragedy was averted when the police arrested the distressed preacher. Within a month, Cooke would be placed in an insane asylum and expelled from the ministry, his name "blotted from the records of the Conference and consigned to infamy."[35]

If Cooke's name was removed from church records, it was not easily forgotten by the press, although the coverage of the case was not universally celebrated either. After all, it was not until 1875, with the sensational adultery trial of Henry Ward Beecher, that the press fully gave itself permission to cover Protestant sex scandals with meticulous, exhaustive detail. Cooke's elopement occurred five years earlier, when journalists still felt conflicted about covering pastoral scandals. The press was negotiating how much reporting was too much, what was at stake in publicizing the immoral acts of the nation's moral leaders, and whether public virtue suffered when the press covered pastoral sins. Six to ten newspapers devoted daily columns to Cooke's elopement, but the attention it received also had its critics.

The *Philadelphia Day* and Godkin's *Nation* condemned the intense coverage of the case and alleged impure motives behind its proliferation. *The Nation* dismissed Cooke's elopement as a story barely worth reporting and bemoaned the fact that a "petty scandal [swelled] to the dimensions of a public calamity."[36] The *Philadelphia Day* concurred: "The light, flippant tone, and the reckless disregard of the feelings of innocent parties involved, which characterizes the reports in the offending journals, fastens upon their conductors a vicious motive to put money in their purses, at the expense of truth and decency." Without doubt, the editors reasoned, if Cooke had committed the crime of which he stood accused, he needed to be punished. But their issue with the journalists who covered his case was that "in place of acting as the conservator of public morals, the offending press alluded to has done its utmost to shake popular confidence in every profession of religious faith."[37] The *Philadelphia Day* foresaw with keen insight how stories like Cooke's would be used by critics of religion. But even as the paper attempted to plead with fellow journalists to scale down the coverage of pastoral misdeeds, it was fighting a losing battle. The persistence of scandal persuaded newspaper editors that exposing religious hypocrisy might, in fact, be not only consistent with, but essential for preserving public morality. Calling out corruption would ultimately become secular newspapers' sacred duty.

If the newspapers of the 1870s reported on only thirty-one pastoral elopements, in the 1880s that number would swell almost twofold to fifty-seven. It peaked at eighty-two in the 1890s—an especially elopement-prone decade—and remained steady at seventy-eight in the first ten years of the twentieth century. One explanation for the tendency of pastors to mysteriously disappear rather than legally separate from their spouses lies in family law. Through most of the nineteenth century, divorce was difficult to obtain. Not only was it an undesirable blemish on one's reputation but it was also often a legal impossibility. Since marriage fell under state jurisdiction, there was little uniformity in laws across the country.[38] At midcentury, most states permitted divorce only on the grounds of adultery, cruelty, or desertion. As a result, some enterprising Americans flocked to states and territories that had looser regulations, such as Indiana and Nevada.[39] The 1880s were the first decade that saw a significant spike in divorce rates: one in every fourteen to sixteen marriages.[40] In some cases, ease of mobility and lack of systematic state surveillance enabled extralegal separation. As newly added states competed for laborer-citizens, it was not particularly difficult for a resourceful man to move west, declare himself a widower, and remarry, leaving his previous spouse behind. Ministers may have chosen this route since the possibility of divorce, even when it was legally viable, came at a cost. As self-proclaimed moral guardians of the nation, pastors ran the risk of losing credibility if they chose to divorce. At stake was more than the legal status of their marital state. Divorce demolished reputations. So pastors kept running.

In 1881, the *New York World* began featuring a regular column titled "Elopement Eccentricities." The February 1882 installment noted that the "elopement market this winter has been rather more active than usual."[41] The column listed twenty-two latest elopements: five in Great Britain, one in Canada, and sixteen in the United States. One of the latter involved Jesse Way, an Indiana Disciples of Christ minister, who eloped with his daughter-in-law. His name was swiftly struck from denominational records, but no amount of internal church censure could assuage the rise of public skepticism in response to poor behavior among the clergy. As the *Chicago Tribune* put it, Way's actions brought "discredit upon the whole theological flock."[42] The editors of the *Tribune* understood that constant reports of ministerial misdeeds hurt the reputation of Protestantism.

Even as churches began to take the threat of scandal seriously by rushing to disassociate from erring ministers, journalists employed increasingly harsh language to discuss the reverend runaways. When the married Methodist pastor David Seymour eloped from Janesville, Minnesota, with the wife of a local editor in 1887, fellow newspapermen were outraged. "The Janesville Sinners," one reporter called the elopers, explaining that "the cloak of Christianity did not cover up all the deviltry in this world, not even all within the pale of the church."[43] Another paper dubbed Seymour "a naughty parson."[44] Yet another publication labeled him a "reverend Lothario."[45] When Seymour and his married companion were captured in Liverpool and returned to the United States, the newspapers were satisfied to learn that the Methodist conference expelled the pastor from the church.[46] Scandal, as reporters understood by the late nineteenth century, could accomplish something: it could remove immoral ministers from their posts. In this new age, morality would be maintained not by refusing to publish the scandalous but by leaning into it—so long as the salacious exposés led to real change in the composition of the nation's clerical cadres.

Despite this consensus, some newspapers maintained their reluctance to employ scandal reporting as a means of instigating social change. In 1883, the *Los Angeles Times* denounced sensationalism, castigating it as deplorable and pleading for a change of tone (or profession) for journalists who embraced such coverage.[47] In 1885, the cover of the satirical magazine *Puck* portrayed the explosion of sensationalism in the press. In the cartoon, the courthouse features a prominent notice banning reporters. The caption reads, "For decency's sake! The reporters of incorrigible scandal-mongering journals must be kept out of the criminal courts, or we shall have to keep the newspapers out of our homes." In the illustration, the reporters are holding publication badges for such fictional newspapers as *Police Horror, Daily Shock, Evening Scavenger, Morning Mud-Hole, Daily Garbage Barrel, Sunday Skunk,* and *Daily Sewer.*[48]

Christian editors were likewise concerned about the rise in sensational reporting. An 1885 *Christian Union* article titled "How to Cure the Plague" identified sensational journalism as a menace to public morality and asked Christians to stop buying newspapers that dealt in scandal. "Millions for intelligence, but not one cent for scandal," the *Christian Union* implored. The article encouraged readers to withdraw support "from the venders of scandal" so that their business might "be greatly restricted."[49] But putting the money where Christian morality was did not always work, especially as Christian morality itself continued to be undermined from within.

Not everyone diagnosed this period in American religious history as a crisis. Plenty of men (and they were almost always men) defended the reputation of Protestant pastors in print and pleaded with the public to view pastoral scandal as a product of its age and a hazard of the ministerial profession. James Monroe Buckley, the concerned editor of the *Christian Advocate,* penned a long essay on "The Morality of Ministers" for a New York journal in 1887. Although he agreed that the "immoral minister" was an inherently dangerous figure due to his easy access to American families, Buckley cautioned readers not to give in to the anticlerical panic that had taken root in the press. The ministerial profession, he wrote, was loaded with opportunity for temptation. A charismatic minister enjoyed both the "warmth of the salutations given to him by men" and the "peculiar, delighted, loving smile lavished upon him by the best of women" and could, therefore, easily succumb to the charms of the attention and flattery he received from both genders. Yet thousands of good Christian men rose above those temptations daily, Buckley insisted; the sensational needed not undermine the quotidian—most Protestant pastors were beyond reproach.[50]

Reporters for fictional publications such as the *Daily Sewer*, the *Sunday Skunk*, and the *Daily Garbage Barrel* are kept outside of the courthouse in order to preserve decency in reporting. As Gilded Age newspapers embraced sensational coverage, they faced criticisms from the public and other members of the press when they engaged in reporting on "indecent" subjects.

Library of Congress Prints and Photographs Division, LC-DIG-ppmsca-28202

Buckley was fighting a losing battle by appealing to contingency. Negative coverage only intensified in the 1890s. In fact, the decade saw the highest number of reports on ministerial elopements—at least eighty-two Protestant pastors were said to have vanished. So frequent were these and other scandals that a Japanese resident of San Francisco purportedly decided to complain to the editor of a local newspaper.[51] Preserving original grammar and capitalization, the *Salt Lake Herald* reprinted his letter as an indictment of the excesses of the age.

> I came from far east a few months ago, and my purpose to see what you civilized nations are doing. Since I arrived in this city I am reading your valuable paper every day, and I am much surprised because the MURDER is almost daily occurrence in this country besides this Robber, Rev. Dr.'s robbing, eloping with other man's wife, etc. etc. Such events are occurred every day, shocking! Shocking! Murder in CHURCH that's awful, awful. Where is civilization? Where is christianity?[52]

Christianity, it appeared, could be comfortably found on the scandal pages. A list of contemporary headlines exemplifies the general register of the coverage: "Another Preacher's Weakness: This One Elopes with a Pretty Marietta Girl" (*Atlanta Constitution*, 1891); "Elopers in Trouble: A Canadian Clergyman and His Companion under Arrest at Lansing" (*Detroit Free Press*, 1891); "He Preached Well, But Wound up Running off with a Notorious Prostitute" (*Cincinnati Enquirer*, 1892); "Much Married Divine: A Methodist Minister Said to Have Three Wives Living—He Eloped with Two of Them" (*Washington Post*, 1892); "Another Chicago Scandal: A Prominent Preacher Elopes with a Married Woman" (*San Francisco Chronicle*, 1894); "Fell from Grace: Rev. Lee, D.D., Disappears with One of His Flock" (*Los Angeles Times*, 1895); "Flees with a Minister: Waterloo, IA., Girl of 15 Elopes with Her Preacher" (*Chicago Tribune*, 1896); "In Sheep's Clothing: A Kansas Wolf Captured in State of Washington—Baptist Minister Eloped with Another Man's Wife—His Own Family Subsisting on Charity" (*Los Angeles Times*, 1899).

Paradoxically, the proliferation of the genre of elopement articles helped decrease their sensational rhetoric. Overall, the tone of scandal coverage became increasingly dismissive and sarcastic—a testimony to how commonplace these stories had become. This was especially true for the anti-religious press, as exemplified by the freethinkers' *Boston Investigator* story on a Methodist minister's elopement in 1893:

> The Rev. Leigh Vernon, evangelist, has been conducting a series of revival meetings in Joplin, MO. He met with such phenomenal success, and the power of grace was poured out in such a flood, that it drowned Mrs. J. E. Pearson's affection for her husband and home. Whereupon the Rev. Leigh Vernon, evangelist, revived her affections to such a degree that she eloped with him, and now the good people of Joplin are wondering at the increase of crime.[53]

This was the entirety of the story: bare on details and full of humorous juxtapositions. The tone, language, and allusions to spiritual themes placed in the corrupt reality of the carnal served to undermine religion. By the mid-1890s, freethinkers did not have to cry "sensation" at a new report of a runaway pastor. These stories had become ubiquitous, and they required only a gesture—a small, dismissively sarcastic remark—to make their point.

Vernon's case would be covered differently in mainstream publications. Though now unavoidable, scandal coverage was still a matter of concern for those who feared that pastoral misconduct could undermine Christianity. Vernon was a respected evangelist who frequently toured the Midwest. His testimony of abandoning "infidel" ways and finding salvation through meticulous study of the Bible was reprinted in multiple newspapers.[54] Vernon's revival meetings, which urged men to become better husbands by abandoning alcohol and turning to Jesus, drew large crowds.[55] It was on one of these evangelistic trips that Vernon met young Mattie M. Pearson, the recently married daughter of a Methodist minister in Pittsburg, Kansas. In June 1893, shortly after Vernon's wife and child had left to spend the summer in California, Vernon arranged to meet Pearson in Missouri, where he was scheduled to speak. Having delivered the promised lectures, Vernon took off with Pearson in search of a happier life in Canada.

Midwestern newspapers, once celebratory of the minister, covered the case widely and reveled in the hypocrisies of the preacher's career and conduct. The *Wichita Daily Eagle* pointed out the irony of the fact that only two years earlier, Vernon had delivered a sermon titled "Be Sure Your Sin Will Find You Out" at a local church. The newspaper lamented that the minister was able to deploy religion "in the furtherance of his designs for securing the object of his desire." Still, the article about the preacher was titled "A Bad Egg"—thus differentiating the man from the profession whose reputation his elopement might have tarred.[56]

Vernon's coreligionists attempted to spread a similar message: a bad egg did not, they insisted, have to spoil the whole smorgasbord of Protestantism.

A few days after the disappearance, the pastor of Pittsburg Congregational Church delivered a sermon on the scandal: "Shocks threatening destruction come to individuals, communities, and institutions. The church is no exception. Yet the man who concludes, because some standard bearer falls, that her ruin is come and her influence gone, shows not only a lack of confidence in God, but a woeful ignorance of the past."[57] Vernon, the minister advised, was merely a man given to temptation by Satan's machinations. He chose to give up his family and his good work for the allure of newness. God, in turn, would punish the minister by condemning him to eternal damnation. The scandal had nothing whatsoever to do with the church; the only thing at stake, according to this sermon, was the individual salvation of the troubled preacher.

Vernon and Pearson were arrested in Duluth, Minnesota, a month after they disappeared. The woman cited hypnotism as her reason for eloping with the minister, a not uncommon explanation at the time.[58] Vernon, during his extradition to Kansas, was reported to have attempted suicide by jumping out of a moving train somewhere in Missouri. Sustaining only minor injuries, he was quickly recaptured by the deputy who accompanied him. When asked why he tried to end his life, the minister allegedly replied, "I realized that my influence for good as an evangelist was gone. The shame of coming home manacled and in charge of an officer was more than I could bear....I heartily regret the circumstances, and trust they will not conspire to destroy whatever influence for good I may have been able to exert in the past."[59] Whether Vernon actually gave this interview to an *Emporia Gazette* reporter cannot, of course, be established with absolute confidence. At the time, journalists were not terribly opposed to making their stories more colorful by fictionalizing certain sections of their reporting. Indeed, the concern for the work of evangelism and for the reputation of religion more broadly that comes through in the quotation may reveal more about the priorities of Kansas newspapers than about Vernon's own sentiments regarding his predicament. One thing seems clear: ministerial elopement scandals were an extremely delicate matter, and the press reported on them according to their own particular leanings. After all, with the rise in pastoral scandals, the reputation of Protestantism itself was at stake.

At the end of the century, elopement stories were both uncomfortably familiar and still deeply divisive. If the 1870s saw the press disagree on whether journalists should even be devoting space to publicizing preachers' downfalls, after Beecher's trial, scandal was there to stay. The new dividing line among the press was not with regard to the existence or volume, but to the tone of coverage. If reporters who were critical of religion used scandal to undermine Protestantism, those who sought to protect the status quo learned to cast elopement scandals in the light of personal—not institutional—failure. Defenders of the church portrayed the erring divines as mere humans who, being exposed to the privileges and temptations of ministry, proved too weak in their constitution to resist the desires of the flesh.

In the early twentieth century, disappearing got trickier. Changing legislation and new social conventions led to elopements' eventual decline. Of the ninety-six ministers who eloped between 1900 and 1914, fifty-two either returned home voluntarily or were eventually located by pursuers. Twenty-two of the fifty-two were arrested. As the government, informed by the advocacy of reformers, responded to the elopement epidemic by introducing harsher punishments for wife deserters, many of the runaway pastors suffered the consequences of their choices through arrests, fines, and imprisonment. An important piece of legislation, the so-called White Slavery (or Mann) Act of 1910, criminalized transporting women across state lines for "immoral purposes." The law purportedly sought to protect white women from sex trafficking, but in effect served as a poorly disguised attempt to curb interracial relationships and police women's sexual agency. Simultaneously, divorce was becoming easier to obtain, and many people found marital separation an increasingly viable option. New ideas about romantic love and the malleability of familial composition allowed the press to paint eloping pastors as tragic figures, not villainous predators. By the mid-1910s, some newspapers would begin portraying eloping pastors as sympathetic victims of unlucky marital arrangements.

The twice-eloped Mexican American minister Joseph Francisco Cordova endured arrest and imprisonment before he could finally be united with the young lover who was not his wife. Cordova was a Methodist pastor from South River, New Jersey. His first elopement took place in May 1904, when he disappeared with an eighteen-year-old member of his church choir, Julie Bowne. The thirty-nine-year-old pastor left behind a wife and three children. His young companion left her job at the local handkerchief company and her grieving parents. Rumors about Cordova paying disproportionate attention to Bowne had circulated for some time, and when the girl's father confronted the pastor about the gossip, the couple decided to run in search of a better future. The decision to escape was no doubt made easier by the fact that Cordova's wife had recently inherited $1,500 and deposited the money into the minister's bank account. Cordova withdrew the cash shortly before taking off with Bowne. Soon detectives were on the chase for the girl and the money.

Within a month, Cordova and Bowne were spotted in Canada. In Brampton, Ontario, Cordova checked into a hotel room, telling the clerk that Bowne was his niece. They then traveled to Toronto. Trying the same strategy in Toronto failed, and the suspicious couple was turned away from the hotel. Eventually, at another establishment, Cordova and Bowne registered as husband and wife, securing their room at the inn through a false assurance of matrimony.[60] By July, apparently repentant, the couple had made their way south to New York City. From there, Bowne returned home to New Jersey.

Cordova, whose trial for removal from ministry had been scheduled in absentia, attempted to defend his reputation by talking to the press and explaining that the fear of scandal—not the desire to sin—forced him to elope. The New York Evening World's article was titled "Preacher Tells Why He Eloped" and featured a prominent subtitle that read: "Cordova Says Unwarranted Scandal Made Him Board Trolley-Car and Go Further than He Had Intended." Cordova swiftly penned a letter of defense and mailed it to several newspaper editors. In the letter, he explained that while he had always enjoyed Bowne's company and thought highly of her as a parishioner, the two of them had never been more than friends. The fateful evening when the couple disappeared had been tumultuous. Bowne's father, a deacon in Cordova's church, had heard the rumors about his daughter and his pastor. In despair, Cordova panicked. "I was dazed," the minister explained, "and by the time I reached the trolley track my only thought was that none would believe any explanation I might give; that all was necessarily lost, even my children; that all the world was against me, that I must leave at once." In this state, he ran into Bowne, who had been confronted by her father about the rumors of the affair as well. Feeling similarly desperate, she agreed to run away from the town about to explode with scandal. "We felt hunted," Cordova wrote, "persecuted, chased by anger and vengeance, and so went far, further than we had intended." When they read newspaper reports of the elopement, the couple became even more distressed. Eventually, letters urging them to return home reached the elopers in Canada, and they decided to come back, hoping for forgiveness and understanding.[61]

Cordova's account failed to persuade his critics. To avoid the impending church trial, he submitted his resignation in July. The Freemasons, another organization to which Cordova belonged, voted to remove him from their ranks in September. By November, Cordova's wife left him and moved in with her parents.[62] Back in South River, things remained quiet for a few months—until late February of the following year, when Bowne once again disappeared from her father's home. Cordova was missing as well.

The second elopement was halted much quicker than the first. Cordova and Bowne were arrested in Washington, DC, three days after their escape. Detectives apprehended the runaways using a photograph of Cordova. The five-foot-tall bespectacled forty-year-old man and the nineteen-year-old beauty were not difficult to spot. The pair was soon extradited back to New Jersey—Bowne as a witness, and Cordova as an accused wife deserter. Bowne stuck by her lover, refusing to leave the jail on bond and go home to her worried parents. Cordova, in the meantime, attempted to fix his situation by writing to his wife and asking her to initiate divorce proceedings.[63] The abandoned spouse refused to comply, and the minister was arraigned on two charges: desertion and domestic assault, which his wife alleged took place in April of the previous year, shortly before the first elopement. Cordova pleaded not guilty to both.[64]

The crime of desertion had become a serious social concern at the turn of the century. Between 1890 and 1915, every state enacted legislation that made spouse desertion a crime.[65] In fact, the grounds of desertion accounted for 39 percent of the 945,625 divorces granted in the country between 1887 and 1906.[66] Urban areas were most affected, and social relief organizations struggled to keep up with the demand for assistance from deserted wives and children.[67] With their husbands gone and charitable aid exhausted, abandoned wives turned to the state for relief. The government, in turn, introduced harsher punishments for deserters.

Fear of imprisonment failed to dissuade would-be deserters, as burgeoning ideas about the importance of romantic love inspired new critiques of traditional family values. In urban centers in particular, the new generation began to date without chaperones or supervision. They engaged in previously taboo premarital sexual behaviors. And they began to seek partners for emotional intimacy and companionship—undermining the old-fashioned notion that marriage was a lifelong contract whose primary function was procreation.[68] Divorce, followed by a new union based on love and intimacy, was no longer a heretical idea celebrated exclusively by free lovers and infidels.

Even some pastors embraced this new philosophy. Already in 1900, one Congregational minister, George D. Herron, began preaching the doctrine of divorce. "I do not believe that the present marriage system is sacred or good," Herron postulated. "I believe that union is made by love alone and that it is terminable at the termination of love." If love was the basis of marriage, Herron reasoned, then when the love expired, the marriage needed to end as well. "Love marries us and, as long as our love lasts, love will keep us together," Herron concluded. "I think it wrong to obey a law that would keep us together when love has ended."[69] Four years earlier, as he was developing this new theology of turn-of-the-century romance, Herron told his wife that his love for her had ceased, and he promptly began dating another woman. The Congregational Church remained unpersuaded by the divine's philosophy and behavior. Herron was dismissed from ministerial ranks in 1901.[70]

As the now defrocked Herron preached his gospel of romantic love, the New Jersey Methodist Conference met to discuss Cordova's case. To punish the minister for unbecoming conduct, it refused his request for resignation and instead expelled him from the church.[71] As one reporter put it, "The vote was unanimous, even the minister who came here to defend the divine voting yes."[72] Within a week, a secular jury of his peers found Cordova guilty as well. He was sentenced to three years in prison for assaulting his wife and to an additional year for deserting the family.[73] Upon hearing the verdict, Bowne, who was in attendance, fainted. Cordova was downtrodden, but not despondent. According to one newspaper, "Rev. Cordova, the eloping parson of New Jersey, says he is guilty and glad of it. Even if his religion is a little frayed his optimism is admirable."[74]

Perhaps it was optimism that sustained Cordova during his time in prison. In 1909, the ex-minister and Bowne got married in Welland, Ontario. The surviving marriage certificate reveals important details about the couple's story. Cordova listed his occupation as bookkeeper, his place of residence as Flint, Michigan, his denomination as Presbyterian, and his marital status as "widowed." (His ex-wife would follow suit and list herself as "widowed" in the 1920 census as well; being listed as "divorced" still carried some amount of stigma, despite the growing cultural acceptance of marital separation.) That Cordova had changed professions was to be expected, but the denominational shift is curious. Did he adopt Presbyterianism in prison? Did he denounce religion altogether, but the bureaucratic rigidity of Canadian marriage officials forced him to claim some—any—denomination as his own? Whatever the case, ideas of romantic love and companionate marriage won in the end. With Canada's stamp of approval, the American couple that survived a scandal, two elopements, and four years in prison were finally united in matrimony.

Even as some eloping ministers found happiness through romantic love, their collective choices continued to undermine the public's trust in the profession. In 1907, when yet another elopement scandal unfolded in New York, a freethought Kentucky newspaper reported on the scandal with weariness: "The Old, Old Story," the article's headline complained. The Reverend Winfield B. King, the piece sneered, had eloped from his Methodist post in Arcade, New York, with "his favorite choir girl." The pair were arrested within two weeks in Ohio, where they had picked up work at a chicken farm. The moral of the story, for the editors, was this: "O, fool girls, don't marry preachers! This one may now be in Utah or Mexico or some other safe place ready for another job."[75] As far as this newspaper was concerned, the itinerant passions of Protestant pastors disqualified them from being good husband material.

In fact, in the early twentieth century any unexpected disappearance of a Christian pastor was almost universally assumed to be a scandalous elopement. For example, when the Congregational minister Carl S. Jones mysteriously left his pulpit and home in 1909, a fellow pastor acknowledged the suspicion surrounding his sudden departure. "The natural supposition," the Reverend William B. Forebush said, "is that something is wrong. I have my own ideas, but I have no proof. There is no woman missing from the parish. We hope the matter will be dropped and forgotten for the sake of the church."[76] Forebush's words appeared in an article titled "Search for a Pastor Who Abandoned Family Dropped for Fear of Scandal." The fear of scandal seemed to be omnipresent. By 1909, a Christian minister could not disappear without inspiring rumors about his extramarital activities.

The first half of the 1910s saw a significant decrease in the reported number of runaway ministers, in large part due to developments in state and federal legislation. Newspaper accounts indicate that at least three pastors who eloped in the early 1910s were prosecuted. The African American minister R. H. Hightower eloped with a married woman from Kansas in 1910. Upon his capture, he was sentenced to thirty days in jail and ordered to pay a fine of fifty dollars.[77] Two years later, the Reverend William F. Dunn eloped from Granite City, Illinois, with his eighteen-year-old organist. Having made it only fifty miles south, he was arrested, convicted of "immoral conduct," and sentenced to ninety days and a $200 fine.[78] Another Illinois minister, the Lutheran J. D. Lewis, would face similar charges for eloping in 1913. Having become infatuated with seventeen-year-old Elizabeth Kohl, a member of his congregation, he stole $500 of his wife's money and $15 of his daughter's piggy-bank savings. He used the cash to buy a car and drive away with Kohl.[79] The couple were eventually captured in Davenport, Iowa, where the minister was arrested for violating the Mann Act, since he and his female companion had crossed state lines. Eventually, both Lewis's wife and Kohl's family dropped the charges against the Lutheran runaway, and the scandal dissipated.

Although Lewis avoided punishment, the fear of prosecution under the Mann Act was growing more palpable by the month. Most infamously, the African American boxer Jack Johnson was charged with violating the act in 1912, when he was arrested for interstate travel with his fiancé Lucille Cameron. Cameron, who was white, refused to testify against Johnson, and the charges were dropped. Johnson's arrest exposed the Mann Act for what it was: a racist attempt to punish Black men for engaging in interracial relationships. But the threat of the implications of the Mann Act also extended to white elopers traveling across state lines with their lovers. In the *Caminetti v. United States* decision of 1917, the Supreme Court ruled that the Mann Act applied not only to legitimate cases of trafficking but also to any interstate transportation of women whatsoever—including for consensual sex.

Perhaps this is why when the Reverend Charles Huffman of Ohio was arrested in Denver in 1917 for eloping with seventeen-year-old Gladys Marie Overlander, he insisted that nothing sexual had occurred between them. "It was all my fault," Huffman swore. "Gladys is pure and innocent— but we loved one another so." Love convinced the minister and the girl to leave in order "to escape the scandal." Still, Huffman asked the public to blame him and forgive Overlander. "She has not sinned nearly as much as she has been sinned against," Huffman urged. "I hope it can be arranged to send her back to her people."[80]

As harsher punishments were introduced to prevent the dissolution of marriages through desertion laws and the exploitation of young (white) women through the Mann Act, divorce laws were simultaneously becoming more liberal and the practice more socially acceptable. The Episcopal minister Jere Knode Cooke left his wife to elope with Floretta Whaley, a seventeen-year-old heiress and member of Cooke's Long Island congregation, in May 1907. A warrant for Cooke's arrest for abduction was issued within days, but the couple were not discovered until eight months later—living in San Francisco with a newborn baby. Having been deposed from the ministry, Cooke became a painter. In an interview, he explained how his unhappy marriage led him to give up his life of comfort for love.

> I awoke to love and everything else was worthless. You know the end. On the one hand was a loveless life with honor and position and wealth, and on the other, love and poverty. I chose this....I don't praise myself for the step I took. It was weakness, it was unmanly, but I was only human, and as I am to be judged by humans, it is but right that they should know that I gave up all—all that I had—for this. I am doing a man's work. I have sinned, but I have suffered. Now I beg the world to let me alone with my wife and child. I can live the life of a good Christian. I am a good decorator....I asked the world to let me be a painter, nothing more—to do a man's work and enjoy the average sorrows and happiness of the average man.[81]

In the new century, the average man, according to Cooke, could choose love over tradition—leaving his respectable job, moving to the other coast, living under an assumed name, and being on the run from the law. At least for this Episcopalian, the change in his marital arrangement did not automatically undermine his religion.

The average woman struggled to accept this new disposition. Cooke's wife Miranda read his interview and became enraged. She told reporters that she had shielded Cooke from rumors of infidelity for years and that his callous denunciation of their nine-year marriage was now pushing her to sue him for divorce and to speak out against the ungrateful spouse. "It was an interview that only a coward could utter," she said, "with clear, malicious purpose, so I am forced to believe, he struck with contemptible innuendo at the wife who had crucified her heart to shield him."[82] Although divorce seemed to be the perfect solution for Miranda Cooke's problems at first, she soon realized that it would in fact punish the ex-reverend more if she remained married to him: as long as the Cookes were still legally wed, the deserter could not marry the woman with whom he eloped.

Eventually, time cured Miranda Cooke's desire for revenge. She divorced Cooke in 1913, six years after his elopement. By then, the defrocked minister, Whaley, and their two children had moved back to Brooklyn—to claim

Whaley's inheritance and to be closer to family. According to one newspaper, when Cooke received his divorce papers, he "fell on his knees, and, with tears running down his cheeks, expressed his thankfulness in prayer" for finally being able to wed Whaley and to claim his sons as his own in the eyes of the state.[83] Pictures of the Cooke-Whaley children were reprinted in newspapers with the headline "These Two Little Boys Can Have a Name Now."[84] For the time being, the news of a peaceful divorce resolution for the sake of the new family seemed to overshadow the scandal of years past. Divorce, at least for the sake of children, was now seen as an honorable solution to an unhappy union. Cooke and Whaley were married on June 10, 1913, by a justice of the peace in a Connecticut hotel.

Cooke's ex-wife gave one last interview on the matter. "In spite of the fact that my church does not recognize [divorce]," she said, "I decided after much thought to do the big thing." Her reason for the magnanimity was "to give Jere Cooke's innocent babies a name and their mother the right to call herself his wife." She still disapproved of divorce on theological grounds but admitted that realizing that her union with Cooke had been "only a man-made marriage" made the decision easier. With God one step removed from matters of matrimony, the two Cookes could start new lives. In deciding to grant her husband the divorce, the former Mrs. Cooke could show grace to his new family and, perhaps, even reclaim some self-esteem that his elope-ment no doubt injured.[85]

By the mid-1910s, divorce had become a viable option for families like Cooke's, even as most Christian denominations still refused to recognize it formally. In both the tone and content of coverage, the press softened on clerical elopers. As legislation and social norms changed, elopement stories all but disappeared from the press.

The freethinkers' chronicle of pastoral misdeeds, *Crimes of Preachers*, saw only two reissues in the 1910s, including the book's final iteration in 1914. By then, a separate publication dedicated to tracking ministerial crimes was no longer necessary. The mainstream press was well seasoned not only in reporting on the facts of religious sex scandals but also in pro-viding commentary on scandal's meaning for religion writ large. Scandal had won the day—and the new century. If the press had been hesitant to report on Protestant elopements in the 1870s, reporters became increas-ingly comfortable with scandal over the next two decades. The debate that raged on in the 1880s and the 1890s was about what elopement scandals meant for Christianity and no longer about whether those stories ought to be covered in the first place. By the mid-1910s, with changes in legislation and cultural perceptions of marriage and romantic love, ministerial elopement stories acquired a less sensational bend—with some journalists tacitly accepting the choice to elope even when it came to Protestant pastors.[86]

Although reports of ministerial elopements diminished, scandal continued to be a problem for religion. The preface to the final edition of *Crimes of Preachers* summarized the cumulative findings of the project: the ministers featured in the book collectively committed almost five thousand crimes—with adultery, seduction, and "immoralities with women" being among the most populous categories, followed only by financial crimes, such as embezzlement, swindling, and fraud. North American clergy were not delivering on the promise of religion as a reliable guarantor of sexual morality.

Indiana Baptist Reverend C. M. Dinsmore tried to address this professional crisis in his 1912 sermon "How Preachers Go Wrong." He complained that newspapers compromised the public's faith in the church by publicizing ministerial crimes. Christian pastors, Dinsmore explained, were men first—prone to temptation and sin. It was up to women to minimize those temptations. "When Christian mothers let their daughters go out on the street with dresses cut so low in the neck, as many do, and cut so short at the bottom as many wear them, can they wonder that hell is stirred up in the breasts of every man who sees them?" the minister asked.[87] When a preacher fell, Dinsmore argued, he deserved the punishment that came his way, but an individual pastor's fall did not have to bring disgrace to his entire profession. It was up to the churches, then, to sift through their representatives. "Too many men," Dinsmore claimed, "are getting into the ministry who are weak morally. No man has any business there unless he finds that he is able to fight successfully that [which] is in his own nature."[88] Women's modesty and better vetting for prospective ministers would ensure, the reverend gentleman hoped, that scandal would not destroy religion's credibility. And while there was no easy way to control the length of women's ever-shortening skirts, Protestant churches got to work on tightening their selection criteria for prospective pastors.

4

Institutional Responses

In 1909, the Congregational minister Frederick Eli Hopkins felt frustrated with how Protestants handled scandal. They were too retaliatory. Hopkins wanted more grace, less stringency, and unconditional forgiveness for all kinds of sinners—lay and ordained. It was unfair, he argued, that the church offered salvation to "some man who has been a drunkard, thief, liar, and all-around villain all his life" while refusing the same generosity to the occasionally impious Protestant ministers. Hopkins decried the typical response to pastoral indiscretion, which, in his characterization, went like this: "We will pin the scarlet letter on your breast. We will wear our shoes out running from one house to another to tell what we have heard you have done. We will demand that you surrender your license to preach."[1] Forgiveness had to extend to the redeemed, too, Hopkins insisted. Preachers' sins did not have to end in disgrace.

The public and the press disagreed. Sex scandals had become such a persistent feature in religion coverage that even some ministers began to defend sensationalism. William Evans, vice president of the Bible Institute of Los Angeles, argued that newspapers were "perfectly justified" in publicizing pastoral scandals. "There is more talk about an eclipse of the sun," Evans said, "than there is about the sun shining day by day throughout a whole day. So there is more talk about a minister who falls into sin than over one who keeps on doing good for a whole year, and therefore the newspaper is perfectly justified in putting on the front page the account of the minister who falls."[2] Unlike Hopkins, Evans recognized scandal's universal appeal.

In giving newspapers license to advertise pastoral problems, Evans was in the minority of Christian elites. Yet the juxtaposition of his and Hopkins's attitudes is indicative of larger debates in this era. The first quarter of the twentieth century saw a reckoning with the persistent threat of scandal. Ongoing revelations about the sexual habits of the nation's clergy threatened Protestant hegemony. Worse, familiar scandals of the heterosexual variety were now supplemented by tales of queer intimacy and same-sex desire. These developments necessitated the introduction of new measures

Disgraced: How Sex Scandals Transformed American Protestantism. Suzanna Krivulskaya, Oxford University Press.
© Oxford University Press 2025. DOI: 10.1093/oso/9780197599686.003.0005

intended to prevent—or at the very least conceal—scandal. Fundamentalist institutions started to tighten their selection criteria for prospective students and to discipline ordained ministers whose sexual proclivities deviated from orthodoxy. Churches began to prosecute erring pastors in secret trials held behind closed doors. All the while, interdenominational dialogue about the crisis of Protestant representation in the press led to the creation of church publicity departments, which attempted to find sympathetic allies among secular journalists. Some of these efforts succeeded; others failed in humiliatingly public ways. In the end, this era taught Protestants to be more vigilant about what information they allowed to escape their sanctuaries, seminaries, and offices. The best bet for dealing with sensationalism was intensified secrecy and a conscious construction of an elaborate system of silencing meant to protect the church from scandal's reach.

At the turn of the twentieth century, Christian institutions began to take proactive measures to prevent scandal in their midst. Moody Bible Institute (MBI), a Chicago training school for ministers, took the threat of scandal among its students seriously from its founding in 1889. MBI was the product of the work and ambition of its namesake, the famed revivalist Dwight L. Moody, whose career transformed the landscape of religion both at home and abroad. Charismatic and unwearied, Moody traveled the globe to preach the gospel, held evangelistic revivals across North America, and ran a successful Christian publishing company until his death in 1899. His message was simple: God desired to have a personal relationship with every individual.[3] To guarantee that this divine plan for the world could unfold, Christian workers were needed to evangelize the lost and spread the news of salvation. Moody and his associates would undertake the work of training evangelists to take the gospel to the farthest reaches of the earth. MBI soon became one of the largest evangelical institutions of higher learning in the world.

From its inception, MBI was central to building a network of the country's leading evangelists. The institute's early mission did not end with spiritual salvation; it also extended to the material concerns of the day. Specifically, MBI sought to convert working-class people in order to elevate their economic condition and bolsters the ranks of middle-class Protestants.[4] Social stability and middle-class respectability were incompatible with scandal, so MBI faced the difficult task of weeding the applications of numerous potential recruits to eliminate any bad fruits with otherwise lofty aspirations for Christian ministry.

Before applicants were admitted, MBI subjected them to meticulous screening. Form letters asked the writers of recommendations to comment on the personal qualities of prospective students. For female applicants, questions about submissiveness, malleability, and teachability were central. For example, the form asked whether the applicant was "a thoroughly converted woman." Was she "unselfish," "teachable," and "willing in manner"? Additionally, MBI wanted to know if the applicant had "any peculiarities or eccentricities that would unfit her for Christian work." The last page of the form provided space for the reference writer to comment on anything that "would specifically qualify or disqualify her."[5]

Recommendation forms for male applicants demanded even more minute scrutiny. In addition to asking whether the applicant was "teachable," the form queried whether he might be "conceited," "fault-finding," or "indolent." Further questions about the applicant's personality, habits, and leanings escalated in intensity. "Do you believe him to be a converted man, and if so, on what grounds? Has he ever to your knowledge backslidden? If so, how long since and what were the circumstances? Has he good sense? Any bad habits?" Finally, and perhaps most significant: "Is he discreet in his conduct toward women?"[6] Sexual impurity—or, at the very least, indiscretion—was a disqualifier for MBI ranks.

Along with sexual impropriety, MBI also wanted to prevent any potential disruptions to doctrinal orthodoxy. Some of the men who would be at the forefront of the new fundamentalist movement were leading the MBI hierarchy. They wanted to shield their students from the theological temptations of modernity. MBI asked each applicant three questions. "Are you in agreement with the doctrinal teaching received at the Institute? If differing, state your point of disagreement and give scriptural reasons therefor." And finally, "Is there any point of our teaching upon which you are not clear?"[7] With confirmed assurance of good character and discretion as well as self-professed conformity to MBI doctrines, a signature and a postage stamp put the prospective student's application in the pool.

A clean application packet did not always guarantee unproblematic admits. Faculty meeting minutes from MBI's early years (1903–5) demonstrate the level of scrutiny that the people in charge of the school applied to future religious leaders. The faculty watched students closely—monitoring their activities and disciplining those whose questionable life choices could undermine the institution's reputation. This was no simple task. By 1903, MBI enrolled almost 500 full-time students: 273 men and 226 women.[8] The gender parity of the student body was due, in large part, to the efforts of Emma Dryer, a prolific Christian evangelist who had founded several Chicago ministries and who first persuaded Moody to open a training school for both men and women.[9] While the faculty expected only a minority of male students (and none of the women) to become ordained at the end of training, most graduates would end up representing Protestantism in some form. Of the 132 men who graduated in 1903, for example, 82 would be engaged in religious labor—including missionary work, evangelism, and ministry—by the following year.[10] Female graduates' career trajectories differed. Many became homemakers or preachers' wives. Some continued with Bible teaching, missions, or rescue home administration.

Gender differences affected more than just vocation. On September 5, 1903, the faculty voted not to admit men under the age of twenty-one or women under the age of twenty to the institute. The original practice of admitting younger applicants had apparently created problems within the student body. The decision to implement a one-year difference based on gender suggests that the students' level of maturity was taken into consideration in admissions decisions. Even though MBI leaders believed that women were not fit for ordination, they apparently trusted them more than young men in matters of conduct. This was a time when Victorian notions of Protestant spirituality being the domain of women gave way to a decidedly masculine gospel.[11] By the end of the Progressive Era, most fundamentalists would come to view women as psychologically and spiritually inferior to men, but at the start of the century, women were still trusted more when it came to decorum and discretion.[12]

Gender determined how MBI faculty functioned as well. In 1903, a special male-only panel was convened after the regular September 5 faculty meeting had concluded. This gender-segregated cohort investigated charges against two students. The investigation revealed the institution's profound concern with the public image of the school as reflected in the moral character of its students. Fred Leroy Enslow, a twenty-four-year-old Baptist minister-in-training, had been suspended from MBI because of an unspecified allegation by an anonymous source. The faculty voted to continue his suspension until "he had cleared himself of the charges."[13] Though no other details about Enslow's case survive, he appeared to have succeeded in doing so. Five years after the investigation, MBI's journal the *Institute Tie* celebrated Enslow's evangelistic work.[14] A Nebraska city directory also reveals that a missionary by the name of Rev. F. Leroy Enslow was active in Kearney that same year.[15] Having somehow been reinstated, Enslow was cleared to serve God as a worthy public representative of MBI.

The other case under investigation was that of Jacob M. Harris, a married student accused of "immoral conduct" by a Mr. Edson of Lake Odessa, Michigan. The unspecified charges were apparently grievous enough to warrant Harris's suspension from ministry. In the words of MBI faculty, Harris was "advised to refrain from doing public Christian work for the present for reasons known to Mr. Harris and the Faculty."[16] Two weeks later, the faculty deliberated about whether Harris's wife could be admitted to MBI and decided that "it would not be wise" to accept her. Almost two years later, however, Harris wrote to the faculty asking to be reinstated as a student, and his request was granted.[17] Like Enslow, Harris eventually became a minister despite a temporary setback in his religious training.

MBI's efforts to carefully evaluate prospective applicants' potential for moral slippage and to quickly censure unsavory behavior proved successful, at least initially. Early records reveal the institution's preoccupation with students' character and a concern with tracking their whereabouts, behaviors, and doctrinal dispositions both during their time at MBI and long after they left the school.[18] MBI faculty were right to be concerned. For decades, secular critics of the church had tried to use scandal to undermine religion. As other organizations' reputations were being challenged in newspaper exposés, MBI leaders hoped that their proactive strategy of careful screening and swift discipline would produce scandal-free ministers for years to come.

MBI's plans for cultivating a scandal-free environment were soon thwarted from within. Two prominent MBI men—a one-time assistant superintendent and a former student turned teacher—were involved in highly publicized sex scandals in 1912 and 1922 respectively. The scandals revealed the lengths to which MBI and the Chicago Moody Church were willing to go to keep the cases away from the press. When secrecy failed to protect the institution's reputation, MBI learned to quickly disassociate from problematic ministers.

It began at the top of the school's administration. William R. Newell was the son of a minister, a graduate of Princeton Theological Seminary, and a skilled exegete of the Bible. In 1895, Dwight Moody personally invited Newell to become MBI's assistant superintendent. Newell accepted. The next year, he married Mellicent M. Woodworth, albeit after an unusually lengthy engagement that was due, according to newspaper speculation, to the bride's hesitation on account of an unspecified quarrel with the groom.[19]

Newell became one of the most famous Bible instructors of his age. By 1901, he was teaching the largest Bible class in North America. For a while, the preacher's weekly schedule looked like this: after a Sunday class in Chicago, Newell traveled to Detroit to teach on Monday, to Toronto on Tuesday, then back to Chicago for the Thursday class, finishing in St. Louis on Friday. About eighty-seven hundred students came to learn from Newell every week, and the demand kept growing.[20] Even after he had transitioned from running MBI to being a full-time traveling preacher, he still maintained close ties to both the Institute and the Moody Church, where he served as an elder. Preaching the Bible, going on international missions, and rousing audiences across the continent, Newell appeared to be unstoppable.

In the fall of 1912, newspapers broke the revelation of a sex scandal that MBI and the Moody Church had attempted to conceal for nearly half a decade. Newell, it turned out, was addicted to women and prescription medication. He was partial to female missionaries and chloral hydrate.[21] For these sins, the Moody Church banished him from membership after a secret internal investigation and trial in 1909. Few details of the alleged misbehavior survive, but Newell had apparently confessed them to fellow evangelists in the midst of a mental breakdown in 1905.[22] When the confession became public among the Moody leadership, Newell tried to retract it, which might have worked had he not also made the same confession to former MBI superintendent R. A. Torrey in 1907—that time, in a perfectly lucid state.[23]

In 1909, a group of Moody Church elders brought the Newell affair to the attention of the church's executive committee, which conducted an ecclesiastical trial. The charges of lying, substance abuse, and "exceedingly indiscreet conduct toward women" Newell denied vehemently—obfuscating, blaming his inability to recall the events of the previous several years on his mental health problems, and undermining witnesses' testimony by scrutinizing their choice of words in recalling the alleged confessions. As Torrey mournfully complained after reading the trial transcript, "Mr. Newell at this very trial uttered things that, as it seemed to me, he must have known to have been untrue, that he practiced deception and resorted to subterfuge and sought to throw dust into the eyes of the committee."[24] Newell's machinations were not persuasive. The committee, comprised of twenty-eight men, found Newell guilty and unfit for Christian ministry.

The verdict notwithstanding, the Newell matter would remain confidential. The leadership of MBI and Moody Church worked tirelessly to keep the subject out of the newspapers. Their correspondence referred to the case as "the N. affair" and discussed it in coded language.[25] The men in charge understood that institutional reputations could be crushed by scandal. Lyman Stewart, cofounder of the Bible Institute of Los Angeles, confessed to being afraid that the "controversy between the Moody Church and Mr. Newell will react against both the church and the institute."[26] In response, Moody Church pastor Azmi C. Dixon, assured Stewart that the case would not become a sensation and explained that the church had succeeded in keeping the story out of newspapers. Three reporters had apparently asked Dixon to confirm the rumors of an internal investigation, but he "finally prevailed upon them not to publish anything." Dixon's remarkable admission suggests that at least in Chicago, Christian leaders may have held some sway over reporters. To further alleviate Stewart's fears, Dixon assured him that few people knew anything about the affair. Besides, the investigative committee left no printed evidence of the Newell case and "circulated only the typewritten copy of its finding, where it was called for by people who had a right to know."[27] Those with a right to know were a select few men at the top of the leadership—not the newspapers or the public.

The scandal still broke in September 1912. Despite Protestant elites' best efforts, information traveled—sometimes even internationally. A Toronto church had apparently closed its doors to Newell after his trial. When a Methodist church in Chicago invited Newell to speak, information from Toronto "was furnished certain officials," who decided to un-invite the speaker, thereby causing inquiring minds to wonder about the reason behind the action.[28]

Newspapers were all too happy to cover the case. "It was the original intention of the Moody Church authorities to keep the whole scandal under cover," reported the *Chicago Tribune*. "The hearing was in 1909," the article continued, "but so carefully was the scandal hushed that although the church following had a fair idea of what had taken place, no inkling of it was permitted to become generally public." The *Tribune* then provided some details of the Newell hearing, thereby revealing that reporters had gotten hold of the evidence in the case. Quotations from the article came directly from Moody Church insiders. One church official even offered a quasi apology: "Well, we preferred to keep it to ourselves. We kept the newspapers from learning anything about it." Fortunately for eager consumers of titillating sensations, the leadership's success at keeping the scandal from the press was only temporary.[29]

Once the story broke, the coverage exploded. It helped that reporters liked Newell, and Newell loved publicity. The *St. Louis Post-Dispatch* had for years covered any event in which Newell took part in Missouri—praising the preacher's ability to reach thousands with his Bible lessons. When things got rough for the minister, the *Post-Dispatch* came through. A week after the scandal broke, the paper published an extensive defense of Newell, accompanied by an exclusive interview and a large photo of the preacher. In recounting the story for the *Post-Dispatch*, Newell's memories appeared more lucid than they had been in his trial testimony. He stood by the claim that his confessions about women and drugs were false—mere side effects of his fragile mental health back in 1904. He also accused Moody associates of abuse. Two evangelists, Newell claimed, had removed him from the sanitarium where he was being treated after a mental breakdown and took him to an abandoned home in the woods of Wisconsin. There the ministers allegedly kept him prisoner. The purpose of that imprisonment, Newell said, was to "pray the devil" out of him—to heal his mental health through isolation and intercession. In practice, the attempt at curing what ailed Newell only made him more fragile, melancholy, and self-deprecating, which is why, he now claimed, he had falsely confessed to the crimes he never committed.[30]

Newell's story was compelling. Other newspapers reprinted the interview with headlines like "The Rev. William R. Newell Says Pastors Tortured Him" (*Chicago Tribune*), "Preacher Charges Inhuman Treatment" (*Inter Ocean*), and "Minister Tells How Colleagues Persecuted Him" (*Evening News*). Within days, the Moody Church responded to the allegations by publicizing Newell's drug addiction and refuting all charges of treating the erring preacher unfairly. For good measure, the executive committee of the church also unanimously voted to excommunicate Newell. (Back in 1909, he was only censured and declared unfit for ministry; excommunication, after all, would have brought unwanted publicity to the case.) With that, in October 1912, Newell's relationship with all Moody-affiliated institutions was finally dissolved.[31]

Newell dismissed the excommunication as an "outgrowth of spite and malice on the part of a small clique of men in that body" and defended his version of events. He also threatened a libel suit against the Moody Church as well as against the *Chicago Tribune* and the *Toronto World*, both of which reprinted the church's statement on the excommunication. All the while, Newell continued to preach at churches across the country. During a revival in Owensboro, Kentucky, he gave an interview about his troubles. The interview exhibited the ambivalent relationship Protestants like Newell had with the press. On the one hand, Newell needed his version of the story to dominate press coverage. But he also wanted to suppress all negative publicity—threatening lawsuits and even warning the *Owensboro Messenger* that it "would incur a great liability" if it mentioned the scandal. It was, of course, already too late for suppression. Newell ended the interview with a request to not print the story, which the *Messenger* ignored. The piece did, however, conclude by quoting Newell's threat to "comment on the moral responsibility of the newspaper and the misuse of its power in a community." The reputations of all involved depended on the right kind of publicity.[32]

Remarkably for Newell, the threats appeared to have worked; or, perhaps, the Moody elites did more behind-the-scenes work to minimize negative publicity. No archival records survive to determine precisely what happened, but the story died quickly. Over the next four decades, Newell continued his work as an evangelist and enjoyed immense popularity on the traveling preacher circuit. Already in 1914, the *Chicago Tribune* was once again advertising the revival meetings of "William R. Newell, America's Foremost Bible Teacher."[33] The foremost teacher also began composing church hymns and publishing books on biblical interpretation. Due first to the silence imposed by the Moody Church and then to the threat of libel suits, Newell re-emerged, mostly unscathed by the crisis.

Melvin (Mel) Trotter, who likely crossed paths with Newell in Chicago, also made an inconvenient confession whose consequences forced Protestant leaders to reckon with another scandal. Trotter was the son of a village bartender in rural Illinois. Drinking became Trotter's pastime. By his early twenties, he developed a serious addiction. His firstborn died when Trotter was on a binge, and at the boy's funeral Trotter swore to never drink again. The resolution was soon broken. In 1897, Trotter took a train to Chicago, where he found himself penniless and in need of a drink. He decided to sell the shoes off his feet and get the fix. Drunk and barefoot, he stumbled into the Pacific Garden Mission, a city rescue that had come to replace the site of Pacific Beer Garden, a drinking establishment. Legend has it that Dwight Moody himself came up with the new name—dropping the beer but keeping the drunks in hopes of leading them to redemption.[34] In this saloon turned sanctuary, Trotter found grace.

Trotter's sanctification progressed swiftly. For an entire year he spent an hour each day attending Bible classes at MBI. He quickly became Moody's personal friend. Three years after his shoeless landing at the Chicago mission, Trotter became the superintendent of his own ministry in Michigan. The City Rescue Mission of Grand Rapids, established to combat homelessness and alcoholism, grew to be the largest operation of its kind in the country. There, having reconciled with her recovering alcoholic husband, Trotter's long-suffering wife Lottie started a ministry of her own. The Martha Mission helped poor women acquire trade skills.[35] By 1905, Trotter would be ordained in the Presbyterian church and become more successful than he ever imagined he could be.

Things went smoothly for the Trotters for years. Then, in 1917, Trotter's young secretary Florence Moody (no relation to Dwight Moody) gave birth to an out-of-wedlock child. In 1922, Lottie Trotter, emboldened by strong suspicions that her husband was the father, sued the evangelist for separation and division of their significant marital property.

Lottie had a strong case against Trotter, and the testimony was damaging. A fellow mission worker testified that Lottie had confided in her about Trotter's confession of paternity. Another mission worker recalled Lottie divulging the details of once forgiving Trotter for infidelity. There was more. A widow revealed that Trotter had once given her an unwanted kiss in his office.[36] A local painter and a Detroit barber both testified to having witnessed Trotter and Moody exchange kisses.[37] A Grand Rapids businessman, "one of the staunchest of local church pillars," reported that after Moody gave birth, Trotter's mission board began an investigation, in the course of which Trotter confessed his paternity.[38] A former servant in the Trotter household told the court about the many arguments that she had witnessed between the spouses, including physical altercations. Less tangible, but just as damning, was her recollection of a sarcastic prayer that Trotter once offered. "God bless this home, if you can call it a home," he reportedly uttered while saying grace before a meal for which he was not particularly grateful.[39]

Despite the damning testimony, Trotter continued to enjoy local support. Most of the men on the board of his mission stood by him. All three major local newspapers—the *Grand Rapids Press*, *News*, and *Herald*—united in refusing to publicize the trial, citing their desire to protect Trotter's reputation should the charges against him be proven false. "We believe in the mission work and we believe in Trotter," one editor told the *Detroit News*. "We think he is more sinned against than sinning."[40] Trotter's religious work in Grand Rapids was important enough to be shielded from scandal.[41]

Friends from afar rushed to Trotter's defense. The evangelist Billy Sunday sent Trotter a telegram: "Just read of your trouble. You have my sympathy and confidence."[42] R. A. Torrey, the former MBI superintendent and a key actor in the attempted cover-up of Newell's scandal, traveled from Los Angeles to testify in the trial. Torrey and Trotter were longtime friends and frequent preachers at the biggest revivals across the nation. It was now time for Torrey to lend Trotter a hand. Torrey's task on the witness stand was to discredit the testimony of George T. Walker, former president of the board of Trotter's mission, who claimed that Trotter was the father of Moody's child. Torrey testified that Walker had, in fact, once told him that another man was the father.[43]

If Torrey, now in charge of the Bible Institute of Los Angeles, unequivocally supported Trotter, his counterparts and former colleagues at MBI were more cautious. Trotter had been scheduled to teach a summer class at MBI when the leadership decided to cancel the class and remove Trotter's name from the program. As MBI's president James M. Gray explained, "Many lies have been told about Mr. Trotter, but we feel we must protect the public."[44] MBI had learned from past mistakes: quickly disassociating from the potential for scandal was the best course of action.

Trotter, in the meantime, was trying to undermine his accusers' credibility. He called his wife "a scheming, plotting degenerate" who, he claimed, had imagined the entire paternity confession in a spurious spiritual vision.[45] Trotter's minister friends mounted similar accusations. Pastor Charles F. Meyers of Greensboro, North Carolina, defended Trotter as "the finest, straightest man I ever knew" and dismissed his wife as an "insanely jealous" woman who belonged in an asylum.[46] Even some out-of-town newspapers were hastily dismissive of Lottie. As one North Carolina newspaper quipped, "Trotter's subsequent conduct may have been quite correct, but he certainly made one bad mistake when he married."[47]

When Lottie Trotter finally testified, she denied that she had ever had any spiritual visions and reaffirmed her recollection of the confessions that both her husband and Moody had made after the birth of the child.[48] Lottie also introduced another witness with sensational allegations of her own.

Gertrude Smith, a gospel singer, told the court about "kissing games." According to Smith, these games were a regular occurrence at Trotter's mission. Girls would dare each other to kiss Trotter, then line up and proceed to fulfill the dare one after another, planting kisses on Trotter's cheeks.[49] Another woman suggested that the evangelist had hypnotic influence over the women in his care.[50] Moody, in the meantime, denied both Trotter's paternity and having ever confessed to Lottie Trotter. She would not, however, reveal who the real father was.[51]

After months of testimony and a countersuit for separation by Mel Trotter, the preacher was granted a divorce in August 1922. Lottie received a sizable settlement: two houses worth $25,000 and $5,000 in cash. The minister was also ordered to pay attorney fees and court expenses.[52] Yet, in a more significant sense, Trotter emerged victorious. The verdict stated that the charges of adultery and cruelty were not proven.[53] Within days, Trotter was again conducting revival meetings. Although he claimed to be broke, he was also ready to start over with "a clean record."[54] As one newspaper playfully prophesied, "Mel Trotter declares he is broke. Now he will have to start saving again."[55]

Like William R. Newell before him, Mel Trotter gave the leadership of MBI and other evangelical organizations a good scare on account of his scandal but was ultimately able to return to ministry. Ten years after the affair, Trotter could once again be found preaching in Chicago—his sermons broadcast over the waves of WMBI, MBI's radio station.[56] Despite a brief distancing during the summer of the trial, MBI welcomed its vindicated son back into the fold.

While MBI leaders were experimenting with scandal management, a new kind of problem began to plague American ministers. Homosexuality was rapidly becoming a formidable concern among the highly homosocial Protestants. In the early twentieth century, European sexologists' theories about sexual diversity entered the American imagination.[57] Queer sub-cultures thrived in large urban centers.[58] Despite these developments, the culture writ large did not possess a sophisticated understanding of homosexuality and would continue to be hostile to queerness. Part of the difficulty with the concept of homosexuality in this period was the relative illegibility and discursive imprecision of the category.[59] The crime of sodomy, for example, was still widely used to describe both consensual sexual encounters among adults and what would later be understood as sexual assault and pedophilia (fellatio and bestiality also fell under the definition of sodomy in many states).[60] This is why the word "queer," which at the time would have been used as an insult or, at best, an unflattering diagnosis, may be helpful for discussing sexual nonconformity in this period: it encapsulates a multiplicity of acts and identities.

Nomenclature is secondary, however, to what occurred on the ground. As ideas about sexuality changed, new kinds of sexual misconduct entered the genre of religious scandals. The press had grown increasingly comfortable with publishing queer rumors. If in 1898, newspapers found it sufficient to report that a Methodist minister was found "guilty of offenses similar to those of which Oscar Wilde was convicted in England," within a few years, they would start reporting on the previously unprintable crime of homosexuality in less coded language.[61] And if other kinds of scandals did not always succeed in ruining ministers' careers, rumors of homosexuality would become a full-proof strategy—leading some of the accused to joblessness, asylums, and suicide. By publicizing accusations of sexual deviance among the clergy, the press compelled the Protestants' reckoning with a new kind of sex problem in their midst.[62]

When the Peoria Baptist minister George H. Simmons drank a bottle of cyanide in 1906, newspapers linked his suicide with the accusations of sodomy that had recently surfaced. Although Simmons's suicide note did not mention the allegations of inappropriate conduct with the young men in his congregation explicitly, it contained a telling sentiment: "I have preached the truth, but conditions beyond my control have prevented my realizing it." A boy from Simmons's congregation had recently testified against the pastor before the district attorney and, in one newspaper's estimation, "dispelled all doubts as to the truth of the rumors." The article also noted that Simmons had "won the confidence" of his congregation by his work with the boys—taking them "camping, coasting, hunting, and swimming," all while enjoying an unusually casual relationship with the young men. Simmons reportedly insisted that the boys called him "George," not "Reverend" or "Mister."[63] The overt attachment to youth ministry and unusual familiarity with the boys marked Simmons as a likely deviant.[64] The *Los Angeles Times* concluded that Simmons was a "moral degenerate," who ruined not only his life but also the lives of several young men in his spiritual care.[65]

The slippage between allegations of inappropriate sexual behavior with "boys" and "young men," combined with a lack of evidence outside of newspaper reports, makes it difficult to assess Simmons's unfortunate life and death in terms legible for today's students of human sexuality. Still, his case demonstrates how homosexuality would come to be associated with concepts like sickness, disease, and insanity just as the subject finally began to appear in print.[66] Ideas about homosexuality emerged at the same time as the psychological sciences developed the concept of adolescence.[67] As scientific theories of human development embraced the dichotomy of normalcy and deviance, healthy male adolescents were defined, in part, by their rejection of effeminacy. The corruptible vulnerability of youth became a problem to be fixed. Homosexuality assumed the place of the "abnormal," in contrast to the desired normalcy of virile masculinity. When Simmons's fellow Baptist minister E. L. James of the First Baptist Church in Decatur, Illinois, pleaded guilty to charges of criminal assault, newspapers called him a "moral degenerate" and attributed his derangement to unspecified vices."[68] No further details were supplied, but an attentive reader would have assumed some form of deviant sexuality. Queerness and degeneracy were not disparate diagnoses.

As the subject of irregular sexual behaviors became more printable, accusations of this nature multiplied. Few strategies for ruining reputations were more bulletproof than casting a minister in the light of sexual deviance. As Protestant denominations competed for followers and prominence, some of their representatives deployed this strategy to discredit their competitors.

Such accusations of homosexuality played out in the inter-religious campaign against the nascent pentecostal movement and one of its leaders Charles Fox Parham. Along with William J. Seymour, Parham is generally considered the founder of pentecostalism. The story of the relationship between the two men is more complicated, however. Parham, a white Midwesterner, was a Ku Klux Klan enthusiast who supported, promoted, and endorsed anti-Black racism and Jim Crow segregation. When Seymour, who was Black, attempted to attend Parham's classes, for example, Parham allowed him to listen in on one condition: Seymour had to remain outside the classroom door.[69] Despite enduring inhumane treatment, Seymour managed to extract valuable lessons from Parham's flawed teaching on sanctified life. It was Parham's theology that first connected the experience of being baptized in the Holy Spirit with receiving the spiritual gift of glossolalia—or speaking in tongues—as described in the second chapter of Acts and popularized in Seymour's 1906 Azusa Street Revival.

Parham enjoyed immense evangelistic success until the summer of 1907, when he was arrested on charges of committing "an unnatural offense" with twenty-two-year old J. J. Jourdan of San Antonio, Texas. The details of the arrest are sketchy at best.[70] Between the murky facts and the seemingly untraceable identity of the codefendant, the nuances of Parham's sexuality are not easily recoverable in the historical record.[71] What is clear is that his contemporaries apparently had serious reservations about his fitness for ministry due to his sexual proclivities, and his wife appeared to have known about the problem.[72]

In contrast to the fragmentary nature of the surviving evidence in the case, Parham's own calculated denunciations of any unsavory sexual behavior were certain. From the start, the minister categorically denied all accusations. Fortuitously for the embattled preacher, the charges were dropped in a matter of weeks. Secular newspapers quickly moved on to other matters, but Christian publications refused to let the story die. Parham's coreligionists latched on to the sensational arrest and exploited it for their own purposes.[73]

The *Zion Herald*, pastor Wilbur Glenn Voliva's church newspaper, was the first to report on the matter—embellishing the story with false claims and invented details. Voliva had begun spreading rumors about Parham a year earlier, after the preacher, once a frequent visiting speaker at the Illinois church, suddenly distanced himself from the establishment. Voliva's *Herald* reported that Parham confessed to impropriety, which the minister denied and no other publication mentioned. In the aftermath of rumors and speculations, Parham's ministry survived, but the evangelist's reputation was tarnished by rumors of queerness.[74]

Over the course of the following decade, accusations of deviant sexual conduct against Protestant pastors multiplied. Episcopal clergymen were a frequent target. A native of Troy, New York, Robert Morris Kemp was ordained at age twenty-nine and served New York City parishes for most of his career. In July 1907, Kemp accepted a call to pastor St. Chrysostom's Episcopal Church in Chicago. Just a year into his tenure, Kemp resigned amid allegations by eight of his choirboys. Newspapers were initially hesitant to print the details, but readers likely understood that the matter involved sexual impropriety. "The offense with which they charged him," reported the *Des Moines Tribune*, "is a penal one under the new code and were he to be convicted he would be sent to the penitentiary for an indefinite term."[75] Kemp denied the allegations, which included both the unspecified offenses against the choirboys and an "indiscreet" relationship with the wife of the church's sexton.[76]

Church leadership met to discuss the allegations three days after Kemp rendered his resignation. "Several church officials," reported the *Chicago Tribune*, "refused to believe the truth of the accusations, while others declared that the evidence was sufficient" to accept Kemp's resignation. The congregation decided to drop the matter, keep the details secret, and simply part ways with the pastor. Some of the choirboys' parents seemed satisfied; others considered seeking criminal prosecution where ecclesiastical justice failed. Officials at St. Chrysostom's were careful to supply only the vaguest details of the case, telling journalists that "the publicity has hurt the church and aroused dissension in the parish, and we believe every effort should be made to forget the whole trouble in the interests of harmony and Christianity." Forgetting allegations of abuse was quickly becoming church officials' preferred remedy to ongoing challenges to Protestantism's reputation. [77]

It proved difficult to forget sensational accusations when they continued to manifest in eerily similar ways in other congregations within the scandal-plagued Episcopal Diocese of Chicago. Less than a month after Kemp resigned, Alfred William Griffin, rector of St. Peter's Church, who, like Kemp, moved to Chicago from New York only a year earlier, was accused by his choirboys of offenses similar to Kemp's.[78] Newspapers, on their end, discussed the two cases in similarly opaque ways. That the charges were unprintable suggested that they were, almost certainly, sexual in nature.

Despite the ambiguity in coverage, Griffin's case offered new revelations about the dynamics of clerical abuse in this period. The category of choir "boys," it turns out, was less straightforward than the designation might suggest. The *Chicago Inter Ocean* listed the identities and ages of the "boys" who provided affidavits: "Walter Anderson, 19 years old; George Nicholas, 20 years old, and Robert Powell, said to be 33 years old."[79] The designation of "boy" was thus not always indicative of the person's actual age, but it did not mean that all alleged victims were eighteen or older, either. Kemp's accusers, for example, included teenagers between sixteen and eighteen years old.[80] Still, Griffin's case complicates the otherwise seemingly straightforward—and tragically familiar—story of child sexual abuse. This is not to say that the church responded in a manner that was sympathetic to the victims. On the contrary, St. Peter's fired the accusers—a tactic that other religious groups would continue to employ for silencing whistleblowers.

The choirboys' removal did not resolve the problem. The victims demanded that the rector be formally investigated. Griffin agreed and requested that the Chicago bishop oversee the ecclesiastical proceedings. Members of St. Peter's congregation were divided. Some expressed unequivocal trust in the pastor's innocence; others stopped attending services in the wake of the affair.[81]

Within a month, the Episcopal Church exonerated Griffin. The internal investigation resulted in three findings: the charges against Griffin were of immoral but not criminal nature, the alleged victims failed to prove the charges, and Griffin was, therefore, vindicated and restored to ministry.[82] "Now let us turn an intellectual somersault," said Bishop C. P. Anderson, "and get our minds on something else."[83] With semi-vindicating findings and attendant intellectual gymnastics, St. Peter's was ready to move on from the scandal.

Meanwhile, three miles south, St. Chrysostom's was still dealing with the fallout from the Kemp affair. With the pastor's resignation, the church was ready to erase the episode from its annals, but the victims kept pressing the issue. In late October 1908, the diocese called a special secret commission that interviewed the boys who accused Kemp. Two weeks later, the committee exonerated the resigned pastor, though not without a dissenting vote from one of the investigators.[84] Kemp, in turn, told the bishop that he wanted to undergo a full ecclesiastical trial in order to erase all doubts of his innocence.[85] The bishop, tired of dealing with cases of this nature, declined Kemp's request and refused to grant him a trial.[86]

After the church washed its hands of the affair, the state got involved. Kemp was arrested on Christmas Eve in 1908 and released on bond the same day.[87] The preliminary hearing began in January 1909. Testifying on his own behalf, Kemp proved to be a colorful witness. He blamed the accusations on an internal congregational conspiracy designed to force his resignation. He admitted to having taken church boys to a cafe but claimed that it happened only once and that, on that occasion, the conversation centered on "the immaculate conception and the infallibility of the pope."[88] Kemp also stated, though not without hesitation, that he knew the boys to be "immoral" because they had revealed as much to him in confession.

The presiding judge was not convinced by Kemp's defense; the testimony of the boys regarding the apparently unprintable details of what occurred in the pastor's parlor proved detrimental. "Knowledge of this sort of crime," Judge Freeman Blake noted, "shows that the offense is not alone prevalent among the low and degraded, but is committed by persons of high station and supposed high ideals."[89] Homosexuality afflicted all kinds of people.

Kemp was initially indicted on three counts of immoral conduct.[90] Within three months, two more indictments were added. The most sensational charge came from outside the pastor's former church. George Nelson, who had worked as a bellboy at a downtown hotel, alleged that in February 1908, Kemp invited him and several other bellboys out to drinks. Kemp then had Nelson accompany him to another hotel.[91] The story of the buzzed bachelor clergyman and the bellboy renting a hotel room suggested impropriety, especially in light of the other complaints against Kemp.

The trial was set for June 1909. Newspapers reported that Kemp was going to plead "not guilty by reason of insanity." To help his chances, Kemp, who was out on bond, checked himself into a sanitarium and claimed that he had a mental breakdown—a strategy other ministers in his situation would continue to employ.[92] It is possible that Kemp's internal distress was entirely sincere. In July, the former pastor was arraigned "on a charge of drunkenness that grew out of a visit he made last night to the home of a friend who was a former choir boy at St. Paul's."[93] St. Paul's was Kemp's last place of employment before he moved from New York to Chicago, and issues with choir boys apparently extended to both congregations. Neither of the parties pressed charges, so the incident resolved quietly. Still, Kemp's drunken interactions with younger men appeared to constitute a pattern.

Kemp's first trial finally began in March 1910, more than a year and a half after he resigned. The defense's strategy worked: jurors sided with the minister who cried conspiracy in his former congregation. Within a week, Kemp was acquitted of two charges.[94]

Kemp stood his final trial in June 1910, and newspapers were now offering a few more details about the case. The prosecution argued that Kemp "formerly had a boy with him whom he introduced as his son," despite being a bachelor.[95] But even that detail did not persuade the jury of the pastor's guilt. Kemp was acquitted of immorality.[96] He moved back to New York City and eventually returned to ministry, serving as the assistant rector of Manhattan's Saint Thomas Church until his death in 1940.[97]

Cases like Kemp's would continue to plague the Episcopal Church, even as the denomination was refining its strategies for dealing with queer pastors. In 1912, Alfred Garnett Mortimer, rector of Philadelphia's Saint Mark's Church, was suddenly asked to resign from the pastorate due to such rumors. Initially, the reason for the development was kept secret from the public and the press. "From vague reports today," announced the *New York Times*, "it was understood that it is in the intention of all concerned to let the affair die out as quickly as possible."[98] But the affair refused to disappear either quickly or quietly. The *Chicago Day Book* prefaced the story with a provocative headline: "Rector of Exclusive Church Resigns—Scandal?"[99] The article reproduced the gossip around the case and contributed to the speculations about why Mortimer was being removed from his post. One rumor accused Mortimer of an inappropriate relationship with a married woman; another pegged him as a homosexual. Within days of the article's publication, Mortimer left the country for his childhood home in England to avoid scandal. "I have been charged with doing many things against the church as well as against the set rules of morality," the minister explained. "Some of these charges may be true; others are false. I am not the degenerate that I have been pictured."[100] Mortimer's use of the word "degenerate" provided a clue to the likely charges against him.[101] At the time, the word would have been regarded as synonymous with "sodomite" or "homosexual."[102]

Three years later, the public fall from grace of an anti-vice reformer would further confirm that even the most outwardly orthodox pastors were apparently highly susceptible to queer temptation.[103] Kenneth G. Murray was a Methodist minister who served on the board of the Baltimore Society for the Suppression of Vice. In 1915, he was accused of making sexual advances toward young men at the YMCA, where he frequently ministered and socialized. One evening, residents caught Murray in the act of oral sex with an eighteen-year-old man.[104] Murray resigned his position and even voluntarily entered a sanitarium, but the alleged crime was egregious enough to cause a citywide scandal. Journalists like H. L. Mencken used the story to dismiss religious anti-vice crusaders as deviant hypocrites.[105] As newspapers disparaged Christianity on account of its representatives' queer proclivities, denominational bodies became increasingly sensitive to the formidable predicament in their ranks. Over the following decade, Protestants would experiment with various strategies of managing the problem.

Presbyterian fundamentalists would attempt to hide their queer scandal from the press in 1916. That August, four copies of an anonymous letter were mailed to ministers in Elmira, New York, alleging that John Balcom Shaw, president of the Elmira College for Women, was guilty of "the crime of sodomy."[106] The story did not become a national scandal, newspaper headlines did not reproduce the accusations, and reporters did not seek comments from either Shaw or his denomination. The case was handled internally and with the greatest degree of secrecy. Despite initially dismissing the claims in the anonymous letter, the ministers involved in handling the problem continued to hear rumors about Shaw's sexual proclivities. Eventually, in early 1918, an investigative committee advised that Shaw "cancel all speaking engagements and go away quietly, possibly to a sanitarium" to seek help for his condition.[107] Shaw's fellow clergymen seemed to believe that he was ill with the plague of homosexuality and wanted him to disappear. To avoid scandal, Shaw was expected to make himself scarce. He resigned from Elmira College and remitted the ministry in April 1918. The Presbyterians succeeded in handling Shaw's case internally and relegated his sexual proclivities to the realm of mental health.

The following year, the Episcopal Church would face similar accusations against one of its representatives. In 1919, the US Navy received reports of homosexual activity among the men stationed in Newport, Rhode Island.[108] At the helm of the alleged deviant ring was the Episcopal chaplain Samuel Neal Kent, who was accused of paying sailors for sexual favors.

World War I flooded Newport with new recruits. Whereas the station normally housed two thousand enlisted personnel, the war brought in between fifteen and twenty thousand young men annually.[109] Some of the newcomers were, according to the report, "persons of low morals" who incited "demoralization among the enlisted personnel."[110] Rumors of "sexual perverts" soon reached Secretary of the Navy Josephus Daniels and Assistant Secretary Franklin D. Roosevelt. With great speed and determination, if unusual zeal, the local naval officers decided to investigate the scandalous reports by soliciting volunteers who would infiltrate the ring and engage in homosexual acts to establish that the rumors were true. In the summer of 1919, Roosevelt issued an order to enlist men to go into Newport "and to allow immoral acts to be performed upon them, if in their judgment it was necessary for the purpose of running down and trapping or capturing certain specified alleged sexual perverts."[111]

With the evidence obtained and seventeen sailors apprehended, Reverend Kent was implicated as well. Five men accused Kent of having engaged in sexual acts and advances. The chaplain was arrested on two charges of immoral conduct. During his trial, details of the government-sanctioned investigation by means of engagement with the alleged homosexuals shocked the public. One operative testified that he was instructed to allow the minister to "play with [his] penis" until he "had an emission."[112] Details like this made the press and the public question the navy's integrity. Whatever Kent did or did not do with other men's genitals was based on strange evidence and unconventional methods of obtaining the damning reports. Kent was acquitted.

The navy was embarrassed and determined to try Kent again, this time in federal court. The Episcopal Church supported Kent ideologically and financially. The Diocesan Church War Commission, which voted to fund Kent's defense, expressed "its gratitude to the Rev. Samuel Neal Kent for his service as Chaplain, its absolute confidence in him, and also its regret for the unfortunate situation into which he was brought by the charges preferred against him by the Navy Department."[113] Despite the denomination's professed confidence in Kent's innocence, he was soon transferred from Rhode Island to Warwick, Pennsylvania, to serve a local congregation far from the drama of Newport. There the minister was arrested for the second time.

Fourteen clergymen testified on Kent's behalf. Kent denied all accusations of impropriety and insisted that his conduct in the chaplaincy had been nothing short of exemplary when it came to Christian standards of hospitality and care for fellow men. When sailors needed shelter, Kent invited them to room with him at the rectory. When they were hungry, Kent cooked them dinner. If they needed transportation, Kent offered them rides. Kent's defense team successfully recast what would otherwise have been interpreted as sexual interest in sailors in terms of Christian service and brotherly affection.[114]

Although the chaplain was acquitted, he did not remain a minister much longer. Kent left religious work in 1921 and occupied secular professions until his death in 1943.[115] It was easier for the Episcopal Church to dismiss a clergyman of questionable sexual affinities than to deal with public disgrace. At least when it came to deviant sexuality, Protestant denominations were learning to minimize the damage scandal caused.

Protestants were also finally realizing that they had to do something about their public image in the press.[116] "This is preeminently the age of newspaper readers rather than of church goers," wrote one advocate of better church publicity in 1915. "It is time that someone led the way to a modification of the training of future religious leaders so that they may influence men through the press."[117] Already in the early 1910s, the Men and Religion Forward Movement (M&RFM), an evangelical association formed to counteract the perceived feminization of Protestant churches, identified this crisis of mutual distrust between secular journalism and religious work.[118] The men in charge of M&RFM lamented journalists' disregard of religion as a positive agent of social change. The "alienation between the newspapers and the churches," they argued, was the result of "mistaken and short-sighted views on both sides." They agreed that bad behavior by clergy deserved publicity but cautioned that the overemphasis on scandal undermined the overall positive impact the church had on the world. To ensure balanced reporting, newspapers needed to bolster positive church publicity and eschew "the exploitation of the occasional scandal."[119]

Persuaded by this logic, Protestants attempted to rebuild their reputation through the press. In 1913, Methodist minister Christian F. Reisner published a book that advocated church publicity and outlined a strategy for compelling people to join churches through newspaper ads and positive media exposure. Reisner argued that Protestants needed to invest in newspaper advertising to cultivate an image that would appeal to "the modern man."[120] Two years later, Presbyterian editor and publicity manager Herbert Heebner Smith published a book that provided practical guidelines for utilizing various kinds of advertising—including paid listings in secular newspapers—to generate popular interest in religion.[121] By 1916, most major Protestant denominations had established church publicity departments. Their representatives participated in national ad men's conventions, hoping to make friends in the publishing world and improve their reputations through commercial means.[122]

This was a necessary development for the rapidly fracturing world of modern Protestantism. The 1920s saw the height of the fundamentalist-modernist crisis, in which Protestant denominations split along theological lines on issues of biblical interpretation and modern scientific theories of evolution. As the controversy intensified, sex scandals marked one possible way of adjudicating what kind of religion was going to prevail. This tension played out in the sensational 1922 double murder of the Methodist minister Edward Hall and his lover Eleanor Mills. The married pastor and his choir singer had been in a romantic relationship for years. When their bodies, riddled with gunshot wounds, were discovered, they were positioned so that they "lay in embrace, with steamy letters scattered around them," revealing the truth of adultery even in death.[123] Fundamentalist Protestants hastened to use the story to discredit their modernist counterparts. The fiery evangelist Billy Sunday, the same man who had expressed unshakable confidence in his friend Mel Trotter's innocence two months earlier, led the charge. Sunday's diatribes focused on Hall's moral hypocrisy, as he excoriated the late couple's loosened sexual mores. Incongruity between belief and praxis had long been used to discredit religious leaders, but this particular moment of division among Protestants marked a new turn in the crisis of representation, as they turned to newspapers to discredit each other.

In response to such challenges, Protestant denominations came together to devise new publicity strategies. In 1922, the Chicago Church Federation (CCF) organized the first National Conference on Church Publicity. With five hundred attendees, the gathering's pithy central message was "Co-operate with the newspapers."[124] Collaboration quickly bore fruit. In 1924, the Associated Press (AP) addressed the CCF with an acknowledgment of the common goals of religion and the press. "We endeavor to avoid scandal and chit-chat, the divorce court and the gutter," the AP manager Frederick Roy Martin wrote in his address to conference attendees.[125] Urging churches to promptly report religious news to local editors, the AP extended a helping hand to Protestant organizations that were desperately trying to redirect newspaper coverage away from sensationalism and toward positive publicity.

Church-press collaboration was supposed to be mutually beneficial, and, for a while, it appeared to be working. The timing was fortuitous. In 1923, the American Society of Newspaper Editors adopted a new code of professional ethics. The "canons of journalism" included responsibility, freedom, independence, sincerity, truth, accuracy, impartiality, fair play, and decency. A newspaper, the organization posited, could not "escape conviction of insincerity if while professing high moral purpose it supplies incentives to base conduct, such as are to be found in details of crime and vice, publication of which is not demonstrably for the general good."[126] Ninety years after the penny press revolution, during which the sensational propelled newspapers to the top of political influence and cultural power, editors were reconsidering their role in shaping public morality.[127]

In that spirit, the press began to treat religion with more reverence. In 1925, the *New York Times* introduced a weekly religion column, headed by editor Rachel McDowell, a fundamentalist Presbyterian whose office nickname was "Lady Bishop."[128] A contemporary observer concluded that if, prior to World War I, newspapers "scorned to print a line of Church news— except scandal—unless it was paid for at the regular advertising rates," by 1925, coverage had changed to cater to readers who were "increasingly interested in the activities of the Church, and religion in general."[129] For the time being, the press and the church were getting along more harmoniously than they had in almost a century.

This alliance was short-lived. The year 1926 would see one of the biggest religious scandals of the twentieth century: the sensational disappearance of Aimee Semple McPherson and the drawn-out saga of subsequent legal investigation and journalistic probing. The scandal would shake the foundation of the nascent harmony achieved by church publicity departments with the press. Like Henry Ward Beecher's drama from half a century earlier, McPherson's disappearance became a case study in the legitimacy of religious authority and disrupted the fledgling alliance that had been forged between the pulpit and the press.

5

Vanishing Acts

The mysterious disappearance of a female celebrity evangelist from a public beach would have been surprising for any other time or place, but 1920s Los Angeles was the perfect setting for such a stunt. The city had recently become the birthplace of pentecostalism and the movie industry—two institutions that would fundamentally transform religion and popular culture.[1] It buzzed with innovation and thrived on sensation. The charismatic revivalist at the center of the mystery was uniquely suited for the role of the most compelling protagonist of her era.

Aimee Semple McPherson was Canadian by birth and American by calling and disposition. Raised in a Salvation Army household, McPherson was always interested in religion. In 1907, she converted to pentecostal Christianity during a revival near her hometown in rural Ontario. At seventeen, she felt eager to devote her life to ministry. The next year, she married Robert Semple, the young preacher who had issued the altar call. The couple moved to Chicago to pursue evangelistic work. In 1910, pregnant with her first child, McPherson accompanied her husband on a mission trip to China, where he died after contracting malaria. Less than a month after burying her spouse, McPherson gave birth to her daughter Roberta, and the fractured family returned to the United States.

Having once committed to Christian ministry, the young widow struggled to envision a life of service amid the tragedy of losing her first love. Besides the support of her mother Mildred "Minnie" Kennedy, whom she joined in New York, McPherson saw few opportunities to pursue evangelism as a single mother. In 1912, she solved the problem of insufficient financing by marrying a businessman, Harold McPherson, with whom she had a son. The new family arrangement helped with McPherson's material circumstances, but spiritual matters remained unresolved.

McPherson would later liken herself to the biblical prophet Jonah, whom God violently compelled to answer the call to ministry, and the comparison was not without merit. Depression and melancholy had distracted the would-be preacher from her spiritual path and made her feel like a burden

Disgraced: How Sex Scandals Transformed American Protestantism. Suzanna Krivulskaya, Oxford University Press.
© Oxford University Press 2025. DOI: 10.1093/oso/9780197599686.003.0006

on friends and family. While she avoided active ministry and attempted to play the part of a contented housewife, her health began to decline. In 1913 and 1914, McPherson underwent two serious surgeries. So bad were her pain and depression prior to the second surgery that she prayed that God would take her life. When she recovered from the operation, McPherson became convinced that God had spared her in order to commit her to full-time evangelistic work. "Oh, don't you ever tell me that a woman cannot be called to preach the Gospel! If any man ever went through one hundredth part of the hell on earth that I lived in, those months when out of God's will and work, they would never say that again," she concluded.[2] Experience and conviction—not exegesis or theology—cemented in McPherson's mind her ministerial calling. Like other female preachers, McPherson located spiritual authority in her relationship to the divine and refused to seek validation from a culture that largely upheld the New Testament injunction for women to "keep silence in the churches."[3]

Despite her chosen occupation, McPherson was far from an advocate for women's liberation. In fact, the preacher unapologetically placed the blame for the sin of the world on women, while simultaneously using it to justify her own ministerial calling. Eve, McPherson argued, was responsible for the entire mess; it was therefore up to women to undo the damage.[4] So she got to work. Abandoning marital duties, McPherson left her second husband on the East Coast in 1915. (He would eventually file for divorce on the grounds of desertion—an offense most often committed by men—in 1921.) With two children in tow, this "miracle woman" drove around the country in her gospel car plastered with the words "Jesus Is Coming Soon—Get Ready," preaching and healing the sick. By 1920, most cities struggled to secure venues large enough to contain the crowds yearning to see the "female Billy Sunday," as newspapers dubbed McPherson in a flattering comparison to the most successful male evangelist of the era.[5] Though McPherson never figured out how to undo the consequences of original sin brought on by a woman, she had succeeded in becoming the nation's favorite female preacher.[6]

The timing was fortuitous. The decade marked a break with Victorianism and ushered the country into modernity.[7] Economic prosperity and technological innovations presented some Americans with unprecedented opportunity for material flourishing. For the first time in history, more than half of the population lived in urban areas.[8] Large cities buzzed with new forms of entertainment and socialization. Writers and artists mounted

Aimee Semple McPherson, holding a Bible, reaches out her hands in prayer in an early publicity photo. McPherson is wearing a white outfit modeled after Red Cross nurse uniforms, which she used to signify her spiritual calling as the "Bride of Christ."
Library of Congress Prints and Photographs Division, LC-DIG-ggbain-31648

newly articulated critiques of orthodoxy and advocated for radical transformation of society and culture. The "roaring" twenties were bursting with creativity, innovation, and change—at least for the upwardly mobile.

The break with Victorian norms most potently affected young people—single white women in particular. For generations, the burden of sexual purity had been laid on their shoulders by the Victorian ideal of women's "passionlessness," as historian Nancy Cott has labeled it.[9] Women had been socialized to behave as innately more pure, more spiritual, and more sexually restrained than men. By the 1920s, the established sexual consensus had fractured. The new "flapper girl" cut off her hair, went out dancing, and kissed men. One contemporary observer of these developments, Frederick Lewis Allen, would later recall the overwhelming concern with women's appearance:

> In July, 1920, a fashion-writer reported in the *New York Times* that "the American woman...has lifted her skirts far beyond any modest limitation," which was another way of saying that the hem was not all of nine inches above the ground. It was freely predicted that skirts would come down again the winter of 1920–21, but instead they climbed a few scandalous inches farther.[10]

The length of women's skirts as well as women's newfound distaste for corsets were symptoms of a larger epidemic. Women, it appeared, were abandoning the sexual norms instilled in them by their elders. Increasingly, they were turning instead to the seductive glow of the silver screen for role models.

Los Angeles, where independent women like McPherson made their home, was central to propagating the sexually liberated spirit of the 1920s. "Thousands of girls receive their first thrills of sex knowledge in the movies," complained one critic. "Every step taken, showing the unfaithfulness of women, [is] vividly portrayed. This showing gives girls and wives the idea, and belief, that they are, and will be, immune from punishment, for this immorality."[11] At the time, Hollywood produced 80 percent of all films worldwide, and the early days of the movie industry exploded with on-screen explorations of previously taboo topics like sex.[12] Idolized by the public, screen actors became celebrities in the modern sense of the word—and inspired enterprising evangelists like McPherson to comport themselves with similar flare. McPherson's signature look was a simple white outfit modeled after Red Cross uniforms and chosen, in part, to embody her theological emphasis on the church—and herself—as the virginal "Bride of Christ."[13] But the simplicity of McPherson's fashion did not translate into orthodoxy. Her charismatic sermons, accessible message, and undaunted enthusiasm for the gospel attracted mesmerized followers wherever she went. By 1923, contributions from supporters and admirers across the nation enabled McPherson to erect a worship center of her own—the stunning fifty-three-hundred-seat Angelus Temple in Echo Park. McPherson's spiritual empire found a comfortable home in the heart of the City of Angels.

A smiling Aimee Semple McPherson (*center*) poses with a group of women who dress and wear their hair in the popular 1920s "flapper" style. McPherson's ministry attracted young people, including Hollywood actors, and drew criticism from conservative rivals who feared that McPherson's embrace of secular culture compromised her commitment to traditional Christianity.
Library of Congress Prints and Photographs Division, LC-DIG-npcc-16475

McPherson's decision to settle in Los Angeles was strategic. In less than a decade, she had traversed the country on the preaching circuit multiple times. As one Kansas newspaper put it, "Although only 31 years old she has probably spoken to more people than has any other woman in the world's history."[14] The demand for the dazzling evangelist was not subsiding, and McPherson's proto-megachurch in Los Angeles allowed the spiritually hungry masses to come to her.[15] The strategy paid off. In addition to show business, oil discoveries and industrial manufacturing in and around Los Angeles ensured a steady supply of newcomers, who arrived in search of sunnier, more prosperous lives.[16] Between 1920 and 1930, the population more than doubled from 577,000 to 1.24 million, and the city expanded its sprawling boundaries by eighty square miles.[17] With opportunities for newness and prosperity along with the allure of celebrity, Los Angeles embodied the promise of the 1920s.

It was not just Southern California that was undergoing this cultural shift. When the sociologists Robert and Helen Lynd decided to conduct their ethnographic study of a typical municipality, they settled on Muncie, Indiana—a majority-white, industrial, Protestant town of about thirty-five thousand. This was the heart of the nation. It was, as the Lynds aptly dubbed it, "Middletown, U.S.A."[18] By the time the Lynds got to Muncie in 1925, innovation was infiltrating tradition in all areas of life, including religion. Although Muncie was heavily Protestant (the town had only one synagogue to its forty-two churches, and Protestants outnumbered Catholics fifteen to one), religion faced fierce competition from other forms of community engagement and entertainment. Church membership rates were high, but the residents were increasingly lured away from the pews by weekend leisure activities. Sunday morning "motoring," picnics in the park, baseball, golf, and shooting ranges compelled potential church attendees to skip the tabernacle for more tantalizing pursuits. In Muncie, the Lynds concluded, religious observances appeared to be "a less spontaneous and pervasive part" of life compared to the previous generation, despite the ministers' best attempts to modernize their methods of engaging the public.[19] Even the most conservative Christians understood that to compete in the Sunday marketplace of leisure, they had to revolutionize their outreach efforts.

The most enterprising religious leaders were the most successful. During one revival, the publicity manager of a local church sent out newspaper notices advertising a meeting devoted to the subject of "follies of 1924." The attendees would likely have understood the double meaning of the word "follies." The 1913 edition of Webster's dictionary defined "folly" as a "foolish act" or "scandalous crime; sin; specifically as applied to a woman, wantonness." Muncie residents would have also been familiar with New York's Ziegfeld Follies, which had taken Broadway by storm, and likely associated the word with secular entertainment of the vaudevillian variety.

The night in question promised to be "the hottest meeting" on the revival route. With tickets that resembled theater passes in hand, spectators crowded the church. The men took over the tabernacle. The women gathered in the basement to listen to an address by the pastor's wife. For the men, the sermon painted a picture of "a fine crop of chorus girls" who were "positively indecent in their over-exposure." Their names were Godlessness, Hypocrisy, and Flippancy. These were the vices of the secular world, the minister asserted, hoping to stir the crowd toward godliness. The sociologists observing the event were less convinced. The Lynds remarked, "It is noteworthy that the appeal used both here and in the women's meeting to get out the crowd, by this church which condemns dancing, card-playing, and the theater, was identical with that used by the more sensational local movies."[20] Even as conservative Protestants outwardly eschewed secular culture, they incorporated and exploited its allures. The world that the 1920s ushered in was full of such contradictions.

For Protestants, contradictions begot confrontations. For decades, tensions had been escalating between theological traditionalists, who sought to protect their churches from the influence of modern scientific thought, and progressives, who believed their tenets were capacious enough to accommodate the theological challenges modernity had wrought.[21] The two groups came to be known as fundamentalists and modernists, respectively, and they sprang up among all major Protestant denominations. In the long list of fundamentalists' complaints about the modern age were moral laxity, consumer culture, women's dress, and loosened sexual ethics.[22] As historian George Marsden explains, "The fundamentalists' most alarming experience was that of finding themselves living in a culture that by the 1920s was openly turning away from God."[23] To counteract the liberalizing tendencies within their denominations, fundamentalists emphasized the centrality of personal, experiential salvation and reaffirmed their commitment to the doctrines of biblical inerrancy and the virgin birth.

A prime example of the fundamentalist-modernist controversy was the struggle over the legality of teaching Darwin's theory of evolution in public schools. After all, if the Bible contained no errors or contradictions, traditionalists asserted, then Genesis had to trump Darwin. In March 1925, the Tennessee legislature passed the Butler Act, which prohibited the teaching of evolution in public schools.[24] Two months later, high school science teacher John Scopes was charged with violating the act. The Scopes trial quickly became a national sensation. As hundreds of reporters crowded the Dayton courthouse to document each day's proceedings, thousands of outside observers descended on the town to witness the drama unfold. The cast of characters in the case warranted such attention. The folksy presidential candidate and conservative Presbyterian William Jennings Bryan served on the prosecution team. The nationally renowned American Civil

Liberties Union attorney Clarence Darrow represented Scopes. The two great orators spelled out the cultural anxieties of their generation as they battled it out in the stuffy courtroom for eight days. At the end of the ordeal, the jury found Scopes guilty and sentenced him to a fine of $100, but the verdict was soon overturned on a technicality.[25]

The real significance of the case lay not in its resolution, but in what evolution represented for the rapidly modernizing country. At its core, the Dayton sensation concerned questions that had been hotly contested for decades: separation of church and state, freedom of religion, and freedom of speech. Scopes's defenders saw his right to teach evolution as a key principle of democratic education. His detractors, by contrast, emphasized another kind of freedom: that of local communities to make autonomous decisions about their children's education. The trial revealed the dynamics of a complicated struggle over religion's place in the new century, and both sides employed the logic of modernity to argue their case.[26]

Although the anti-evolution side technically won, their opponents and secular media critics used the trial to mock fundamentalists and to portray them as the worst examples of out-of-touch anti-intellectualism. As Nunnally Johnson, who covered the trial for the *Brooklyn Eagle*, explained, "Being admirably cultivated fellows, [the newspapermen] were all of course evolutionists who looked down on the local fundamentalists."[27] Johnson was not exaggerating. The outspokenly secular *Baltimore Sun* reporter H. L. Mencken, for example, referred to Dayton fundamentalists as "the local primates," "the poor half wits," "yokels," "simple folk," and "morons" who foolishly mistook William Jennings Bryan for a prophet.[28] When Bryan died just five days after the trial concluded, Mencken celebrated his passing, describing Bryan as an "ignorant, bigoted, self-seeking, blatant and dishonest" man whose last weeks on earth were "broken, furious, and infinitely pathetic."[29] Mencken showed no sympathy for the departed because he found the anti-evolution crusade to be a dangerous meddling in public education. Although the Butler Act remained on the books until 1967, fundamentalists lost the public relations war in 1925—due, in large part, to hostile reporting.[30]

Secularism was far from the only threat to religious traditionalism. Fundamentalism was also being challenged by other, less stringent anti-modernist religious expressions. The nascent pentecostal movement, to which Aimee Semple McPherson belonged, represented one such challenge. Pentecostalism emerged out of the Methodist Holiness movement in the first decade of the twentieth century. Adherents emphasized spiritual experiences of entire sanctification (the ability to achieve a sinless life on earth) and baptism of the Holy Spirit, which manifested in speaking in tongues. Pentecostals shared many of the same anti-modernist concerns as their fundamentalist brethren, but the new movement emphasized personal spiritual experiences and was not yet preoccupied with dogma. In the fundamentalists' assessment, this made pentecostals problematic allies in the battle for the soul of the nation.[31]

Racial equality and gender egalitarianism that defined early pentecostalism likewise troubled religious traditionalists. In an era characterized by unapologetic, often violent segregation, pentecostalism allowed for unprecedented intermingling among people of different ethnicities and races.[32] Integrated revivals and worship services served as a sign of God's grace to adherents, even as they scandalized outside observers.[33] Many pentecostals also believed that women could—and had the obligation to, if they were so divinely inspired—preach the gospel. The acceptance of female ministers was far from universal, but the decentralized nature of the early movement prevented pentecostalism from being entirely closed off to women's leadership.[34] When the first formal pentecostal denomination, the Assemblies of God, organized in 1914, women made up one-third of its clergy.[35] The proportion of female pastors would eventually decline, but early pentecostalism embraced women's leadership.[36] McPherson's own denomination, the International Church of the Foursquare Gospel, which she would found in 1927, employed eighteen women as pastors across one-third of its fifty-five branches.[37]

Women like McPherson succeeded because they performed ideal pentecostal femininity in a way that convinced their followers of their claims to authority: they could be both good Christian women and good Christian leaders.[38] By emphasizing Jesus's role as the Bridegroom of the church, McPherson could assume her position as a Bride of Christ.[39] She did this often in illustrated sermons and in her many publications. The *Bridal Call*—a magazine McPherson started in 1917—bore the feminine in its very title.

Regardless of women's ministerial aspirations, they posed a problem for American fundamentalists. In the 1920s, women won the right to vote, entered the workforce at unprecedented rates, swapped their wardrobes for less restrictive clothing, and engaged in new forms of dating, nightlife, and entertainment that had been taboo for the entire gender for generations.

The fundamentalist critique of modernist religion was, at its core, an attack on the new cultural outlook on gender.[40] And although the majority of women remained housewives, and the sexual revolution had not quite arrived, religious traditionalists worried about the state of affairs—especially when some of their own women began to look and behave in virtually indistinguishable ways from the new, modern woman.

Although McPherson was politically conservative, decidedly anti-Darwinist, and in favor of biblical literalism, she embodied fundamentalists' concerns about women's leadership. Her theology prioritized grace and salvation; she was willing to temporarily mute certain dogmas in favor of saving the lost. Like Henry Ward Beecher two generations earlier, McPherson preached a gentler kind of gospel. As one biographer puts it, McPherson "wanted no part of an idea that might exclude people out of hand from the experience of Christianity."[41] To that end, she eschewed the doctrine of sanctification being attainable in earthly life and focused her sermons instead on the cleansing power of the conversion experience. A converted life did not mean a perfect life; it just meant a life full of forgiveness and grace. Relying on her stunning looks and commanding presence, McPherson incorporated her femininity and sexuality into the project of saving the lost.[42] McPherson managed to appear seductive while preaching "the old-time religion," innocent despite being a divorcée, and confident in the face of criticism from Protestant colleagues.[43] For religious traditionalists, who already perceived the "feminization" of American religion as a crisis, this signaled trouble.[44]

Perhaps chief among McPherson's detractors was fellow Los Angeles minister Robert "Fighting Bob" Shuler. Paranoid that McPherson was using her sexuality to distract from the gospel, the Methodist pastor barraged McPherson with unsolicited letters and published his accusations in sensational pamphlets. To critics like Shuler, McPherson replied, simply, "Show me a better way to persuade willing people to come to church and I'll be happy to try your method. But please, please don't ask me to preach to empty seats."[45] For the rest of her career, McPherson did not have to worry about having an empty seat in the tabernacle.

Despite her critics' skepticism, McPherson's ministry flourished. When Angelus Temple became too small to accommodate the endlessly charmed crowds that could not get enough of McPherson, she began broadcasting her sermons over the radio. The broadcasts, like everything else McPherson did, became wildly popular, so she started her own radio station in 1924.

Wanting to work with only the best professionals in the field, she hired a secular engineer, Kenneth Ormiston, to run a state-of-the-art recording studio. By then, McPherson had become one of Los Angeles's biggest stars.[46]

Popularity and insatiable public interest came accompanied by gossip. Rumors about McPherson's close relationship with her married radio technician were persistent. The gossip forced Ormiston to resign his position at Angelus Temple in December 1925.[47] The next month, when McPherson was in Europe, a Hollywood gossip magazine was set to publicize the rumor that Ormiston accompanied the evangelist on the trip, but the article's publication was halted after a travel agency confirmed that Ormiston was not with McPherson.[48] Still, the engineer's marriage was apparently in trouble. Ormiston's wife would eventually blame its dissolution on "a certain prominent woman."[49] Six months after the near-scandal of her European vacation, McPherson mysteriously disappeared from an Ocean View beach. Ormiston was missing as well.

Supporters cried drowning and held vigils. They were convinced that McPherson had perished at sea. After all, this was the story that McPherson's secretary, who happened to be present for the disappearance, told the press: McPherson had swum out too far from the shore and vanished. Hopeful volunteers swept the beach, diving crews combed the ocean floor, and airplanes surveyed the water from the sky in their attempts to locate the body. All efforts proved futile; there was no body to be found. "Aimee Semple McPherson, given to the world in the providence of God, has been promoted to Glory!" opened the June 1926 issue of the *Bridal Call*.[50] Upton Sinclair published a sympathetic poetic eulogy titled "An Evangelist Drowns" in the *New Republic*.[51] McPherson's vanishing act had an air of finality about it.

Then there were rumors of sightings and kidnappings.[52] People from across the country reported spotting McPherson. Ormiston, who returned to Los Angeles in late May, was brought in for questioning but denied having any knowledge of McPherson's whereabouts. After being cleared by investigators, he once again left the city. Journalists, meanwhile, began to speculate about Ormiston's potential involvement with the case.[53] A few fake ransom notes made their way to the Los Angeles Police Department. McPherson's mother Minnie Kennedy, a close associate in all of McPherson's affairs, offered a reward for the safe return of her daughter. When all leads on McPherson's possible location were exhausted, Kennedy held a memorial service on June 20. Three days later, her famous daughter reappeared along the border between Mexico and Arizona.

Aimee Semple McPherson (right) and her mother Minnie Kennedy are seated in a courtroom in 1926, likely during the preliminary hearing to determine whether McPherson would be tried for criminal conspiracy, perjury, and obstruction of justice. The district attorney dropped all charges against McPherson in January 1927.
Los Angeles Times Photographic Archive, UCLA Library Special Collections

McPherson's account of the thirty-six days during which she was missing seemed far-fetched from the beginning. According to the evangelist, two men and a woman abducted her from the beach and held her hostage in a shack in the middle of a Mexican desert. When, at the end of her month in captivity, she was tied to her bed and briefly left alone, she prayed, summoned up the courage to break the rope, and climbed out of the window. She then walked for ten hours through the desert before stumbling into Agua Prieta, where she met a kind stranger who drove her to a hospital in Douglas, Arizona. Her mother and children—accompanied by throngs of reporters who wanted the first scoop on the story—took the train to Arizona to be reunited with the evangelist and to get more details on the abduction.

McPherson's triumphant return was grounds for a citywide celebration. A crowd of thirty thousand people swarmed the railroad station in anticipation of her arrival. The Angelus Temple band played familiar gospel tunes, while shouts of "Hallelujah!" filled the celebratory air. Los Angeles was glad to have its most dramatic character come home. As one newspaper put it, McPherson was "hailed as one risen from the dead."[54]

As the days went by, however, puzzled skeptics began to probe the validity of McPherson's story. For a victim of kidnapping, binding, and captivity, she appeared surprisingly unscathed. Despite claiming to have been frail and weak from eating only canned food for a month, McPherson's physique did not seem to have suffered. Her skin was not sunburned—which would have been a side effect of her purportedly exhausting journey through the desert under the blazing June sun. The soles of her shoes had grass stains on them—an unexpected consequence for a daylong trek through a desert. Her clothing appeared to be in decent shape.[55] McPherson's description of the alleged kidnappers rendered them more believable as movie villains than flesh-and-blood humans. "Steve," "Rose," an unnamed man, and an occasional visitor named "Felipe" lacked any defining characteristics in the evangelist's retelling. Resorting to vague descriptors like "there was nothing particularly distinctive" about them, McPherson was nonetheless suspiciously confident that she would recognize the kidnappers "again in an instant."[56]

McPherson's enemies were quick to reject her version of events. John J. Kershner, author of the sensational book *The Truth about McPhersonism*, sent an alarmist telegraph to the US Department of Justice two days after McPherson was found. Kershner believed that he was "voicing the sentiment of many" when he said that the federal government needed to conduct a "thorough investigation of McPherson [sic] disappearance and doubtful kidnaping [sic] story." As far as Kershner was concerned, it was "quite evident" that McPherson "disappeared voluntarily" and had to therefore be held accountable for her antics.[57]

Kershner was not alone in crying conspiracy. The veracity of McPherson's story had already been challenged by numerous reports of Ormiston sightings in and around Carmel-by-the-Sea, a resort town three hundred miles north of Los Angeles, in the company of a blond woman who bore a remarkable resemblance to McPherson. Although Ormiston would deny that McPherson had been with him, he nonetheless refused to identify the blond, referring to her exclusively as "Mrs. X" in order to protect the woman's anonymity. What added to the spuriousness of Ormiston's claims was the fact that he had lived under various aliases in the months prior to

McPherson's disappearance. The *Los Angeles Times* made sure to report on Ormiston's strange travel habits when McPherson was still missing. The newspaper also supplied this information to the district attorney's office.[58]

At first, District Attorney Asa Keyes continued to pursue the kidnapping case. Who were the people who abducted the evangelist? And why was her story so vague, so sparse on the particulars? What began as an inquiry into who wronged McPherson quickly turned into an investigation of whether McPherson was telling the truth. On July 6, 1926, Keyes issued a subpoena for McPherson to appear before a grand jury and defend her account.

Stirred by the district attorney's incredulity, the press began entertaining new, more compelling versions of the disappearance.[59] On July 15, the Associated Press reported that a witness positively identified McPherson as the woman accompanying Ormiston in his car in Salinas (just north of Carmel) eleven days after her disappearance.[60] Ormiston vehemently denied these accusations. Ten days later, a San Francisco newspaper publicized multiple witnesses' claims that the mysterious couple that had been spotted vacationing at Carmel were indeed the evangelist and Ormiston.[61] McPherson's lawyer issued a statement refuting the allegations.[62] Despite insisting on his client's innocence, however, the attorney said McPherson would not provide fingerprints for comparison with those found in the Carmel cottage.[63] The fingerprints were not the only evidence potentially linking McPherson to Carmel; the handwriting in the grocery list discovered at the cottage looked eerily similar to the evangelist's.[64] The evidence stacking up against McPherson made the outlook grim for the preacher.

By August, the same California newspapers that had celebrated the return of the missing celebrity were openly mocking McPherson. The *Oakland Tribune* ran a joke whose punch line was that the talk of California was an "Aimee Semple McPherson sandwich" made of "boloney and lots of apple sauce."[65] When McPherson told her congregation that investigators discovered four potential shacks in the vicinity of Douglas, Arizona, the *Santa Ana Register* joked that real estate agents would benefit from going into business by trying to bill these properties as "The Aimee Semple McPherson subdivision"—fully equipped lots "with a modern shack and all the comforts of home."[66] A song titled "The Ballad of Aimee McPherson" gained popularity. It told the tale of the disappearance and of how the grand jury "uncovered a lot of spicy information, found out about her love nest down at Carmel-by-the-Sea, where the liquor is expensive and the loving is free."[67]

Journalists began to mount serious criticisms veiled in humorous parlance. In September 1926, Louis Adamic, H. L. Mencken's mentee and fellow critic of religion, wrote a scathing renunciation of McPherson's version
of events. He dismissed all ransom notes sent to McPherson's mother as
fake, castigated the memorial services that Kennedy held for her daughter
as a scheme to defraud parishioners, and cited Ormiston as the most likely
reason for the preacher's disappearance. Whatever the truth of McPherson's
strange story was, Adamic lamented, her downfall would not stop the pervasive power of religious charisma or supporters' ongoing defense of their
pastor. What would become of these people without their preacher, Adamic
asked? "I don't care either way," he wrote, "and it wouldn't matter if I did;
this is a war between the Holy Ghost and Satan, and my caring or not caring would not help either side. I am satisfied to watch and laugh and write
about it."[68] Other journalists continued to watch and laugh and write about
the story for months.

McPherson's drama also inspired contemporary fiction. In *Elmer
Gantry* (1927), Sinclair Lewis based the character of Sharon Falconer on
McPherson. Falconer is a publicity-driven celebrity preacher who builds
an enormous tabernacle with the money raised from her followers. At one
point, she promises the protagonist, with whom she is having an affair,
the same amount of fame: "You will be big! I'll make you! And perhaps
I'm a prophetess, a little bit, but I'm also a good liar."[69] With delusions of
grandeur, Falconer eventually dies in a church fire—all the while falsely
believing that she is a prophet of God who can walk through flames
unharmed.

As McPherson was becoming the laughingstock of secular culture, her
religious foes used the scandal to discredit her ministry. Pastor Bob Shuler,
McPherson's fiercest adversary, declared, "Either a crime of the most terrible nature has been committed against Mrs. Aimee Semple McPherson, or
else a fraud and a hoax that is a shame to Christianity has been attempted."[70]
The fate of American Christianity was once again being linked to a preacher's vindication or demise.

Even the district attorney's office worried about what McPherson's gim-
micks might mean for the future of religion and morality. On September
17, the district attorney issued arrest warrants for McPherson and associates, including her mother and Ormiston, on the charges of perjury and
obstruction. The prosecution's brief read, in part, "Mrs. McPherson and her
mother combined together with the object in view of perpetrating a

gigantic hoax in the name of that which the people hold sacred, namely, religion. Such a thing is a corruption of public morals."[71]

McPherson's defenders also saw the scandal as a test case for the future of national morality. Willis W. Blossom, a dry goods salesman from Madison, Wisconsin, petitioned the president of the United States to intervene in the investigation. Acknowledging that Calvin Coolidge was "a very busy man," Blossom nonetheless urged the president to "take immediate steps to see that a fair and impartial hearing is given to [McPherson]." After all, her case was "a frame up by the enemies of the cause of Christ," and the investigation was "that of tyranny and a pointed challenge pitted against the tenets of the christian religion and the fundamental principles of our government." McPherson, Blossom explained, was an honorable person, a long-suffering missionary, and "a mother of a family." She was, therefore, to be protected by the government, including, if necessary, that "the American army be put in a position to defend the dignity of the stars and striped [sic] and the sacred laws of God which have ever consecrated the constitution and flag of our nation." For Blossom, both God and the country were at stake in the ordeal; no measure of defense was too extravagant.[72]

McPherson herself, like many a scandal-prone evangelist who would come after her, described the ordeal in blunt theological terms. In a series of newspaper columns titled "Saint or Sinner—Did I Go From Pulpit to Paramour?" McPherson argued that any criticism she faced on account of her disappearance was an offense to the Almighty. "It isn't me that my detractors hurt," she wrote; "they do not realize that they are striking at God in their attempt to pull down His temple."[73] Decrying the gratuitous publicity that had come to surround the case, McPherson nonetheless could not help but add to it via various kinds of media that she produced. The cover of the September 1926 issue of McPherson's magazine *Bridal Call Foursquare* featured a woman warrior, with the word "Truth" emblazoned across her chest, slaughtering Lucifer, on whose wings were etched the words "filth, lies, innuendo, calumny, false witnesses, religious persecution, slander." In an accompanying article, McPherson described the proverbial storm that was threatening her ministry. She recounted the abduction story and reproached "the vain and hideous imaginings of evil minded men" who dared question her tale. God was on McPherson's side. "My story remains unshaken," she wrote.[74]

McPherson also utilized the radio to propagate her version of events. If the papers were on the side of the accusers, the listeners who had long enjoyed the familiar voice beaming into their living rooms through daily broadcasts trusted McPherson. As H. L. Mencken, McPherson's newest—if unexpected—defender, wrote, "The local district attorney has the newspapers on his side, but Aimee herself has the radio, and I believe that the radio will count most in the long run."[75] Technology was transforming the nature of media warfare, and McPherson, with her imperturbable perspicacity, appeared to be winning, as her army of supporters multiplied.

The vast majority of McPherson's parishioners unapologetically defended their leader's reputation—occasionally even using actual weapons in the war against sensationalism. When a member of Bob Shuler's church got into an argument with two McPherson apologists a block away from Angelus Temple, passions ran high, and Shuler's parishioner was shot after questioning McPherson's story.[76] He survived the injury. Another McPherson defender, a minister from Baldwin Park, California, wrote letters to newspaper editors to complain about the coverage:

> Shame on Los Angeles for having stooped to the dregs of life to find something with which to discredit Mrs. McPherson and her great work. I am afraid you people back there get only hearsay and newspaper scandal about this case. I am not a member of her church but I do believe that as decent people we must stand together to uphold Christianity and this woman, always ready to bear the burdens of others, especially of the sick and needy.[77]

Many Christians viewed defending McPherson as their sacred duty. Others rejoiced in their anticipation that her imminent downfall would bring Christianity back to a more traditional kind of faith—without women preachers or extravagant church services. As ever, scandal's bearing on religion was no small matter of concern.

In this fight over the meaning of McPherson's disappearance, unlikely alliances began to emerge. The scandal unfolded only a year after the Scopes trial. Since McPherson was an outspoken critic of evolution instruction and a proponent of Bible reading in schools, she became an obvious target for anti-fundamentalist reporters, just as William Jennings Bryan had been for H. L. Mencken one year prior. Indeed, Sinclair Lewis and Louis Adamic used McPherson's scandal in precisely that manner: to mock and discredit her particular brand of religion. Yet, in a development few could have anticipated, McPherson also found several defenders among the intellectual elite. Journalists who would have in the past jumped on the story to point out religious hypocrisy were suddenly defending McPherson in print. The so-called intellectual press sided with McPherson and denounced her detractors.

This unexpected alliance was the product of internal splintering within 1920s journalism. As historian Theodore Peterson explains, the recently emerged intellectual press consisted of iconoclasts who bonded over their collective disdain for "provincialism, prohibition, the Bible Belt, and boobs" (the latter being midcentury slang for "idiots").[78] These intellectuals "assiduously exposed the shortcomings of American life" while disassociating themselves "from the evils they found instead of working to eliminate or to change them."[79] Magazines like *The Nation*, the *New Yorker*, the *American Mercury*, the *New Republic*, and *Vanity Fair* aimed to "tell the truth with novelty, to keep common sense as fast as they can, to belabor sham as agreeably as possible, to give a civilized entertainment."[80] When the *New Yorker's* editor Harold Ross articulated the magazine's mission statement, he described its essence as "sophisticated, in that it will assume a reasonable degree of enlightenment on the part of its readers." The publication aimed to be "interpretive rather than stenographic" and would refuse to "deal in scandal for the sake of scandal nor sensation for the sake of sensation."[81] The object was to provide biting commentary on the political, social, and religious climate of the country while upholding the standards of responsible journalism.

McPherson's scandal created the perfect opportunity for the intellectual press to demonstrate its superiority over sensational publications. *American Mercury's* H. L. Mencken, *Harper's* Sarah Comstock, and the *New Yorker's* Dorothy Parker and Paxton Hibben each wrote about McPherson in the wake of the scandal. Mencken covered the grand jury investigation for the *Baltimore Evening Sun*. His story started with the kind of cynicism his readers had come to expect. "The Rev. Sister in God, I confess, greatly disappointed me," he wrote. Mencken compared the services at Angelus Temple to any other religious revival—entertaining and appealing for the unsophisticated masses. What distinguished this revival, however, was the person at the center of the performance. If Mencken was underwhelmed with her Christian message, he was impressed by McPherson's ability to tap into Los Angeles's marketplace of religious excess. In a town that, according to Mencken, rewarded "osteopaths, chiropractors and other such quacks," McPherson was in a league of her own. She succeeded, Mencken argued, because Los Angeles had "more morons collected" than any other place in the world. Still, even this skeptic could not dismiss McPherson's draw outright.[82]

Mencken may have hated Los Angeles, but he could not bring himself to despise McPherson. His heretofore scathing article changed in tone two-thirds of the way through—when Mencken began to discuss the district attorney's case against the evangelist. He called the investigation "disingenuous" and blamed the preacher's bitter enemies for the fact that there was a case against her in the first place. The town clergy and the Babbitts, Mencken argued, were behind the witch-hunt. The former wanted to take out their greatest religious competitor, while the latter "began to fear that her growing celebrity was making Los Angeles ridiculous." What frustrated Mencken most was the fact that the district attorney's charge against McPherson was perjury—that "when asked if she had been guilty of unchastity, she said no." Women, Mencken argued, could not be prosecuted for insisting on their purity. "It is unheard of, indeed," Mencken wrote, "in any civilized community for a woman to be tried for perjury uttered in defense of her honor."[83]

Writing on the subject again several years later, Mencken would denounce the trial as "an orgy typical of the half-fabulous California courts," in which McPherson was "almost asphyxiated by the smoke of photographers' flash-lights in the courtroom."[84] For the time being, he concluded, God was on McPherson's side. "Unless I err grievously," Mencken wrote, "our Heavenly Father is with her."[85] As much as Mencken detested organized religion, he hated the idea of a manufactured case against an enterprising woman even more. He did not think the evangelist was innocent; she was, as he said, precisely what Los Angeles deserved. For Mencken, though, the problem was jealousy, corruption, and ungentlemanly behavior, not McPherson's private sexual affairs.

Mencken's critique was persuasive. Even Louis Adamic, who had produced sarcastically scathing commentary on the disappearance, began to feel warmer toward McPherson by the affair's end. In late 1926, Adamic published a short book containing several reprinted articles produced by him and other journalists. *The Truth about Aimee Semple McPherson: A Symposium* rehashed some familiar arguments by decrying religious hypocrisy; yet the concluding essay, penned by Adamic himself, assumed a different, softer tone. Like Mencken, Adamic was outraged at the smear campaign that other Protestants were waging against McPherson. It was a "group of high-minded Fundamentalist whoopers," Adamic wrote, that "cooked up a plot against Aimee and her temple." Secular critics did not fare much better in Adamic's estimation. "I have heard," he wrote, "at least a hundred smutty stories, jokes and conundrums invented to reflect upon [McPherson's] character as a woman and as a religious leader, and in most cases I felt a resentment, sometimes a very faint one, it is true, toward the people who seemed to relish telling them around." As much as Adamic despised McPherson's brand of religion, he, like other journalists of his caliber, could not help but feel sympathetic toward the woman at the center of the scandal.[86]

When the New Yorker's Paxton Hibben covered McPherson's visit to Manhattan in March 1927, he did not mention the scandal at all. This was remarkable because Hibben had only recently published his scathing account of Henry Ward Beecher's affair.[87] The book castigated its protagonist as the prime example of the sin of religious hypocrisy. In his rumination on the nature of Beecher's flaws, Hibben wrote,

> Clerical adultery was not invented by Henry Ward Beecher; nor clerical hypocrisy either. But if he was guilty of the adultery, it may be contended, he was also guilty of the hypocrisy. And if he was guilty of the hypocrisy, it may be argued that the scope of his genius should be widened to include the carrying of hypocrisy to greater heights than any other character in history.[88]

In his coverage of the Beecher scandal, Hibben meticulously built his case against Beecher—providing testimony excerpts and citing all the damning evidence against the minister. Yet he was silent on the subject in his piece on McPherson, criticizing only her anti-evolution stance and her fundamentalist reading of the Bible. Consistent with the lofty aspirational mission statement of the New Yorker, even Hibben—the otherwise vocal denouncer of ministerial hypocrisy—chose to forgo the scandalous in his reportage on McPherson.

Harper's Sarah Comstock published her profile of McPherson and Angelus Temple in December 1927. Like other reporters of her ilk, Comstock was won over by the evangelist's gift as a successful entertainer, if not persuaded by her message. "She utters platitudes in a way that gives them the guise of inspiration," Comstock wrote. When discussing rumors of McPherson's lavish lifestyle, Comstock concluded, simply, "For my part I fail to see why one cannot serve the Lord as well in pink silk as in red flannel." And when the article raised the question of whether McPherson was "a messenger direct from God Almighty" or "the most unblushing fraud in the public eye today," Comstock opined that the distinction was irrelevant for the larger significance of McPherson for modern America. "The one fact that stands out," Comstock wrote, "is that her influence is incredible, that it carries as that of few evangelists has ever carried, that she is today one of the most amazing phenomena of power in this feverish, power-insane United States." McPherson, Comstock concluded, was "the most brilliant performer of the century" who would continue to remain relevant and popular "by keeping herself in the newspapers."[89]

The satirist Dorothy Parker had a similar take on the minister. Two years after the scandal, Parker reviewed McPherson's newest autobiography, *In the Service of the King* (1928), for the *New Yorker*. Parker's tone was characteristically biting, but she was not entirely unsympathetic to McPherson. The reviewer seemed charmed by the evangelist's ability to "so lavishly award herself all the breaks" and to create Parker's new "favorite character in fiction" with the purportedly factual autobiography. Parker most certainly did not believe a word of McPherson's personal story—which included yet another apologetic account of the disappearance—but it was not the veracity of McPherson's claims that troubled the reviewer. For Parker, McPherson's greatest fault lay in her disingenuousness, not in whether she ran off with her radio operator in the summer of 1926.[90]

Less highbrow periodicals remained focused on the scandalous. Every day of the investigative hearings brought new developments, and the fact that journalists were allowed in the courtroom made the grand jury investigation the most widely consumed sensation of the year. In 1926, the *New York Times* printed the same number of stories about McPherson as it had about the Scopes trial during the previous year.[91] Serious journalists studied McPherson's persona to understand the power of charisma and the uses of religion in a rapidly secularizing nation. Journalists who lay no claims to being among the intellectual elite continued to spin the sensation for profit.

In the end, money determined the course of the investigation. In early 1927, the district attorney's office decided that further probes into McPherson's admittedly spurious account of her disappearance would incur unjustifiable expenses for taxpayers. The case against the evangelist was exhausted. To have the last word, McPherson published her autobiography. In his review, H. L. Mencken—who had previously predicted McPherson's victory—concluded that although McPherson's book made a good case for her innocence, the evangelist herself "must know very well that Los Angeles will remember the evidence against her long after it forgets the testimony that cleared her."[92] In this assessment, Mencken was prophetic. Although the charges against McPherson were dropped, her credibility post-scandal would forever be in doubt.

In 1933, McPherson, who had thrived on publicity for years, reported that she was beginning to find it exhausting. When asked whether she employed "a publicity man," McPherson emphatically replied, "Never! I need an anti-publicity man!"[93] McPherson was lying—or at least trying to distract from the truth of the matter with a joke. Not only did she succeed in getting some reporters to defend her, she also hired one of them, the *Los Angeles Examiner*'s Ralph Jordan, to be her publicity manager.[94]

For the next decade, the celebrity preacher continued her career—publishing and reissuing memoirs, staging new productions of her illustrated sermons, and marching in parades that promoted the marriage of Christianity and patriotism. McPherson remained a popular, if divisive, figure. She died unexpectedly, at age fifty-three, in 1944.

Although McPherson's influence was immeasurable, her scandal has remained the greatest legacy of her celebrity. For generations, McPherson's disappearance has drawn attention from professional historians and lay observers alike. In the first two decades of the twentieth century, multiple biographies and a PBS documentary attempted to grapple with the scandal and the legacy of the charismatic pastor—all for good reason. McPherson's scandal was key to understanding several cultural and religious developments of her era. It coincided with journalism's division into distinct camps: some outlets eschewed scandal in favor of pursuing more intellectually rigorous cultural criticism, while others remained undeterred in their coverage of sensationalism. And McPherson set a uniquely modern example of a religious scandal protagonist in that she, unlike her predecessors, addressed the crisis head on: multiple times, in different iterations, and while constantly relying on her large media apparatus to push her agenda forward despite the mounting criticism (and considerable evidence) against her. McPherson taught the nation that the energy of scandal could be harnessed to fuel celebrity.

For better or worse, it continues to matter what exactly happened to McPherson in 1926 to both scholarly observers and insiders within her Foursquare church. Long after the evangelist's death, McPherson's denomination has continued its efforts to clear her name of all suspicions of adultery. The 1983 book *The Verdict Is In*, a 250-page apologia, grapples with journalistic assumptions and speculations and seeks to prove McPherson innocent once and for all. The book's late author, Raymond Cox, was a Foursquare minister who served on the board of directors of the National Association of Evangelicals. The book is a fascinating example of the denomination's ongoing fight to defend and revamp the reputation of their founder. Cox opens the preface with a 1976 quotation from the *Washington Post*'s Henry Fairlie, in which the journalist admits that the news "is not what has happened.... It is an account of what a few people, journalists like myself, think has happened."[95] Cox then uses Fairlie's admission to argue that the disappearance scandal was entirely fabricated by the press. Cox also argues that there was a collusion—if not a conspiracy—between the district attorney's office and the press, alleging that District Attorney Asa Keyes admitted that many of the prosecution's expenses were underwritten by the newspapers.[96]

Historians have not found apologetics to be a useful source of evidence. Cox's attempt at mounting a defense has been largely ignored by both professional biographers and amateur bloggers who continue to publish stories about McPherson with renewed enthusiasm every few years. Her legacy still resides somewhere between the flawless and the outrageous.

In 2012, the musical *Scandalous: The Life and Trials of Aimee Semple McPherson* opened on Broadway. It told McPherson's story through song and dance. One number, which featured a group of energetic reporters, summarized the newspapers' role in the scandal: the journalists celebrated publishing unsubstantiated rumors about "Hollywood Aimee" to sell copy.[97] Newspapers, in this retelling, were entirely responsible for manufacturing the scandal. Those who were more familiar with the story may have wondered why the musical portrayed McPherson as completely innocent. The answer came, in part, from the sponsorship of the production. The Foursquare Foundation, the grant-making arm of McPherson's denomination, invested $2 million in the brainchild of Kathie Lee Gifford, the NBC television personality and *Scandalous* lyricist.[98] The musical closed in less than a month due to unenthusiastic reviews and poor ticket sales, yet McPherson did make waves in popular culture once again, this time on Broadway. Almost a century after the disappearance, members of McPherson's denomination were still standing by their leader and funding the efforts to defend her reputation in search of cultural redemption. Yet vindication remained as elusive as McPherson herself during those fateful thirty-six days in the summer of 1926.

6

Queer Silences

Two decades after Aimee Semple McPherson's dalliances were covered in every major newspaper, scandal ceased to be a serious problem for Christians—especially for white Protestants. The genre never fully disappeared from newspaper pages, but it did largely retreat from mainstream media.[1] The tabloids, which had emerged in 1919 and quickly gained popularity, continued printing the sensational and the frequently untrue, but the tone of mainstream media coverage shifted significantly by 1950. If the mid-nineteenth century was characterized by the maturation of the press and the attendant rise in scandal coverage, the mid-twentieth century saw a departure from the genre.

This paucity of scandal coverage is curious considering its upward trajectory in previous eras. Some of this strange silence might be explained by the Great Depression, World War II, and the rising culture of surveillance during the Second Red Scare. Anxieties about the nation's survival amid multiple geopolitical and cultural crises relegated sensationalism to the margins. Already during the Great Depression media outlets began to move away from scandal for reasons both moral and practical. If the industry were to survive, it had to attend to less trivial matters. As Joseph Medill Patterson, manager of the *New York Daily News*, told his staff in 1930, "We are off on the wrong foot. The people's major interest is not in the playboy, Broadway, and divorces, but in how they're going to eat; and from this time forward, we'll pay attention to the struggle for existence that's just beginning."[2] Recognizing that the economy threatened his readership's very survival, Patterson sought to reorient the priorities of his publication.

As dramatic cuts in advertising revenue tightened most operating budgets, new forms of media entered the already oversaturated market, threatening the supremacy of print media.[3] The radio and, later, television transformed the media landscape.[4] The newsreel, first introduced in 1911, reached the peak of its popularity in the 1930s and 1940s.[5] It was a time of consolidation and professionalization. Between 1914 and 1940, the Associated Press grew from about one hundred member papers to over

Disgraced: How Sex Scandals Transformed American Protestantism. Suzanna Krivulskaya, Oxford University Press.
© Oxford University Press 2025. DOI: 10.1093/oso/9780197599686.003.0007

fourteen hundred.[6] The American Society of Newspaper Editors, organized in 1923, emphasized the "canons of journalism," which included responsibility, independence, fair play, and decency. Where these changes failed to stir media coverage away from scandal, threats of libel suits forced the beleaguered press to refrain from publishing unconfirmed reports of titillating gossip.

As newspapers committed to producing more respectable content, Protestant leaders created new mechanisms for shielding their colleagues from public disgrace. With secret investigations, unpublicized defrockings, and calculated denials, conservative Protestant groups assumed a new stance toward scandal. Keenly aware of the wages of sexual sin, they labored to minimize the impact of unwelcome revelations, especially when it came to allegations of deviant sexuality among the divines.

Scandal suppression began at school. Places like Moody Bible Institute had been weathering the storms of scandal for decades. Other fundamentalist institutions—founded, in part, to preserve sexual purity and cultivate moral righteousness—remained sites of turmoil through the 1930s. Just as the leadership of MBI experimented with different scandal management techniques during several close encounters in the previous decades, other Protestant schools were also learning how to prevent private transgressions from becoming public sensations. The key was to act swiftly and to handle problems internally. At least two fundamentalist college presidents successfully kept their sexual indiscretions private with the help of like-minded believers.

In the early 1930s, Denver Bible Institute (DBI) found itself engulfed in controversy that had the potential to create a new publicity problem for the already embattled post-Scopes fundamentalists. The school's president Clifton Fowler appeared to be beloved by all—except his own wife. He accused her of being mentally unstable. She returned the favor by proclaiming that he was a homosexual. Fortunately for Fowler, this story never became public due to the efforts of a well-connected network of white fundamentalist leaders.[7]

Born in 1882, Fowler first heard Dwight L. Moody preach in 1896. He did not convert immediately, but, five years later, Fowler became a devout Christian and was ordained as a Methodist minister. As a zealous new convert, Fowler clung to orthodoxy tightly, alienating some more seasoned adherents. His theology did not align with that of his more progressive brethren, who soon labeled him a heretic. In protest, Fowler joined the nascent fundamentalist movement and poured his energy into founding DBI in 1914.[8]

The school flourished and expanded over the next two decades, but Fowler's personal woes soon drew condemnation from the country's fundamentalist leadership. In 1933, Fowler and his wife Angie separated after he alleged that she was mentally insane. Angie disagreed with the amateur diagnosis and chose to protest it in colorful ways. She would attend DBI meetings and make loud, disruptive remarks, including alleging that her estranged husband had been diagnosed with a "perverted sex complex."[9]

Rumors about Fowler's sexual tendencies spread quickly. When he applied to have DBI readmitted to the Evangelical Teacher Training Association in 1936, national fundamentalist leaders were hesitant to approve the application. To alleviate concerns, Fowler convinced the group to form an investigative committee charged with examining the institute's affairs. The leaders acquiesced but insisted that the investigation be kept secret. According to surviving correspondence, the leadership advised that "it would be best for fundamentalism as a whole if the entire investigation could be kept quiet, so as not to sour the reputation of Bible institutes and fundamentalism in general."[10] Reputations had to be protected. Even a hint of trouble could implicate fundamentalists in yet another scandal.

The investigation revealed disturbing patterns. Fowler was an authoritarian leader who enjoyed controlling his subordinates in all areas of their lives. When students came to Fowler for counsel, he pressured them to confess their sexual sins and later used that information against them. He encouraged married students to abstain from sex. Then there were rumors of Fowler's homosexuality. MBI president Will Houghton, who was charged with interviewing witnesses on the subject of Fowler's moral character, heard several testimonies about a "young man whose 'morals were corrupted in an unmentionable manner by Dr. Fowler.'"[11] The official report of the investigative committee concluded that Fowler was not fit for Christian ministry, though it omitted any mention of the sexual allegations. Keeping Fowler's reputation intact would also serve to protect the reputation of Christian institutions of higher learning.

Passing further responsibility for Fowler's conduct to local fundamentalists, the nationwide investigation came to an unsatisfying end. Fundamentalist leaders worried less about their responsibility to censure a potentially predatory leader than about the reputation of fundamentalism writ large. Having removed DBI from the association's list of approved institutions, the leaders washed their hands off the whole affair.

Fowler technically retired from DBI soon after the upheaval, but he stayed active in the school's governance until 1940. His divorce, finalized in 1937, remains the most scandalous thing about Fowler in DBI's institutional memory. The hundred-year anniversary account of DBI (now Colorado Christian University) mentions Fowler's troubles only in passing: "Clinton Fowler and Angie Fowler divorced in 1936, drawing suspicion from the conservative constituency."[12] No trace of allegations of homosexuality remains. With both national leadership and local fundamentalists conveniently forgetting DBI's troubles of the late 1930s, the school has moved on as well. Fowler is remembered solely as the great visionary founder.

A similar fate befell the Florida Bible Institute, whose name was later changed to Trinity College of Florida due to its acronym (FBI) at the request of the Federal Bureau of Investigation, at least according to campus legend. To this day, the school's greatest claim to fame is its association with alumnus Billy Graham, the most famous evangelist of the twentieth century. Reciprocating the affection his alma mater showed him, Graham always remembered the school fondly as well. After all, Graham's vicarious brush with scandal at the institute taught him valuable lessons for both life and ministry.

W. T. Watson, a fundamentalist tent preacher from North Carolina, founded the school in 1932. Five years later, the institute welcomed a transfer student by the name of William Graham. The young man was promising but distractible. Decades later, Watson would recall that before Graham "got down to business," his two main interests were "baseball and girls."[13] This reminiscence came thirty-four years after Watson's own alleged problem with women became public.

The details are difficult to recover since the institute's archives have been scrubbed of any mention of the scandal. Graham's autobiography, however, reveals important traces of the event. "Dr. Watson," Graham wrote in 2007, "was accused of moral indiscretion—*falsely* accused, I was certain." The indiscretion was likely sexual, since veiled language was rarely reserved for more mundane matters. The certainty in Watson's innocence Graham derived from his belief that Watson was "a man of God," one of his "spiritual fathers." Besides, Graham thought the evidence was circumstantial at best. Because the allegations came from a school's employee who had "himself

Billy Graham, with a Bible in hand, preaches to a crowd of revival attendees in a Washington, DC, amphitheater in 1960. Graham's revivals reached millions of people, and he became the most famous evangelical preacher of the twentieth century.

Library of Congress Prints and Photographs Division, LC-DIG-ppmsca-83220

come under suspicion," Graham speculated that Watson was persecuted out of vengeance.[14]

Still, the accusations were serious enough that, as Graham recalled, a quarter of the student body and several faculty members left the school in protest. The only surviving archival evidence—in the form of yearbooks—supports this recollection. At the end of the spring semester of 1939, nineteen students were heading into their senior year. The yearbook from 1940 reveals that only eleven of them graduated. The junior class shrank substantially as well: from thirty-six to twenty-four students. Despite Graham's unwavering confidence in Watson's moral soundness, a significant number of his students apparently believed the accusations.[15]

Graham, convinced of the innocence of his spiritual leader despite the overwhelming doubt among his classmates, tried to uplift the campus. It was a small, tight-knit community of less than a hundred people. Graham was the senior class president with a passion for rousing crowds. He did what he could, he later wrote, to improve morale. The 1940 handbook is full of inside jokes, anecdotes from class trips, and heartfelt tributes to the school's leadership, including Watson, who remained at the helm of the institution for four more decades.

Graham also extracted an important lesson from the ordeal. "Dreadful as the experience was," he wrote, "I was grateful that the dark cloud passed over Florida Bible Institute while I was there. It was a big learning experience for me in many ways, and it taught me to be very careful myself."[16] Notably, the lesson Graham extracted was not to avoid scandalous behavior altogether, but to "be very careful." In 1948, still likely influenced by the Watson incident, Graham would articulate a new principle of righteous living for himself and other Christian men: never to "travel, meet, or eat alone with a woman other than [one's] wife."[17] Sexual temptation, in the form of women, was everywhere. Graham decided that the best course of action was to eliminate any possibility of scandal altogether.

Other future Protestant celebrities were learning their own lessons in scandal management. Healing evangelist Kathryn Kuhlman had her brush with scandal early in her career. In 1921, fourteen-year-old Kuhlman experienced a spiritual awakening and began traveling across Idaho as a "girl evangelist"—a short-lived trend that was taking the country by storm.[18] By 1933, she had garnered enough support to establish her own congregation, Denver Revival Tabernacle, in Colorado. Two years later, Burroughs A. Waltrip, a handsome and charismatic—if inconveniently already married—itinerant preacher arrived to speak at Kuhlman's church and inadvertently disrupted her career. Kuhlman developed romantic feelings for Waltrip, and the attraction was mutual. Waltrip's son would later recall that on Valentine's Day in 1937, instead of a card, his mother received a letter from his father "telling her he was filing for divorce."[19] With Waltrip's wife and children thus notified, Kuhlman agreed to marry the preacher. Instead of celebrating the news of the union, Kuhlman's Denver congregation rejected her continued leadership on account of the affair. The couple moved to Iowa soon after—fleeing a would-be scandal of their union.[20]

Still reeling from the rejection by her Denver congregation, Kuhlman prioritized her ministry over her new husband, whom she left in 1946 after eight unhappy years of marriage.[21] When Waltrip filed for divorce, he charged Kuhlman with "extreme cruelty" and claimed that 75 percent of their time was spent apart "because of her professional career."[22] Indeed, Kuhlman was resolute in her quest to restore good standing as a Christian pastor. Despite the burden of prejudice that threatened the success of a divorced female evangelist at midcentury, Kuhlman's ministry was

redeemed. She moved to Pennsylvania, where she performed divine heal-
ings and ran a successful radio program. Eventually advancing to television,
Kuhlman produced a weekly show, *I Believe in Miracles*, which aired
nationally between 1967 and 1976—far surpassing the evangelist's early
ambitions. For the remainder of her career, Kuhlman avoided discussing
the Waltrip affair.[23] She focused, instead, on her testimony of divine healing
and grace—things all reputations marred by scandal desperately needed.
Charisma covered a multitude of sins, and Kuhlman's ministry touched
thousands of adherents. By healing the faithful, she repaired her reputation
as well.

With scandals evaded, averted, and forgotten, the 1930s were a relatively
quiet time for Protestants in the media. A sporadic elopement story might
garner some local attention, a charge of immorality would occasionally
spark a closer look into the culprit's prior ministry, and a recently arrived
pastor could rouse suspicions on account of his popularity with the church
ladies.[24] All in all, these stories were rare and not particularly sensational.
Newspapers were dealing with an ongoing financial crisis and an internal
reckoning with their professional mission. Soon, however, another variable
entered the equation of scandal publishing. In 1939, a prominent Chicago
minister rumored to be gay sued a local newspaper for libel. The scandal,
the lawsuit, and the ruling in the pastor's favor made Protestant sex scandals
an even less popular newspaper genre.[25]

Members of Clarence H. Cobbs's First Church of Deliverance and the
wider African American Chicago community likely knew that the pastor
was gay.[26] Indeed, Black working-class urban enclaves often tolerated and
sometimes embraced queerness.[27] As the idea of homosexuality as a distinct, identifiable category cemented itself in American culture, however,
fears of sexual nonconformity challenged the status quo.[28] Theological
denunciations of queerness would not become a staple of American religious culture until the second half of the century, but the view of homosexuality as sinful was beginning to emerge just as preachers like Cobbs
cultivated their celebrity.[29]

Making sexuality a subject for the pulpit was a response to the loosened
sexual morality of the 1920s. In 1929, Adam Clayton Powell Sr., the popular
Black pastor of Harlem's Abyssinian Baptist Church, delivered a sermon
titled "Lifting Up a Standard for the People." In it, Powell denounced homosexuality and accused fellow preachers of sexual degeneracy. He came just
short of revealing actual names, but congregants could have guessed that

Powell was denouncing ministers like Clarence Cobbs. The full text of the sermon has not survived, but its anti-queer message struck a chord with Powell's parishioners and faraway admirers alike.[30] Portions of the transcript were reprinted in the press. The *New York Age*, one of the most prominent Black newspapers in the nation, dedicated the first column of the issue to the sermon. "Dr. Powell's Crusade Against Abnormal Vice Is Approved," proclaimed the headline, with the subtitle reading, "Pastors and Laity Endorse Dr. Powell's Denunciation of Degeneracy in the Pulpit."[31] In his 1938 autobiography, Powell would recall that the sermon focused on "abnormal sins" of fellow ministers because "as every informed person knows, these sins are on the increase and are threatening to eat the vitals out of America."[32] Homosexuality may not yet have become the great threat to the nation that the Christian Right would imagine it to be a few decades later, but it was apparently troubling enough to warrant loud denunciations.

In the meantime, Chicago's Reverend Cobbs appeared to be living his queer life comfortably and relatively openly. Based on the recollections of his contemporaries, the pastor and his associates embodied queerness with some degree of pride—flaunting lavish garments and frequently transferring their energy from church services to nightclubs in the course of a single evening.[33] Cobbs's seven-thousand-member congregation quietly sanctioned such flamboyance. The pastor's charisma translated into missionary effectiveness: his radio broadcasts reached the entire city of Chicago with a message of Christian hope and salvation. In light of these greater achievements, Cobbs's queerness appeared to be almost incidental. It did not require precise articulation or extended commentary. The *Chicago Defender*, one of the most influential Black newspapers in the nation, threatened to disrupt the equilibrium when it publicized rumors of Cobbs's allegedly deviant sexuality in November 1939. In response, the pastor sued the newspaper for libel to the tune of $250,000. The *Defender* was not necessarily trying to create a scandal, but the newspaper was not concerned with protecting the minister's reputation either. The offending article reported on a police probe regarding "widespread rumors of scandalous nature" and then facetiously quoted Cobbs who, in his defense, had claimed that he was a "full man."[34] Readers would have understood that formulation to mean that Cobbs was being accused of sexual deviance.

Cobbs did not take to such characterization kindly. His lawsuit presented the plaintiff as "a law abiding and law-respecting citizen" who happened to be single and resided with his mother. The *Defender*, Cobbs claimed, published false statements and "greatly injured" his name and reputation, thereby causing "hatred, contempt, ridicule, scandal and disgrace."[35] The case was initially dismissed, but in 1941, the Appellate Court of Illinois decided in Cobbs's favor, positing that "there can be no escape from the conclusion that [the *Defender*] tended to injure the reputation of plaintiff and especially to damage him with reference to his qualifications as a minister of the gospel."[36] Rumors of queerness and religion, in the court's estimation, were fundamentally incompatible.

The favorable ruling was vindication enough for the minister, and Cobbs released the *Defender* from liability soon after. As the pastor reportedly told his lawyer, "I am not interested in any money from the *Chicago Defender*. As is told us in Proverbs, chapter 12, 'A good name is rather to be chosen than great riches.'"[37] Cobbs may not have benefited from the lawsuit financially, but his legal victory served as an effective warning to newspapers: questioning the sexual reputation of Christian ministers in print could have serious financial consequences. In the three and a half decades that followed, pastoral sex scandals appeared in newspapers almost exclusively as reports of court cases—providing minimal detail of the scandalous and reprinting only publicly available facts.

It was not just the looming threat of libel suits that kept newspapers from speculating about ministers' sex lives at midcentury. Journalism was also undergoing important structural changes. FM radio revolutionized how information was transmitted and consumed in the 1930s. Competition for audiences and advertisers would only intensify with the advances in television broadcasting in the post–World War II years.[38] These rivalries changed the history of print media in two related ways: through consolidation and professionalization. Mergers became essential for economic survival.[39] As newspapers consolidated, they needed to appeal to broader audiences. The only way for publications to remain competitive and financially viable was to ensure continuous readership and sustained advertisers. Consistency—not capricious sensationalism—would ensure reliable sales.

At the same time, formal education in journalism became the gold standard for media outlets set on delivering trustworthy reporting. Colleges had begun granting journalism degrees in the early twentieth century. In the

1930s, these programs' graduates matured into establishment professionals.[40] Journalistic ethics would be institutionalized during the following decades. Media professionals formed press associations, whose self-proclaimed mission was impartial reporting.[41] The biggest of these organizations was the Associated Press. Formed in the mid-nineteenth century, it expanded its reach and influence in the first half of the twentieth. Members contributed dues, supplied local news to the national organization, and used the shared content in their publications in exchange. Other professional media organizations formed in the era emphasized impartiality, truthfulness, and decency in reporting. This newfound commitment to fact over sensation fundamentally transformed the profession. Some newspapers and magazines still relied on sensationalism, but overall the genre suffered a setback.

While mainstream newspapers retreated from scandal coverage, the state resorted to its own program of surveillance. Beginning in the late 1930s, the government began to systematically monitor the private lives of citizens due to rising fears of "un-American activities"—an intentionally vague term used to denote any deviation from conformity as well as any degree of disloyalty to the nation.[42] Accusations of sexual deviance—which, conservatives argued, threatened to destroy the social fabric of the country—could result in dire consequences for those who did not comply with the demands of compulsory heterosexuality.[43] Rumors of homosexuality could now not only undermine reputations but also lead to loss of employment and, in some cases, criminal prosecution. State surveillance rendered fringe religious communities of color especially vulnerable to prosecution.[44]

The evangelist Father Divine, who was likely born George Baker in 1879, learned intimately that leading a new religious movement that did not conform to the social, racial, and sexual norms of his age came at a price.[45] Growing up in an impoverished Maryland neighborhood of formerly enslaved people, Baker was attuned to Christian influences since childhood, but his participation in the Azusa Street Revival and his interests in New Thought philosophy inspired him to create his own brand of religion. By 1912, Baker was convinced that by achieving harmony with the divine, he had become God and taken on a new name to reflect the development. His small but committed group of followers agreed. They helped Father Divine build the multiracial Peace Mission community in Sayville, New York. Adherents abandoned old ways of living, pulled their resources, and moved to cooperative properties purchased by the organization. Relocating to Harlem in the early 1930s, the group emphasized racial equality and focused on serving the poor—including hosting extravagant free banquets that attracted thousands of new followers who needed the material help during the Great Depression.

In return for teaching, housing, and feeding his adherents, the married Divine demanded, among other things, that they remain celibate. This unusual approach appeared suspect to outside observers.[46] Ironically, the mandate of celibacy inspired rumors of wild sex escapades as Divine's ministry gained a mass following.[47] Fears of integration, political liberalism, socialist leanings, and strange religiosity prompted conservatives to scrutinize the group and accuse it of excess and impropriety. The Ku Klux Klan sent letters threatening violence because the Peace Mission sheltered white women.[48] The nation's most powerful publishing mogul, William Randolph Hearst, spearheaded a media campaign against the group through his newspaper empire.[49] The FBI engaged in several operations designed to besmirch Divine. Such seemingly inappropriate use of government intelligence resources was explained, in part, by the Bureau's leadership. J. Edgar Hoover, the FBI's long-serving director, was committed to white Christian nationalism and worked fastidiously to discredit religious movements that threatened the dominance of evangelical Protestantism as the bedrock of the nation.[50] During World War II, FBI agents infiltrated the ministry in order to find evidence of Divine's anti-American activities.[51] In the late 1940s, the FBI investigated Divine's personal affairs in an attempt to charge him with violating the Mann Act.[52] Both campaigns failed, but not without bringing negative publicity to the fragile interracial movement.

Discrediting new African American religious communities was often easier if it involved allegations of queerness. By midcentury, homosexual acts were felonious in every US state.[53] Protestants began to place these sins high in the hierarchy of carnal offenses.[54] In cases where the presumed offender's theology deviated from the white Protestant norm, punishment would be swift and severe. James Francis Jones, the charismatic founder of Detroit's largest Black church, who went by "Prophet Jones," learned this lesson the hard way. A nonconformist in preaching and practice alike, Jones was used to criticism from the mainstream as he rose to popularity in the mid-1940s. Known for his lavish lifestyle and outlandish religious claims, Jones had always lived on the margins of Protestantism. By the mid-1940s, with the support of his followers, he could afford a well-appointed mansion with a staff of twelve domestic servants.[55] His extravagant clothing, exclusive home decor, and expensive tastes earned him an extended profile in a

1944 issue of *Life* magazine.[56] Jones boasted of his prophetic ability and claimed to receive predictions for the future, including revelations about the results of presidential elections and deaths of important civic leaders, in a "private language" dictated directly by God. He did not drink alcohol or date and urged his congregants to remain celibate. He also happened to be queer, which ultimately helped his detractors undermine his success.

In 1955, an undercover vice officer infiltrated Jones's congregation, gained the leader's trust, and eventually accused the minister of making sexual advances toward him.[57] Jones was arrested on "morals charges" for allegedly propositioning the officer in February 1956 and tried that summer.[58] Largely retaining the support of his parishioners, Jones was acquitted, but his reputation suffered. Other religious leaders had made tongue-in-cheek comments alluding to Jones's sexuality for decades, and the trial seemed to confirm fears of sexual depravity among fringe religious movements.[59] In the competitive marketplace of midcentury religion, "good" Protestants distinguished themselves from "bad" religious actors in part by promulgating an image of sexual purity and right family living that stood in contrast to new religious experiments in the realm of sexuality.

This monogamous heterosexual ideal turned out to be difficult to uphold in practice. When sexual morality failed them, Protestants employed secrecy to protect their reputations. Maintaining the allure of respectable sexuality would become especially important for Christian denominations in the era of midcentury Protestant schisms.

Although the United States never had an established national religion, Protestantism came closest to claiming the mantle. In public, the "tri-faith" consensus of Protestant, Catholic, and Jewish traditions was touted as the great achievement made possible only in a democratic God-fearing nation.[60] Privately, political leaders understood which religion held the most power. As President Franklin D. Roosevelt said in 1942, the United States "is a Protestant country, and the Catholics and Jews are here under sufferance."[61] The postwar years brought new challenges to Protestant supremacy. The nation was becoming at once more secular and, at the other end of the spectrum, more religiously conservative, as evangelical and fundamentalist Christians attempted to combat what they saw as dangerous liberalizing forces. The same conflicts that had pushed fundamentalists and modernists to draw battle lines in the 1920s continued to produce fractures. In the postwar era, the membership in the "Seven Sisters" of mainline churches (Congregational, Episcopal, Evangelical Lutheran, Presbyterian

(USA), United Methodist, American Baptist, and Disciples of Christ) saw a steady decline, while evangelical influence expanded.[62]

Billy Graham captivated the nation with a message of both eternal and temporal salvation soon after earning his Florida Bible Institute degree.[63] If Americans returned to religion, he promised, God would bless them with safety and prosperity. Graham's 1949 West Coast crusade came on the heels of the Soviet government exploding an atomic bomb. In this context, Graham warned Americans of imminent doom—unless they returned to the faith of their forefathers.[64] Shaken by the trauma of World War II, the uncertainties of the Cold War, and the threat of a nuclear holocaust, Americans embraced Graham's message with trepidation and enthusiasm. Good old-fashioned gospel appealed to millions of people trying to make sense of the tragedies modernity had wrought. Communism abroad and lawlessness at home could be overcome, they reasoned, if righteous spiritual forces united with conscientious political effort. The Billy Graham Evangelistic Association, founded in 1950, swiftly grew into a media empire—with radio, television, newspaper, and magazine outlets that attracted millions. Between 1940 and 1960, membership in mainline churches declined by 23 percent, while evangelical ranks rose by 13 percent.[65] This trend would only intensify in the following decades.

Religious coalitions allowed individual denominations to unite against common adversaries. Mainline Protestants attempted to combat membership losses by joining professional associations. The first of these organizations, the Federal Council of Churches (FCC), had been founded in 1908 in response to the social concerns of the new century. In 1950, FCC members joined other church bodies to create the ecumenical National Council of Churches. Conservative groups unified as well—in part to combat the organizing efforts of their mainline foils. The National Association of Evangelicals formed in 1942 in opposition to the FCC. The fast-growing pentecostal communities came together under the banner of the international Pentecostal World Fellowship in 1947. But religious association rarely meant theological agreement or harmonious fellowship. By 1959, the Yearbook of American Churches listed 267 denominations—a telling statistic of Christianity's continued splintering.[66] In some cases, switching denominational allegiances in the chaos of broader fracturing enabled problematic pastors to remain in ministry despite questionable sexual behavior.

Born in turn-of-the-century Wales, Bertram M. Crocker moved to Pennsylvania as a teenager and became a Baptist minister in 1924. For the next two decades, he pastored both Baptist and Congregational churches—apparently finding it easy to transcend denominational differences. During World War II, Crocker joined the military as a chaplain and specialized in counseling "abnormal" men—a common midcentury term for homosexuals. He would later claim that this was the first time he found himself "thinking seriously about and discussing the problems of homosexuality," though his behavior in the postwar years cast some doubts on the assertion.[67]

After being discharged from the military due to an injury in 1944, Crocker returned to civilian ministry. He first pastored a Congregational parish in the nation's capital but was swiftly transferred to a Baptist church in the village of Massena, New York. In 1945, Crocker published a pioneering article on spiritual counseling for homosexuals, in which he criticized Protestants' "smug and cowardly frame of mind" with regard to "the abnormal," by which he meant the homosexual.[68] He pleaded for a more compassionate approach to queerness.

One year after the publication of the article, Crocker found himself accused of sexually assaulting a teenage boy. The incident took place in the vicinity of the church tabernacle. After midnight on July 24, 1946, fourteen-year-old Francis Gerald Breyette asked the minister to give him a ride to a nearby farm. According to the complaint, when the pair got into Crocker's car, the pastor "committed an act of sodomy upon the boy."[69] It allegedly happened again inside the parsonage. Afterward Crocker drove Breyette to the farm.

Whatever occurred that night, Breyette did not report it to law enforcement immediately. Instead, the police brought him in for questioning twelve days after the incident. There was no apparent reason to interview Breyette—a fact that Crocker's defense would later emphasize. The boy was interrogated from 4:00 a.m. to 8:00 a.m. on August 5. Under pressure, he rehearsed the details of what had happened at the parsonage. Crocker was arrested on August 21. That same night, the First Baptist Church at Massena conducted a special leadership meeting, during which Crocker was "relieved of his duties as pastor" in absentia.[70]

During the trial, Breyette testified against Crocker, though not without Crocker's objections on account of the boy's likely intellectual disability. Breyette had been committed to a state institution "as a mental defective," and two psychiatrists claimed that Breyette had "a mental age of six years." Still, the teenager was permitted to take the stand after the prosecution deposed a psychiatrist who attested that Breyette "was a low grade normal individual."[71]

Crocker took the stand as well. His strategy was to appear more reliable than the wayward youth. The minister recounted his military service and explained how his PTSD (then known as "shell shock") contributed to insomnia. This was why, Crocker explained, he was outside during that fateful night in the first place: not as a predator prowling for easy prey, but rather a victim of a disability and, now, a tale manufactured by a delusional boy.

Crocker did not deny giving Breyette a ride, which he said was simply a neighborly favor. The pastor was merely practicing Christian hospitality, he explained. Indeed, the entire strategy of Crocker's defense lay in appeals to his Christian character by virtue of his vocation—a tactic also used in Samuel Neal Kent's 1919 trial. During his testimony, Crocker recalled his childhood in Wales, where he was known as "the Welsh Boy Preacher." When asked to name the date of his ordination, Crocker responded that he could not "remember a time" when he was not a minister.[72]

In his testimony about the night in question, Crocker denied that a sexual encounter of any kind occurred. He said that he had been so shocked to hear about the charges that he asked Breyette's mother to explain why the boy would have given the false story to the police. The mother, he claimed, told him not to believe anything Breyette said due to his intellectual disability. Crocker hoped Breyette's family's doubts about the veracity of his claims would undermine his accuser's testimony.

Despite the impassioned pleas of innocence, Crocker was found guilty. His military record earned him some favor with the judge, even as his ministerial vocation rendered his alleged behavior all the more scandalous. "The nature of your life's work," said the judge, "makes the crime named much more serious than as if you were a common man but I am not going to use that against your service and against the good Christian work which you have shown."[73] Crocker was sentenced to three and a half years in prison.

After the conviction, Crocker's former ministerial associates needed to decide what to do about his status as an ordained pastor. The Massena Baptists had parted ways with the clergyman soon after the arrest, but other churches with which he had been associated were just beginning to catch up. What they knew for sure was that the charges against Crocker were serious. The Reverend Howard Stone Anderson, Crocker's former colleague at the First Congregational Church in Washington, DC, sent a letter to the chief probation officer of St. Lawrence County in New York to inquire about the nature of the crime. The officer confirmed that the offense was sodomy and added that he knew of "several affidavits from boys whom [Crocker] had apparently been abusing, but of course he was only tried on one charge with one boy."[74]

The Reverend Frederick W. Alden, chairman of the Committee on Ministerial Standing for the Rockingham Association of the Congregational Church, pursued the matter further. He discovered that back in December 1944, several clergymen questioned "the fitness of Mr. Crocker to continue in the ministry." There had apparently been accusations "of an affair with a boy" that involved Crocker, but the case was dismissed. A pattern had clearly established itself in the eyes of the Congregationalists, and they decided to part ways with the minister for good. Crocker, Alden wrote, "should be informed at his present address, Clinton Prison, of the action of the Association." Crocker was defrocked in absentia on May 8, 1947, but, as he would later emphasize, no one formally informed him of the censure.[75]

Ignorant of the defrocking, Crocker took his criminal appeal to the Supreme Court of New York. His attorney argued that Breyette was not a reliable witness and that there was insufficient corroborating evidence to support the charges. The Albany court reversed the original judgment and ordered a new trial in December 1947. In the appeal hearing, Crocker's former military glory and ministerial career were once again touted as pertinent to the case. "Defendant is apparently a man of education and culture with a distinguished war record," read the majority opinion, "The alleged pathic, a boy of 15 years of age if not a moron was unquestionably of low grade mentality."[76] Crocker's education and service stood in contrast to Breyette's alleged incompetence. "His mental weakness," the ruling continued, "coupled with his vagrant habits would not indicate a normal degree of responsibility, or lend weight to his testimony."[77] With that, Crocker's case was referred back to St. Lawrence County for a new trial, but the district attorney hesitated to retry the case.[78]

The key witness in a potential retrial was facing legal troubles of his own. Just a few weeks after Crocker's conviction was vacated, Breyette was arrested on charges of theft in Plattsburgh, New York.[79] During his arrest, Breyette claimed to be fifteen, and his case was referred to a juvenile court. Further inquiry into the boy's background revealed that he was sixteen and eligible to stand trial as an adult. A month later, Breyette escaped from the Clinton County jail. He was recaptured in Massena and convicted for burglary and petit larceny.[80] Shortly after his release from prison in 1952, Breyette died in a car accident. He was only twenty years old.[81]

Crocker, meanwhile, returned to ministry—not exactly vindicated, but not terribly inconvenienced either. In early 1949, he moved to Radnor, Ohio, where he was hired on a temporary basis to pastor the First Congregational Church. At first, Crocker appeared to be an excellent fit for the position, but the Radnor church leaders soon learned that the new pastor might have been deposed from ministry. They reached out to the Rockingham Association for clarification.[82] Crocker himself found out about his defrocking around the same time: in late May or early June. "Had it not been for my present ministry," he complained to the registrar of the governing body, "I might never have learned of the Rockingham Association action."[83] Embittered, Crocker added, "Thank you for addressing me as Reverend, but I wish you wouldn't."[84]

The Ohio Congregationalists held a meeting on the Crocker matter on February 14, 1950. H. George Robertson, pastor of the First Christian Church in Mount Sterling, attempted to get to the truth of the matter, but Crocker refused to cooperate or provide straightforward answers. He scoffed at the indignity of being interrogated by the leadership. His new Ohio church was thriving, he said. They were even considering leaving the denomination to become a community church—a comment Robertson interpreted as a threat. "Whether he could be broken down to the point of confession, I don't know," Robertson concluded in his report to another Congregational minister in Columbus.[85]

Instead of confessing, Crocker doubled down on denial, to which he also added a litany of accusations against the Congregational association in New Hampshire. Taking a voluntary leave of absence from his Ohio church in the winter of 1951, Crocker traveled to New York to investigate his own case. Quoting the manual of the Congregational Church on proper defrocking procedure, Crocker accused the association of "grave injustice." Not only was he never informed of the charges against him, but he was also denied the chance to mount a defense. "Your actions not only violated every principle at the heart of Congregationalism, but also every rule of human decency," charged Crocker.[86]

In response—though not without hesitation—the Congregational association proposed arranging a new hearing for Crocker in New York. Frederick Alden, the head of the New Hampshire Congregational

Conference, explained that the suggestion was largely inspired by fears of legal retaliation. "It is to my mind," Alden wrote, "part of Mr. Crocker's scheme to get someone to put into writing answers to a series of carefully framed questions, which answers may be the basis of some legal action against the person who replies either in his personal or official capacity."[87] Christian principles aside, a potential lawsuit loomed large in the minds of the organization's leadership. The new hearing was scheduled for late October 1951.[88]

Not willing to wait for the official verdict, Crocker's Ohio church held a meeting to determine Crocker's fitness for ministry in early October. The minister in question was present and in rare form: argumentative, combative, and self-aggrandizing. He was convinced of his righteousness on the question of appropriate procedure, if not on the issue of sexual morality. Refusing to discuss the sexual assault charges, Crocker defended his character and assured the attendees that the Rockingham Association hearing would clear his name. Feeling persecuted and treated unfairly from all sides, Crocker accused a small group of disgruntled parishioners of conspiring to destroy his reputation. Passions ran high, but no decision was reached that evening. The attendees of the Radnor meeting voted to table the motion to dismiss Crocker until the annual meeting of the congregation the following January.[89]

The lack of a speedy resolution frustrated Ohio's Congregational leadership. Everett Babcock, the superintendent of the Ohio Conference of Congregational Churches, wrote to the Rockingham Association in a desponded tone in late October 1951. Apparently now fully convinced of Crocker's guilt, Babcock called Crocker "seriously mentally ill" and accused the minister of having "absolutely no control or restraint over his disposition or what he says." The accusation of sodomy—and Crocker's removals from prior positions—was reason enough to fire Crocker, Babcock concluded.[90]

The archival evidence of Crocker's Ohio ministry ends in October 1951—with promises of further deliberation but an unsatisfying lack of resolution. It appears that Crocker resigned or was forced to resign soon after, but his ministerial career was far from over, though he supported himself mainly through teaching (he had earned a graduate degree in sociology from Columbia University in 1948).[91] By 1958, he was teaching sociology at Monmouth College (now Monmouth University) in New Jersey. The next year, Crocker was named associate minister at the Unitarian

Fellowship in Monmouth County.[92] Between leaving his Ohio church and settling in New Jersey, Crocker managed to secure teaching stints at the University of Dubuque, Ricker College, and Polytechnic Institute of Puerto Rico.[93] In 1962, Crocker was invited to give a lecture on "crime, delinquency, and treatment" in front of New Jersey's West End Teacher Association in his capacity as an associate professor and acting chair of Social Sciences at Monmouth.[94] A newspaper account of Crocker's ministry from 1967 identified him as "an ordained minister" in an announcement of a Methodist service featuring the preacher.[95]

For Crocker, shifting denominational allegiances was key to sustaining a career in ministry. He was a likable man (the letters of support that poured into the Rockingham Association from his Ohio parishioners attested to his effectiveness as a pastor), and finding part-time church appointments as a veteran preacher with a graduate degree was easy. The people who hired Crocker—first in Ohio and then again at various churches and communities across the country—trusted that the minister's affairs were in order. Someone like Crocker could thrive in the chaos of constantly shifting denominational alliances and secret defrockings.

Another way to escape scandal was to forge relationships of brotherly protection with powerful Christian leaders. Having faithful friends in high places could ensure that scandal-prone Protestants could retain power and salvage reputations despite overwhelming evidence of unorthodox—and even criminal—sexual behavior. Edgar C. Bundy was a retired air force major who, like Crocker, dedicated his post-military career to ministry. Despite being ordained as a Southern Baptist pastor, Bundy devoted his efforts to parachurch work. He especially excelled in anti-communist propaganda. Carl McIntire, the prolific fundamentalist architect of the Christian Right, hired Bundy as his organization's publicity director in the early 1950s. In 1956, Bundy became the chairman of the conservative Church League of America, whose mission was to investigate and expose socialist leanings and communist influences in religious communities. Bundy repeatedly accused fellow Christians of being secret agents of the Soviet Union. As the unsubtle title of his *Collectivism in the Churches: A Documented Account of the Political Activities of the Federal, National, and World Council of Churches* (1958) suggests, Bundy believed that all but the most conservative Christian organizations were in danger of a communist takeover.[96]

Paranoid in his fear of communist sympathizers, Bundy also saw himself as a collaborator with the FBI—a sentiment not shared by the Bureau.

Bundy often wrote to J. Edgar Hoover with unsolicited reports on alleged communist activity. In October 1958, for example, Bundy asked Hoover whether the rattlesnake found in his friend's suitcase upon returning from a trip was a communist warning.[97] The letter received no response. The FBI generally ignored Bundy as an attention-hungry zealot who sought cheap publicity. By 1961, the Bureau was set on dismissing Bundy's project entirely, especially after he attempted to impersonate an agent.[98]

In 1963, the FBI would learn a detrimental secret about Bundy. "The disgusting truth," read an internal memo, "is that Bundy is a sexual pervert." Worse, Bundy allegedly favored "satisfying his perverted desires with young boys." The source of this information was an Ohio minister who maintained "a comprehensive file containing information about Bundy's homosexual activities." This unnamed informant was apparently close enough to Bundy to have confronted him with the evidence, after which Bundy "readily confessed but begged forgiveness." The minister also reported that hundreds of other Christian pastors were aware of Bundy's predicament.[99]

Within the Christian anti-communist movement, it had indeed long been rumored that Bundy had a problem. Already in 1954 McIntire had learned of Bundy's sexual proclivities but retained Bundy in his position. Bundy had apparently made unwanted sexual advances toward two Christian boys in 1946 and 1947—incidents that resulted in his removal from youth ministry.[100] There were additional rumors that he had propositioned several men and a high school boy.[101] Although McIntire was advised to fire Bundy in order to protect the reputation of his organization, he refused. McIntire was involved in the ambitious project of getting the Republican Party to support the agenda of the Christian Right and needed Bundy's considerable gifts of persuasion to support this effort.

Still, the rumors persisted. In 1964, the FBI received further evidence of Bundy's homosexuality. A confession Bundy produced in 1954 suggested that he had both admitted his sexual orientation and seriously considered leaving Christian ministry because of it. Bundy's letter, with names redacted by the FBI, bears quoting in full.

Dear [name redacted],

Out of the anguish of a broken heart and a crushed spirit I am crying to you. I am beaten, defeated and wrecked. I have withdrawn from all Christian work. I have been unable to eat or sleep for the past three days. I have vomited until I cannot do it anymore.

I am sorry for all the misery and heartaches I have caused anyone. I cannot express myself more. All I ask is forgiveness and something or someone to heal. If I were there in your presence I would offer myself to be tramped on.

Please [name redacted], ask all concerned to stop writing and talking about the situation from now on. I am going to try to live my life with my wife by making a living in the secular world. Don't blame anyone in the ACCC or ICCC for me.[102] I am not a member anymore of my own free will, and I don't want any of them to take the blame for me.

God alone knows my heart. I must depend on Him. All I ask is some relief from the suffering which is mine. I must find rest somewhere, somehow. Please try to remember me kindly in your prayers. Again, all I can say to you and all the rest is: I am sorry from the bottom of my heart. There is an ache there which at times seems as if it would consume me. I do not know to whom to turn for help. I have cried to God until I can't cry any longer.[103]

Bundy evidently attempted to grapple with the reality of his predicament—a problem that he viewed as incompatible with his faith. Then again, the minister was not entirely sincere in his confession. He resumed the work of Christian anti-communism in no time and would, in fact, soon utilize the weapon of "sex perversion" allegations against others. Ten years after he penned his anguished letter, Bundy would contact Florida senator George A. Smathers and tell the politician that Martin Luther King Jr. was "a secret Communist and pervert to boot."[104] Seeing no apparent contradiction in making allegations of sexual deviance against others, Bundy proceeded to advance in far-right circles. The FBI may have dismissed Bundy as a "pious hypocrite," but this characterization would do little to impede Bundy's career in conservative recruiting.[105] And unlike Martin Luther King Jr., whom the FBI harassed for years, Bundy enjoyed multiple layers of protection.[106] His whiteness and his connections to other powerful Christian men allowed him to remain in positions of influence long after the allegations of his homosexuality first surfaced.[107]

Bundy persisted in his career for decades. In 1982, a new wave of allegations of homosexuality forced his resignation from the Church League of America, but it did not stop the minister from continuing to labor alongside other fundamentalists. By the late 1980s, he was again officially employed by McIntire as a publicity director. And it was not until 1990 that Bundy resigned—not due to any sort of scandal, but rather to take care of his ailing wife. To console his friend in retirement, McIntire awarded Bundy an honorary doctorate degree.[108] Christian connections protected Bundy for the majority of his career; his legacy stands unimpeded by scandal in evangelical circles.[109]

The fracturing of denominations, the protective secrecy of fundamentalism, and the professionalization of the press behooved scandal-prone mid-century Protestants. Another contributing factor was the shifting focus of the media away from critical coverage of mainstream religion to a newfound fascination with the so-called religious fringe.[110] Cultural anxieties of the postwar era positioned mainstream religion as inherently American, while groups that practiced new communal arrangements or engaged in unusual practices were deemed scandalous by comparison.[111] And since journalism's survival depended on appealing to populist audiences, newspapers focused on inoffensive reporting and occasional fascination with fringe phenomena.[112]

It was not until the early 1970s that scandal returned to the pages of mainstream periodicals. The revival of scandal's prominence had several causes: the re-emergence of investigative reporting, the ongoing competition for profit in the ever-expanding marketplace of news media, and the public's loss of confidence in the nation's institutions.[113] By the early 1970s, television had become so popular and the printing costs for magazines so prohibitive that publishing became a risky investment.[114] Print media began to look once more to the material they knew would sell best: human-interest stories and sensational exposés. One study of *Time*, *Newsweek*, CBS's *Evening News*, and NBC's *Nightly News* found that reports on crime and scandals increased dramatically between 1967 and 1975.[115] Media professionals were revisiting the lesson whose truth their penny press predecessors established back in the 1830s: scandal sold.

The profit-motivated increase in scandal coverage coincided with another development: the public's diminished confidence in democratic institutions.[116] In 1972, burglars entered the offices of the Democratic National Committee at the Watergate complex in Washington, DC. The people responsible for the break-in were members of the Republican President Richard Nixon's re-election committee, and their mission was to wiretap opponents' phones and photograph Democratic campaign documents. Probing the connection between the Watergate burglary and the incumbent White House, the *Washington Post* journalists Carl Bernstein and Bob Woodward uncovered the extent of the crime and the subsequent cover-up by Nixon. In the end, sixty-nine people were indicted, forty-eight people were convicted, and Nixon resigned from the presidency. Summarizing the role of the media in his downfall, the disgraced former president would later speculate that had it not been for the media's dislike of his policies, "Watergate would have been a blip."[117]

Nixon exaggerated the political power of the press. Any celebration of a free press capable of overthrowing corrupt presidencies through diligent investigation arrived with a sense of caution. As the *Washington Post* empire heiress Katharine Meyer Graham recalled, "The press after Watergate had to guard against the romantic tendency to picture itself in the role of a heroic and beleaguered champion, defending all virtues against overwhelming odds."[118] Watergate was an aberration, Meyer insisted, and ought not to have translated into conspiratorial reporting on other matters. *Time* magazine editor Henry Grunwald concurred: "Despite the accomplishments of the past two years, newsmen have ample reason to feel besieged, and many are torn between self-congratulation and self-doubt."[119] Accusations of the press waging a political war against Nixon's administration abounded. Still, the leading investigative outlets insisted that it was the primary function of the press to demand the truth of the people in power. As with the Gilded Age political corruption exposés a century prior, the 1970s media began to actively wrestle with how to maintain the challenging balance between objective reporting and impassioned demands for just politics and responsible religion.

In 1979, President Jimmy Carter labeled the erosion of the public's trust in its institutions "a crisis of confidence."[120] Christianity was not exempt from the crisis. One survey showed that confidence in organized religion had fallen from 41 percent in 1951 to 35 percent in 1973.[121] The political, cultural, and economic upheavals of midcentury may have shielded Protestants from unwanted publicity, but by the mid-1970s, a newly revitalized press community was dedicated to keeping public leaders accountable.

The new media would shift its attention to Protestants of the evangelical variety, a group that was rapidly gaining political and cultural cachet. A 1966 *Time* magazine cover asked, "Is God Dead?" A decade later, *Newsweek* would proclaim that 1976 was the "year of the evangelical."[122] With unprecedented political power and expanding religious empires that attracted large audiences, evangelicals were thriving. But the public and the press, wary of the tendency of the powerful to abuse their privileges, were watching them closely. After four decades of silenced sensations, private sins would once again become fair game for public consumption.

7

Public Relations

In the late twentieth century, a striking number of Protestant pastors were wrong: self-admittedly, regretfully, repentantly wrong. Hoping for a chance at public redemption, they televised their tearful apologies. In addition to publicized confessions, the disgraced ministers published books that projected contrition and humility: Billy James Hargis's *My Great Mistake* (1985), Jim Bakker's *I Was Wrong* (1996), and Marvin Gorman's *The Road to Repentance: The Story of a Televangelist from Ruin to Restoration* (1996). Through these media campaigns, ministers caught misbehaving performed carefully orchestrated public confessions.[1] They understood that the only way back to power was through a ritualized performance of repentance. Whether they meant it or not, disgraced preachers began to proclaim their brokenness in hopes of redemption.

By the late 1980s, the clerical sex offender had become a species. Sex scandals involving ministers seemed ubiquitous. Abuses and adulteries abounded. In 1989, journalists Kenneth Woodward and Patricia King described the proverbial religious abuser based on an academic study of sexual misconduct among religious professionals:

> In some ways, he is not all that different from other predatory Lotharios. He's usually middle aged and disillusioned with his calling. He is neglecting his own marriage. He's a lone ranger, isolated from his clerical colleagues. And he's met a woman who needs him. What makes the clerical seduction different from those of secular counselors is the God factor: unlike other therapists, the minister's power and authority are perceived as ultimately derived from the Lord.[2]

In the late twentieth century, there was no shortage of men who claimed to derive their authority from God while abusing power in ways both subtle and grand.

Sex scandals had been an ongoing source of trouble for Protestants who were struggling to find their footing in a world that was, in their view,

Disgraced: How Sex Scandals Transformed American Protestantism. Suzanna Krivulskaya, Oxford University Press.
© Oxford University Press 2025. DOI: 10.1093/oso/9780197599686.003.0008

quickly secularizing. For evangelical descendants of early fundamentalists, saving the secular world from eternal damnation was mandatory.[3] Despite competition from both mainline denominations and countercultural alternatives to traditional religion, evangelicals were winning some hard-fought battles for adherents. With Billy Graham's crusades, Billy James Hargis's radio sermons, Jerry Falwell's political lobbying, and Jim Bakker's and Jimmy Swaggart's Christian television programming, charismatic, media-savvy preachers were reaching unprecedented numbers of people who were nervous about the realities of life in a more diverse, cosmopolitan world.[4] Communism, homosexuality, juvenile delinquency, free love, and the rise of new religious movements threatened the stability of the social order that conservative Christians sought to preserve. The men who would lead them into the battle for the soul of the nation were uniquely gifted to rouse their passions and arm them with the spiritual tools needed to succeed in this new world.

Sometimes these same men failed them profoundly. The most powerful Christian leaders turned out to also be the most vulnerable to sexual temptation. The carnal overtook them in private, even as they exalted the virtues of restrained heterosexuality from their pulpits. Billy James Hargis, Jim Bakker, and Jimmy Swaggart would all be accused of engaging in extramarital encounters. Two of the men, Hargis and Bakker, were alleged to have had sexual contact with both women and men. When their respective scandals broke, the press and the public had to confront the difficult questions of what it meant for Christian morality that its loudest defenders regularly appeared to violate the very tenets they espoused.

Billy James Hargis was perhaps the most zealous crusader in the anti-communist religious Right until a sex scandal undermined his career and reputation. A devout fundamentalist, Hargis was born and raised in interwar Texas. After World War II, he became convinced that the nation was facing existential threats in secularism, godlessness, and loosened morality. Hargis's message was simple, if not free of wordplay: "Jesus Christ is the hope of the world, and America is God's greatest nation under the living Son."[5] With his catchy slogans, folksy charisma, and media savvy, Hargis quickly rose to prominence as the most outwardly patriotic born-again evangelist of the postwar era.

Hargis's rise to popularity was not conventional by any means, yet perhaps his claim to being the ultimate outsider was precisely what propelled his success.[6] He was, as he liked to remind his followers, a simple orphan boy from Texarkana. Ordained by the Disciples of Christ at seventeen,

Hargis left the group only a few years later and swore never to join another formally organized religious community. The young man had come to believe that true Christianity could not be contained within any one denomination. Headstrong and defiant, Hargis refused to ever again be subject to arbitrary sectarian rules and regulations. He briefly attended Ozark Bible College but dropped out after only a year to become a full-time pastor in Oklahoma. Four years later, Hargis left that position to focus on "warning the churches of America, over a small network of radio stations, of their deadly enemy before it was too late."[7] The deadly enemy was communism, and wary Americans were ready to listen to the alarmist message of the preacher of doom. Hargis was only twenty-four years old.

In 1950, at age twenty-five, Hargis founded the Christian Crusade, a parachurch organization under whose banner he distributed religious literature, produced radio shows, solicited charitable donations, and sponsored missionary outreach. At the heart of the organization's mission was a single issue: Satan was using communism to bring on Armageddon, and the Christian Crusade's job was to rouse patriotic God-loving Americans to fight against the destruction of their nation and the world. Marrying conservative politics with fundamentalist theology, Hargis preached a far-right agenda even as he veiled the message in eschatological parlance. Hargis was a segregationist who proudly belonged to the extremist John Birch Society. He despised other religions and led a zealous crusade against sex education.[8] Publishing pamphlets with titles such as *Is the School House the Proper Place to Teach Raw Sex?* (1968) and *The Sex Revolution in the United States* (1970), Hargis denounced the purportedly Dionysian excesses of his age. Through every arm of his ministry, Hargis promoted a radical-right political agenda, even as he presented his concerns as purely religious, cloaking them in the language of a cosmic battle between good and evil. The Internal Revenue Service (IRS) eventually caught on to this and revoked the organization's tax-exempt status in 1960. At the time, the ministry was a million-dollar-a-year enterprise.

Hargis used the IRS debacle to cry martyrdom at the hands of the godless state. Unable to rely on public education to produce God-fearing citizens, Hargis joined the separatist fundamentalist university movement, which rejected secular institutions of higher learning.[9] With little formal education and no experience in college administration, Hargis nonetheless appointed himself president of his American Christian College, based in Tulsa, Oklahoma, in 1971. President Hargis conceived of the school as a training ground for "God and country" believers who would fight "for Christ and against Communism." He was soon disappointed to discover that running an institution of higher learning meant having to allow for differences in opinion and theology among its faculty. Some of the instructors did not share Hargis's most extreme fundamentalist views yet were protected by the principles of academic freedom and what Hargis would contemptuously refer to as tenure "privileges." The college was not the piece of fundamentalist paradise that Hargis had envisioned.[10]

Still, Hargis enjoyed his new venture. Charismatic and gregarious, the minister formed unusually close relationships with the students. The school's band, the "All American Kids," toured the country and the globe with President Hargis at the helm. Back home, he had an open-door policy and often held private office meetings with students. Later, he would lament forming such close relationships. "While traveling with those young people," Hargis wrote, "I really thought I had become one of them. Today, I wish that I had never ridden the bus with them, never laughed at their jokes, never heard their confessions, and never related to them on a one-on-one basis."[11]

Five years into Hargis's tenure as president, allegations of sexual immorality surfaced. Perhaps most shocking was the accusation that Hargis had engaged in inappropriate sexual relationships with both female and male students. *Time* magazine broke the story in 1976 in an article titled "The Sins of Billy James."[12] The epigraph quoted Hargis's recent fundraising appeal to juxtapose the minister's ideology and praxis.

Dear Friend:

After years of shock and sorrow over the decline of morals and decency in our country, I thought I had become shockproof.... Can you believe it: complete color films of sexual acts between women and men, including homosexual acts, using your children. Unless you and I act today...our children and our children's children will be exposed to perversion so sinister that good will become evil and evil will become good.[13]

The focus on children in Hargis's fundraising campaign was part of the broader strategy of the Christian Right to undermine the growing acceptance of homosexuality. Most famously, soon after Hargis's sins became public, the Christian singer turned activist Anita Bryant spearheaded the anti-gay "Save Our Children" campaign in response to a Florida ordinance that outlawed discrimination on the basis of sexual orientation. Bryant claimed that because gay people could not reproduce, they sought to recruit children into their lifestyle.[14] Through Christian activists like Bryant and Hargis, these ideas became standard arguments for discrimination against LGBT people. It was all the more scandalous, then, that Hargis's alleged sins included not only inappropriate relationships with young people but also homosexuality.

According to David Noebel, the vice president of Hargis's college, the first student to accuse Hargis came forward in 1974.[15] Hargis had officiated at the student's wedding. During the honeymoon, the couple discussed their respective relationships with the minister. It was then that both the bride and the groom confessed that they were not virgins—having each lost their virginity to Hargis.[16] Eventually, three more students, all of them male, told Noebel that they, too, had been intimate with Hargis. And it was not just the open-door policy of his office that facilitated these encounters. The "trysts" also allegedly took place at his farm in the Ozarks and during the All American Kids tour. Noebel recalled that when Hargis was confronted with the allegations, the evangelist "admitted his guilt and blamed his behavior on 'genes and chromosomes'"—presumably trying to explain both his sexual orientation and predatory behavior by assigning responsibility to genetics.[17]

Whatever happened during the confrontation between Hargis and his associates, the allegations printed in *Time* changed the course of Hargis's life. The publication, started in 1923 by Henry Luce, the son of Presbyterian missionaries, had been soft on Protestantism in years past, but the grace *Time* usually afforded other pastors eluded Hargis.[18] He was too right-leaning, too radical in his positions, too zealous in his politics. As the theological and ideological divide between mainline and fundamentalist Protestants grew, so too did *Time*'s commitment to promoting more progressive kinds of religion while dismissing others as fanatical. A decade earlier, the magazine had scolded Hargis's "blatant melding of fundamentalist faith to extreme right-wing politics." The 1962 article, titled "Heavyweight Champ," used less than subtle insults of Hargis's physique to undermine his message, describing him as covered "in rolls of fat that start at his jowls and balloon into an elephant-sized waistline" and dismissing his alarmist sermons as money-grubbing schemes.[19]

The disparaging tone with which *Time* covered Hargis highlighted a tension within late twentieth-century journalism. As stories about religion and sexual morality proliferated, news outlets experimented with finding the appropriate tone of coverage.[20] Despite its Christian origins, *Time* had long championed moderate religious and political views. Even so, in the quarter century between 1950 and 1976, the editors covered many conservative Christian leaders with whom they had serious theological disagreements: Billy Graham, Francis Shaeffer, Oral Roberts, Robert Schuller, and Kathryn Kuhlman. None of these ministers were criticized as harshly as Hargis. One study of *Time's* religion coverage during this period suggests that, unlike other purportedly secular publications, *Time* could not be characterized as hostile to religion, both because of Luce's own religious commitments and because the majority of the middle-class, college-educated subscribers were themselves religious—most often mainline Protestant, but also Catholic and evangelical.[21] It is perhaps this focus on mainstream, upwardly mobile, middle-class sensibilities that rendered less refined, extremist figures like Hargis easy targets for ridicule.

In addition, *Time's* editor-in-chief Henry Grunwald openly distrusted all manner of charismatic authority and religious excess. Back in 1966, Grunwald had commissioned the iconic "Is God Dead?" cover of the April 8 issue. Seven years later, Grunwald penned an unprecedented editorial calling for the resignation of President Richard Nixon, then in the midst of the Watergate scandal—to spare "the country and himself [the] agony" of the impeachment process.[22] The following year, Grunwald published an editorial on the role of the press in sustaining American democracy. The piece, titled "Don't Love the Press, but Understand It," attempted to exonerate the profession of charges of undue sensationalism, partisanship, and bias. Journalism, Grunwald contended, was an inextricable part of any functioning democracy. "The audience will have to learn, or relearn," Grunwald reminded critics, "that printing optimistic pap is no service to the country, while exposing the dark side of a society or a government can indeed be an act of love and loyalty."[23] The editor continued publishing exposés for the duration of his tenure at *Time*. In 1976, it was Hargis's turn to be exposed.

Hargis dismissed the allegations. He denied having admitted to any wrongdoing and claimed that what he had confessed was not that he had sinned, but that he was—in an existential sense—a sinner, with some general, more ambiguous type of sin than the sexual impropriety of which he stood accused. Hargis would prevaricate in interviews: "I am not guilty of all the sins that I have been charged with. However, Christ died to save sinners of whom I am chief."[24] In his autobiography, the minister would double down on the unsatisfying non-confession that he had furnished: "If I had said, 'I am not guilty of *any* sin,' then I would have been lying unto man and God. I couldn't live with that. I had sinned, in many ways that no one but me knows about. God knows I have repented of my sins."[25] Admitting to vague, proverbial sinfulness conveniently freed Hargis from having to fess up to any specific wrongdoing.

This strategy of claiming full responsibility for sin while denying any culpability in the actual charges was a relatively new invention. Ministers such as Ephraim Avery, Henry Ward Beecher, and Aimee Semple McPherson from decades past insisted on complete innocence. Like Hargis, they believed they were sinners, yet none of them tried to obfuscate when asked about alleged sexual improprieties. They simply denied all accusations. Sin had nothing to do with it; their reputations had to be defended unequivocally.

Hargis was trying a different approach. Unlike those who came before him, Hargis did not have many supporters on the inside. His vice president and former friend David Noebel brought the story to *Time*. His students no longer trusted him. In a refrain that he would repeat time and again, Hargis blamed other Christians for his troubles. "I have found that some Christians are the most unforgiving people in the world," Hargis complained.[26] He also lashed out against the "secular media" and firmly held on to the I'm-a-sinner-but-not-in-any-specific-way line of defense. While it is unlikely that Hargis pioneered this particular strategy of obfuscation, he was an early adopter. Thirty years later, when evangelical megachurch pastor Ted Haggard was accused of having a long-standing relationship with a male sex worker, he would give the *New York Times* a statement that was eerily similar to Hargis's: "The accusations that have been leveled against me are not all true,…but enough of them are true that I have been appropriately and lovingly removed from ministry. I am so embarrassed and ashamed. I caused this and I have no excuse. I am a sinner. I have fallen."[27] Haggard would eventually admit to much more than simply being "a sinner," but in the early days of the scandal, his public relations strategy mirrored Hargis's.

In the early months of the district attorney's investigation into Hargis's relationships with students, the preacher appeared on Tom Snyder's show on NBC to warn the country about communism and to defend himself in the process. Snyder was gentle with Hargis, focusing most of the discussion on politics and turning to the scandal, which he called "the trouble," only at the end of the lengthy interview.

Snyder: I would be remiss if I did not ask you about the trouble. Now I know there is litigation pending on that. There is things you can say and that you can't say. Some very serious charges were leveled against you involving immoral actions by students at the university. Where does that stand now?...

Hargis: As far as I'm concerned, it's behind me. I can only say this: that I believe with all of my heart that our work is growing, that God is blessing our work, it's prospering. And what I did or what I didn't do, God has forgiven me. And at the time, I felt the charges weren't fair, but in all sincerity, I'm sure I've done things far worse than I've ever been accused. We've all sinned and come short of the glory of God. I went through a period of emotional distress. It was the most traumatic experience of my life. But it's behind now. I've got a job to do, and I don't have nothing else to say.

Snyder: I understand that, but I want to ask you one more thing. Considering that problem and whatever happened, as you say, is passed. After it was all over, now do you have a little bit more flexibility in your...how can I say this?

Hargis: May I say it for you?

Snyder: Yeah.

Hargis: I'm more sensitive to people that are being accused falsely or truthfully.

Snyder: But I mean, when you stand and you preach the Bible, can you now understand the plight of sinners more than you have been able to before?

Hargis [*interrupting*]: I can. I can. I can. I can. I can. I say yes. And I say to you in all sincerity, if this experience has done anything to me, it's made me realize that the Christians are the only army in the world that kill their wounded. Everybody else binds the wounds of their wounded and helps them. But the Christians are quick to believe whatever they hear without hearing the other side. I can only say to you this: I hope and pray to God that I will never in my life attack a man on such charges, whether they are true or they are false, because I know the hurt that comes for him—not just the hurt to him, but everybody that loves him. What about my wife? What about my four kids? What about my ministry? I am more sensitive now. I really am. I really am.[28]

Hargis refused to take responsibility for his alleged improprieties and shifted the focus instead to how supposedly unforgiving—and therefore un-Christian—his coreligionists were. Future scandal-prone ministers would use the same rhetoric when bewailing their admonishment by fellow believers. The reference Hargis made to his family as the ultimate victims of the affair was another development in scandal management that would take root among Protestant pastors in trouble. The idea that the family occupied the central, sacred role in society dated back to the early republic, but the 1970s saw Protestants unite around this ideal in a new way. As divorce, homosexuality, and premarital sex became more accepted within the broader culture, conservative Protestants organized to counteract the trend. Between 1976 and 1978 alone, the founding of three major organizations—Family Life, Focus on the Family, and Concerned Women for America—signaled a concerted effort among conservative Protestants to turn back the tide of what they perceived to be loosened sexual morals that threatened the very foundations of the nation.[29]

At the same time, ministers' wives, formerly relegated to the background, emerged as formidable actors in both local congregations and national politics—even as they eschewed women's liberation and preached submission to male leadership.[30] Pastors' wives embodied the ideal of female submission at church and at home, as they propagated the message that traditional gender roles were divinely ordained and had to be defended against a culture that embraced egalitarianism.[31] Scandal hurt godly families, Hargis asserted, as he pleaded for the support of like-minded Christians who chose to believe him.

Impatient to move on, Hargis hoped that his appeals to family values and Americans' collective fears of Armageddon would be distracting enough to erase the memory of allegations of extramarital and not strictly heterosexual sex. In some ways, the strategy worked. Although the district attorney's investigation did not culminate in an indictment, the preacher's popularity suffered. Then again, the scandal did not ruin Hargis's career entirely. He was forced to resign from his college, and the institution soon crumbled under financial pressures and the overwhelmingly negative response from parents of enrolled students, but Hargis's ministry did not end. He moved to his Ozarks farm and continued to author anti-communist propaganda until his death in 2004. A small, but faithful flock of supporters continued to heed the fiery preacher, disgrace and all. Their religious and political allegiances galvanized them more than any publicized rumors of their leader's alleged missteps.

Hargis's strategy of obfuscation failed to exonerate the preacher fully, and the new generation of scandal-prone pastors decided, instead, that confession would be key to redemption. They understood that the public needed to hear their leaders describe how they had sinned before they could offer forgiveness.[32] The ritual of confession reassured followers that their leaders were still on the side of the good. A misstep did not have to mean the denunciation of shared morals; it could, in fact, serve as an opportunity to publicly reassert the moral code that the offender had broken. If performed correctly, the ritual of public confession could restore power to the powerful, reassure the public, and reassert proper sexual mores.

Two disgraced televangelists employed this strategy as they attempted to regain the cultural and religious capital squandered in the aftermath of scandal: Jim Bakker and Jimmy Swaggart. Both men were ordained by the Assemblies of God, the largest pentecostal denomination in the world. Both headed enormous multi-million-dollar media empires built in the 1970s and 1980s. Bakker and Swaggart became each other's critics and fierce competitors in the booming marketplace of TV religion. And both fell from grace when their secrets were revealed to the public, which had sustained them with prayers and pocketbooks for years prior.

Jim Bakker and his wife Tammy Faye started out small.[33] They met in 1960 at North Central Bible College, an Assemblies of God school in Minneapolis. Soon the couple settled in North Carolina and began touring the country as healing evangelists. Jim preached. Tammy sang. They entertained the children who came to the meetings with puppets—a compelling medium that brought them to the attention of Pat Robertson, the leading religious television broadcaster in the country. Robertson hired the Bakkers for his Christian Broadcasting Network in 1965. After that, the Bakkers never had to worry about finding adoring audiences again. Modeling their television appearances on secular talk shows like the *Tonight Show Starring Johnny Carson*, the Bakkers quickly became celebrities in their own right. They launched Trinity Broadcasting Systems in 1972. A year later, *PTL Club* (the acronym stood for both "Praise the Lord" and "People That Love") became a hit, and by the end of the decade, PTL television ventures would be among the most successful in the nation.

The Bakkers' ascent as Christian media moguls was remarkable because while Protestants had utilized mass media to propagate their message for generations, television—and early televangelism—was an entirely different venture. As it gained popularity, Jim and Tammy Faye's programming began to resemble secular television entertainment—a development that ran the risk of both alienating conservative followers and drawing derision from secular critics. In the end, the blend of secular entertainment and religious messaging turned out to be the key to the ministry's success.[34] By embracing aspects of secularism, PTL brought televangelism to a national audience.[35]

The success of PTL became impetus for further expansion. In 1978, the Bakkers began construction of Heritage USA, a Christian theme park in Fort Mill, South Carolina. With the new venture, the Bakkers sought to attract believers who eschewed secular entertainment but were still looking for a good, godly time on their hard-earned vacations. Contributions from supporters provided the evangelists with enough capital to continue constant expansion. Prosperity begot greed. Before long, Bakker began lying to his supporters about how much return they were going to see on their investments, as his vision for Heritage USA outgrew his budget and his desire for personal fortune became insatiable. Facing unexpected expenses and inevitable debt, Bakker resorted to speculating in $1,000 "lifetime memberships," on which he knew he could not deliver. He would eventually be convicted on multiple counts of fraud in 1989.

But in the 1970s, with the financial scandal still a decade away, the Bakkers were basking in the glory of their temporary—but lavish—success, even as they struggled with their marriage. By 1980, Tammy Faye had developed a taste for prescription medication and men who were not Jim.[36] Bakker was devastated. In December 1980, he flew to Florida to hold a telethon. There the forty-year-old minister met twenty-one-year-old Jessica Hahn, a church secretary from New York who had been asked to babysit Bakker's daughter while he was away on official PTL business. In his hotel room, Bakker allegedly forced Hahn to have sex with him. Bakker would later deny allegations of assault and portray the entire ordeal as entirely consensual—undertaken, on his part, only to make Tammy Faye jealous.[37]

Whatever the truth of the encounter was, Bakker understood that what happened had to be kept secret. PTL pressured Hahn to stay silent—for the good of the church. PTL tried both monetary compensation in the form of a $265,000 bribe and spiritual intimidation to keep Hahn from going to the press. Recounting the pressure from PTL decades later, Hahn recalled being told, "Just keep your mouth shut, Jess, because this is a *church*." The church, Hahn remembered, was her world: she knew that revealing what happened "would affect millions of people." It did.[38]

After years of investigation of PTL's financial mismanagement by the *Charlotte Observer* and of speculations of marital infidelity by his rivals, Bakker resigned from ministry on March 19, 1987. The few details that came out early on were murky. At first, Jim and Tammy Faye presented the resignation as a consequence of unsubstantiated attacks against the ministry. Stepping down, they claimed, was an act of selfless courage for the greater good of the church—meant to diffuse unnecessary tensions and save PTL.[39] They admitted no guilt.

PTL was indeed in trouble. Evangelical leaders Jerry Falwell, John Ankerberg, and Jimmy Swaggart were summoned to help save the ministry since all three were invested in the broader project of Christian media's success. Falwell and Swaggart were especially worried that Bakker's infidelity would affect their own television ministries. Ankerberg and Swaggart asked Falwell to confront Bakker, and Falwell was happy to oblige, since he had his sights on taking over PTL.[40] The plan worked. When confronted, Bakker confessed to his infidelity and to the payoff that he authorized to keep Hahn quiet. Falwell took over PTL.

Bakker's resignation—first by way of a telephone call to the *Charlotte Observer* and later through a formal letter—blamed everyone but Bakker for Bakker's problems. "I sorrowfully acknowledge that seven years ago, in an isolated incident," he wrote, "I was wickedly manipulated by treacherous former friends and then colleagues who victimized me with the aid of a female confederate." Bakker, not Hahn, was the victim in his retelling. Everything he did in that hotel room, he claimed, was the result of jealous, power-hungry men and a female accomplice who conspired to destroy his reputation. In the aftermath, Bakker said, he "succumbed to blackmail" to save his ministry. Now that this predicament forced him and Tammy Faye to enroll in therapy, the minister hoped for redemption and restoration in some not-too-distant future.[41]

Bakker miscalculated his redemption timeline. The reason the *Charlotte Observer* reporters stumbled upon the Hahn story was because they had been investigating Bakker's finances, which elevated the scandal to a new level.[42] One week after Bakker spelled out his vaguely conspiratorial reasons for resigning, the *Observer* reported that PTL had paid Hahn the infamous $265,000 to stay silent. A few weeks later, the *Observer* revealed the extent of the Bakkers' luxuriously indulgent lifestyles to the public: in the previous year alone, PTL had paid Jim and Tammy Faye $1.6 million in salary and bonuses. Besides, as the reporters had long suspected, Bakker's fundraising

techniques were more than dubious, bordering on fraud. The paper continued to follow the story over the following year, and it won a Pulitzer Prize
for its investigation of PTL.[43]

In light of these revelations, the Assemblies of God deliberated whether
to part ways with the problematic pastor whose celebrity, in less tumultuous
times, was a valuable asset to the broader pentecostal movement. The lead-
erships initially hoped that Bakker could be rehabilitated and restored to
ministry, but anonymous allegations of his bisexuality halted these plans.
"The Assemblies of God church," reported the *Washington Post*, "regards
homosexuality as unpardonable for clergy."[44] In early May 1987, the
denomination defrocked Bakker for the Hahn incident and for "alleged
misconduct involving bisexual activity."[45] No further explanation of the
latter was supplied, but the denomination made it clear that while it was
willing to put up with financial fraud and even alleged sexual assault, queerness crossed a line.

The denomination had worked out protocols for dealing with homosexuality back in the 1950s. The minutes of the Forty-Third General Assembly
included the following recommendation: that the "same ruling apply to
homosexuals as applied to those guilty of adultery and fornication."[46] The
ruling involved revoking ministerial license, disfellowshipping the offender,
and ensuring that he or she could never be reinstated. However, whereas
the status of adulterer or fornicator presumably required a provable physical offense, the General Assembly applied the rule to homosexuals just by
virtue of their existence.

Jim Bakker denied the new allegations. Tammy Faye, feigning peace of
mind in the chaos of the scandal, reassured the public that she had no
doubts about her husband's heterosexuality. In an ABC interview with Ted
Koppel, Tammy Faye testified to Jim's straightness. "I have been married to
this man for twenty-six years," she said, "and I can tell you one thing: he's
not homosexual or [*sic*] is he bisexual; he is a wonderful, loving husband."[47]
With assurances of sexual orthodoxy, the Bakkers looked for the public's
compassion.

It was not immediately clear who had supplied the evidence of Bakker's
bisexuality, but the televangelists who orchestrated Bakker's downfall were
the likely culprits. Jerry Falwell had long preached that the future of
America was being jeopardized by "the homosexual revolution."[48] As the
scandal unfolded, Falwell began to publicly denounce Bakker's sexual appe-
tites. Falwell told the media that a male witness had confessed to having had

sex with Bakker and to having witnessed the minister "in the same act with others." Another man, Falwell alleged, claimed that a naked Bakker had once made sexual advances toward him.[49]

As the rumors spread, Protestants worried about what yet another scandal might mean for their religion's reputation. "The sad part of this whole sordid mess," wrote *Los Angeles Times* reader Patricia A. Kelley, "is that we are 'judged' by the company we keep—and the leader of this gang of crooks is[,] innocent or not, God. His reputation is suffering by the behavior of his leaders here on Earth." Another reader expressed a similar sentiment: "The problem of Christians behaving lovelessly and divisively among themselves is becoming recognized as a serious problem in convincing the public of our message and personal sincerity." Readers with longer memories of Protestant sex scandals predicted that the Bakker affair would blow over quickly. "Sister Aimee Semple McPherson," wrote William R. Osteck of Los Angeles, "had her rendezvous in the desert with her audio station announcer and returned in a triumphant parade, I predict the same for Brother Jim Bakker."[50]

Bakker's triumph would be postponed. Five months after he was defrocked, the disgraced PTL leader was indicted on twenty-four wire and mail fraud charges and on one count of conspiracy to commit fraud. Ten months later, Bakker was sentenced to forty-five years in prison and a $500,000 fine. "I have sinned," a tearful Bakker appealed to the judge, "but never in my life did I intend to defraud." The plea fell on deaf ears, as the minister was marched off to prison.[51]

At the peak of Bakker's unraveling, the press turned to other prominent televangelists for answers about religion and sexual morality. Jimmy Swaggart was an especially sought-after expert. Popular TV news anchors Ted Koppel and Dan Rather interviewed the folksy Louisiana minister to understand one televangelist's disgrace through another's commentary.[52] By the late 1980s, Swaggart had become an expert in disgrace.

The first high-profile case in which Swaggart had direct involvement was that of Marvin Gorman. Gorman was a megachurch pastor who had been rumored to be a bit too intimate with his female parishioners, including church deacons' wives. In 1986, Swaggart confronted Gorman with the rumors and pressured him to confess. While denying other allegations, Gorman admitted to one extramarital affair. He resigned from ministry but held on to a grudge. Determined to repair his reputation, Gorman filed a defamation lawsuit against Swaggart in 1987. The timing could not have been more fortuitous: if the courts were sluggish in restoring Gorman to his prior glory, rumors of Swaggart's own sexual secrets promised a speedy resolution.

It turned out that Swaggart—the tireless crusader who implored Americans to repent of their sins, condemn pornography, and return to Christian morality—had an insatiable appetite for sex workers. A family man, Swaggart had married Frances Anderson in 1952 when they were still teenagers. Thirty years later, the minister grew discontented with his marital state. By 1987, the fifty-two-year-old pastor became a frequent visitor at the Travel Inn Motel in Baton Rouge, Louisiana—an establishment that offered reasonable hourly rates and quick sexual encounters. On average, Swaggart visited the Travel Inn one to three times a month. Twenty-seven-year-old Debra Murphree regularly took care of the man who called himself "Billy" to avoid being recognized as the celebrity televangelist. Murphy charged twenty dollars a visit. Billy, she said, never tipped. Apparently concerned with the deadly threat of HIV and the reputation-ruining prospect of getting caught, Billy asked for penetrative sex only once; the rest of the time, Murphree would pose for provocatively staged photos or perform oral sex on the client—always with a condom.[53]

The New Orleans police were well acquainted with the Travel Inn. As coincidence—or divine justice—would have it, Marvin Gorman's son Randy was an officer on that force. He, too, was intimately familiar with Debra Murphree's work. Murphree would later reveal that she had been seeing Randy Gorman for a few months when he got especially excited at her mention of the fact that Jimmy Swaggart was one of her clients. Soon Randy and his father hatched a plan. During one of Swaggart's sessions with Murphree in October 1987, the Gormans set up a camera in a nearby motel room and let the air out of one of Swaggart's car tires. Once Swaggart realized that he could not get away from the motel quickly, his former colleague Marvin Gorman approached the minister with questions. What, precisely, was the Reverend Jimmy Swaggart doing with a sex worker in a seedy motel room? The answer held the key to Gorman's revenge.

Swaggart knew he had to confess. He admitted to his sex worker habit, which had apparently plagued him for almost thirty years. In exchange for keeping the story secret, Swaggart promised to help Gorman piece together his broken ministry. But Swaggart was slow on the redemptive apology tour on behalf of Gorman, and the disgraced pastor was becoming impatient with the soon-to-be disgraced televangelist. In February 1988, Gorman contacted the Assemblies of God and shared what he knew about Swaggart, complete with photographic evidence of his indiscretions.[54]

Just two weeks earlier, the National Religious Broadcasters (NRB) association convened under the theme "Accountable to God and Man" to address the media crises in their midst—including Jim Bakker's fall and Oral Roberts's suspect fundraising techniques. (During one of Roberts's campaigns, he informed viewers that God had told him that he would die unless the audience raised enough money—$8 million, to be precise—for his ministry.) Like their predecessors in the early twentieth century, NRB members wanted to skip past the scandals and go on to positive publicity, restored images, and successful crusades. To achieve these goals, NRB voted to adopt stiffer ethical and financial codes aimed at greater transparency and accountability.[55]

Swaggart, for utilitarian reasons, was on board with NRB's newly articulated posture toward corruption. He understood what Billy James Hargis and Jim Bakker failed to fully grasp: the only way to redemption was through unambiguous, full, and heartfelt confession. His dramatic apology came with high production values. From a tabernacle filled with his brokenhearted, disappointed (but still adoring) flock, Swaggart aired his confession for the viewing pleasure of millions of followers at home. He opened the confession by promising to speak from the heart in order to fully account for his sin. The preacher insisted that the blame and fault were his alone. While what precisely Swaggart took the fault for was conveniently left unsaid, he seemed genuinely remorseful. Parting from the tendency of other accused adulterers to blame the media for sensationalism, Swaggart even commended the press for its measured coverage.[56]

The part of the confession calculated to have the greatest emotional appeal came next. With all the sincerity he could muster, Swaggart—and the video cameras—turned to his wife Frances. "God never gave a man a better helpmate and companion to stand beside him," the pastor said. The ministry's success, he went on, would not have been possible without "her strength, her courage, her consecration to her redeemer, the Lord Jesus Christ." The camera zoomed in on Frances's face, as her husband's piercing eyes focused on hers: "I have sinned against you and I beg your forgiveness."[57]

Next came the biblical metaphors, carefully selected to portray its protagonists in the most redeemable light possible. Swaggart was a modern, made-for-television King David. God forgave David and forgot his sin; surely, the Lord—and the viewing audience—would do the same for

Swaggart. With the pattern of godly forgiveness established, Swaggart addressed his denomination and fellow televangelists. He regretted embarrassing the Assemblies of God and hurting fellow preachers' reputations by association. At the end, Swaggart turned his confession to God. "I would ask," he prayed, "that your precious blood would wash and cleanse every stain, until it is in the season of God's forgetfulness, never to be remembered against me anymore." The ministry would continue, Swaggart assured his supporters. No sin was big enough to stand in the way of his plans for expansion. The pastor closed by reading Psalm 51—about transgression, redemption, and renewal. With that, Swaggart hoped that his comeback was complete.[58]

Despite the intensity of the confession, Swaggart never actually specified his transgression, which was helpful for rhetorically minimizing the impact of his actions. The Louisiana chapter of the Assemblies of God recommended that Swaggart stop preaching for three months and be put on probation for two years. "We'll be merciful, and he'll be restored," the denomination's representative said.[59] The presbytery, headquartered in Missouri, was slightly less merciful. The men in charge agreed with the length of the probation (two years, during which Swaggart would be required to meet with denominational leaders and committees tasked with monitoring his spiritual and moral progress) but required that the preacher stay away from the pulpit for an entire year. When ABC's *Nightline* asked one of the representatives of the presbytery whether such a light punishment had anything to do with the fact that Swaggart's ministry brought in $10 million a year in donations to the denomination, the representative prevaricated. Enough money was coming in as it was, with or without Swaggart, he assured the incredulous interviewer.

The public was divided in its response to Swaggart's confession. As the *Los Angeles Times* put it, "Some, warmly remembering Swaggart's past ministerial services, will probably react to his tearful confessional candor with a generous readiness to forgive his slip from grace. Others are more likely to find the revelations of his alleged trysts with prostitutes utterly hilarious."[60] It was true that Swaggart endured much mockery in the press on account of his hypocritical conduct. That his fall occurred so soon after Jim Bakker's meant that the conversation about corruption at the highest echelons of evangelicalism would continue. That Swaggart was instrumental in bringing down Bakker only to be disgraced the following year made the ironies of televangelists' problems all the more poignant. "Hands down," wrote the

Washington Post columnist Judy Mann, "the television evangelists are giving us the best entertainment of the year."[61] Commentators poked fun at Swaggart's stances against pornography, homosexuality, and sexual immorality by juxtaposing them with his own secret vices. Here was yet another Elmer Gantry, they wrote—just as the 1970s musical based on the novel was seeing a timely revival on Broadway.

Meanwhile, Protestant preachers were grieving. They worried about the effects of scandals' proliferation on their own ministries. "This could begin to plant seeds in people's minds," worried one clergyman, "'If we can't trust Swaggart, who can we trust?' It could begin to undermine spiritual authority. That's my fear."[62] In an attempt to counteract the negative publicity surrounding religion's most notorious leaders, a new cable station, Vision Interfaith Satellite Network (VISN), launched in the summer of 1988. Based at the Trinity Episcopal Church of New York, VISN aired interdenominational religious programming, which included Protestant, Jewish, Catholic, and LDS offerings. The station was supposed to redeem the clergy in the eyes of the public and address the "concern over the fact that the mainline churches were doing nothing to take advantage of the power of television."[63] The enterprise saw limited success and meager ratings. It eventually merged with other progressive networks before it was bought by Crown Media Holdings to form the Hallmark Channel in 2001. By then, feel-good movies had proved to be more profitable than religious television devoid of such charismatic—if controversial—personalities as Jim Bakker and Jimmy Swaggart.

Jerry Falwell remained optimistic about Protestantism's survival despite his associates' scandals. "You need not be embarrassed by what has happened," he told the members of the National Association of Evangelicals less than a month after Swaggart's scandal broke, "This is a time to regroup, judge ourselves and march on with a greater intensity than before." Scandals, Falwell hoped, would only make Christianity stronger through better accountability, greater commitment, and more relentless morality.[64] After all, Falwell reasoned, just as Watergate led to positive reforms in the government, so too could televangelists' sex scandals unite Christians in their pursuit of holiness.[65]

Swaggart was unsympathetic to the notion that his downfall would merely improve Christian morality. He sought to emerge redeemed, and he wanted the redemption to come quickly. In the end, Swaggart decided that his ministry was too profitable to squander; he could not afford to be away from the pulpit for an entire year. Defying his denomination's order to abstain, Swaggart announced that he would return to preaching on May 22, 1988—just three months after his tearful confession. In response, the Assemblies of God defrocked the pastor. Swaggart, in turn, resigned from the denomination. "We believe that to stay out of the public for a year would totally destroy the television ministry and greatly adversely impact the [Jimmy Swaggart Bible] college," the minister said. "Therefore, I must regretfully withdraw from the Assemblies of God, understanding that they will have no choice except to dismiss me from the fellowship."[66] Having parted ways with the denomination, Swaggart was free to independently seek forgiveness among his captive audience—this time, without the oversight of a governing church body.

For his comeback sermon, Swaggart brought on the stage the two people who served to symbolically reassert his authority as father and husband, thereby making him appear fit to lead his congregation forward, past the hiccup of scandal. Swaggart's son Donnie and his wife Frances each addressed the congregation from the stage. They were thrilled to have Jimmy back—ready and willing to resume the Lord's work. Swaggart opened the sermon with humility: "I have preached, stood before some of the largest crowds in the world but I guess I stand now with more fear and trembling than I have ever before in my whole life." But preach he must, he explained. He would accept any lot God assigned to him. "If He sees fit for me to sweep floors in a…little mission across the track," Swaggart assured his audience, "I would be honored to do anything for Him and do it the rest of my life." The idea that God saw fit for him to hold off on any kind of ministry for twelve months was apparently not convincing for Swaggart. In the meantime, the pastor asked for financial contributions from his congregants—both at home and via television. He ended the sermon with a meditation on the nature of God's forgiveness. "I have suffered the fire of eternal God," Swaggart said. Still, God's response was, "I find no fault in him." Apparently faultless, Swaggart stepped off the stage and turned his energies toward the rest of his career.[67]

In October 1991, three years after the first time he got in trouble, Swaggart was once again caught in a compromising situation involving a sex worker, this time in Indio, California. Rosemary Garcia would later tell the press that Swaggart spotted her from his Jaguar and solicited her services. On the way to their tryst, the police pulled the evangelist over for reckless driving. He received a citation for driving on the wrong side of the road in a car with an expired license plate while not wearing a seatbelt. These were the only formal violations, but reporters who got hold of the story followed up on the circumstances of the traffic stop with Garcia, who told them precisely who she was and why she was in Swaggart's car. As she deftly put it, "It's the same guy who cries on TV...to get people to give him all this money, and for what? So he can give it to us."[68]

Although critics predicted the complete destruction of Swaggart's ministry after this second scandal, the preacher emerged less repentant than the first time. "The Lord told me it's flat none of your business," Swaggart informed his congregation. Frances Swaggart once again stood by her husband. Eventually, Swaggart agreed to step down for "medical and spiritual help" during a short rehabilitation period. But scandal would never again be a deterrent for Swaggart. He was back to preaching in a matter of days.[69]

Swaggart's old rival Jim Bakker would soon be making a comeback of his own. Already in 1988, while Bakker was still under federal investigation, several television networks approached Jim and Tammy Faye with offers to serve as consultants on movies about their lives. The first made-for-TV film was released in April 1990. It starred Bernadette Peters and Kevin Spacey.[70] "There's a moral to this story," wrote Judy Mann in the *Washington Post*. "Scandal sells."[71] But Bakker could not get to the profits from cinematic consulting quite yet. He was dealing with an especially tough judge and an especially harsh sentence for mail and wire fraud. "Those of us who do have a religion are sick of being saps for money-grubbing preachers and priests," said Judge Robert Potter, who sentenced Bakker to forty-five years in prison.[72] Ironically, it would be this blunt comment that would eventually shorten Bakker's sentence and release him back into the world of televangelism. In 1991, an appeals court reduced the sentence to eighteen years, and Bakker was paroled in 1994. Nine years later, he resurrected his religious broadcasting empire, this time with a daily show, on which he would warn Americans about the impending end times and sell them buckets of dehydrated apocalyptic gruel in exchange for $600 donations.

In the wake of televangelist sex scandals, outside observers struggled to understand the peculiar crisis. Newspapers asked what the proliferation of scandal meant for religion. The *San Bernardino County Sun* ran two side-by-side editorials debating the meaning and merits of the PTL debacle.[73] "Sex-and-Money Scandal Brings Much Needed Public Scrutiny," proclaimed the editorial on the left-hand side of the paper. "TV Ministries Should Not Be Judged by Bakker's Mistakes," objected the one on the right. Sociologists conducted academic studies of the public's views on organized religion. They found that while confidence levels declined immediately after a scandal's revelation, they leveled out just 119 days after the event.[74] Scandal's attention-grabbing powers appeared to be diminishing proportionally to the public's attention span.

As disgraced celebrity preachers experimented with obfuscation and confession, they found their footing in the rhetoric of sin. They were wrong, they gladly admitted, which meant that they could now be forgiven and restored to their rightful places of authority. These preachers evoked the reality of sin, the weakness of the flesh, and the responsibility of Christians to forgive one another just as God forgave them. They learned to rebrand their downfalls as evidence of the gospel's effectiveness.

Celebrity ministers also learned that they did not need a church to be successful. If a denomination punished them, they could always resign. And they did. Hargis left his church long before the scandal. Bakker was defrocked. And Swaggart resigned when he judged his punishment to be too severe. These charismatic men needed no earthly authority above them. Convinced that they were right with God, they could continue building their empires undeterred by outside criticism. Their followers did not seem to mind. Charisma covered a multitude of sins. The Christian public was willing to overlook indiscretion if it meant that their values were affirmed in the process. Loyalty overshadowed scandal.[75]

Fallen preachers' emotional televised confessions and repentantly titled memoirs would suggest that their authors were serious about meaningful rehabilitation, yet a genuine grappling with the reality of their power abuses never occurred. Jimmy Swaggart's dramatic performance never actually articulated his faults and was severely undermined by the later "none of your business" retort. Billy James Hargis's My Great Mistake argued that being too friendly with his students and too trusting of fellow Christians— not any manner of sexual sin—was the reason for his troubles. And Jim Bakker's I Was Wrong did not, in the end, refer to his sexually predatory behavior or the fraudulent financial machinations for which he was convicted. While Bakker admitted to regretting his sexual encounter with Jessica Hahn, his being "wrong," according to his memoir, had nothing to do with his guilt. The closing lines of the book read: "I once thought that God had abandoned me. I thought that my days of ministering for the Lord were done. I thought that I would never preach again. I was wrong."[76]

Resolute in their insistence on the right to preach despite being caught in acts they otherwise label immoral, charismatic ministers of the television age appeared to be unstoppable—scandal and all. Perhaps Judy Mann was right when she summarized the meaning of the all-too-quick comebacks of Protestant celebrities in 1988. "The final moral of the story," Mann wrote, "is that there is no such thing as disgrace anymore."[77] Subsequent decades have borne out her lament.

Epilogue

At the turn of the millennium, scandal ceased to matter. Ted Haggard—the disgraced evangelical minister whose penchant for gay escorts and recreational narcotics became public in 2006—returned to the pulpit only four years after Mike Jones exposed him to the press. Shortly after being exiled from Colorado and dismissed from ministry, Haggard set out on a kind of redemption tour. He needed absolution to proceed with his career. When the disgraced pastor emerged from the first round of Christian counseling in November 2007, he declared himself "completely heterosexual"—a label his critics found disingenuous.[1] Newspapers reprinted the headline, pundits mocked the pronouncement, and comedians ridiculed the assertion. Musical satirist Roy Zimmerman wrote a song titled "Ted Haggard Is Completely Heterosexual," whose lyrics read, in part, "He was one in a million, or, more aptly, one in ten. Some folks say he put the men in amen."[2]

The extent to which such mockery propelled Haggard's exploration of his sexual identity is difficult to measure, but the blunder certainly inspired deeper self-reflection. Three years after the scandal, Haggard's testimony took on the shape of something more palatable for secular observers of his demise. In a 2009 interview with Oprah Winfrey, Haggard admitted to having wondered whether he was gay. His therapist, he said, had suggested that Haggard was "a heterosexual with homosexual attachments." When Winfrey pressed Haggard on what that meant, the minister explained: "I do believe I don't fit into the normal boxes. I do think there are complexities associated with some people's sexuality." Haggard's queer theory exploration ended there, but he admitted to having had sexual thoughts about men. He no longer answered the question of whether he was "completely heterosexual" in the affirmative. "I would say I'm a heterosexual with issues," Haggard concluded.[3]

In a subsequent *GQ* profile, Haggard acknowledged his "issues" again, though he would reject any readily available queer identity labels. "I think that probably, if I were 21 in this society, I would identify myself as a bisexual," Haggard told his interviewer Kevin Ross. Ross pressed Haggard

Disgraced: How Sex Scandals Transformed American Protestantism. Suzanna Krivulskaya, Oxford University Press.
© Oxford University Press 2025. DOI: 10.1093/oso/9780197599686.003.0009

to explain why he refused the label. "Because, Kevin, I'm 54, with children, with a belief system, and I can have enforced boundaries in my life. Just like you're a heterosexual but you don't have sex with every woman that you're attracted to, so I can be who I am and exclusively have sex with my wife and be perfectly satisfied."[4] Haggard's age, family, and faith precluded him from embracing the labels that outside observers of his scandal wanted him to adopt.

In 2010, Haggard started a new church in Colorado. He had to change denominations—a small price to pay for a return to his chosen profession post-scandal. Besides, in the twenty-first century, denominational affiliation had come to matter less than the political commitments and personal charisma of Protestant leaders. On his website, Haggard posted a page dedicated to clearing up the "facts" of the 2006 scandal. Citing the results of a polygraph test, Haggard now insisted that he never had more than a single sexual encounter with escort Mike Jones. He also disputed the allegations of sexual contact with anyone affiliated with his former megachurch—a precondition designed to present Pastor Ted as a safe shepherd for his congregation.[5]

In July 2022, new accusations of the old variety surfaced against the allegedly reformed minister.[6] A former colleague told the press that he had caught Haggard in possession of crystal methamphetamine and gay pornography in 2012 but agreed to keep the incident secret. Seven years later, two young men accused Haggard of inappropriate behavior. Both men had been members of the congregation, and one of them was a minor when the alleged incidents took place. In response, church elders asked Haggard to step down in April 2020. The minister complied in his own way: he retained the post of head pastor but moved church services into his home and offered virtual programming instead of in-person worship—citing the coronavirus pandemic and dwindling numbers of regular attendees as the culprits for the change in format. He continued to preach and teach in his home, having, as he put it in in a 2022 sermon, "learned to minister as the chief of sinners."[7]

This bold reclamation of leadership by disgraced ministers is not surprising. As the religious Right aligned with the political priorities of the Republican Party in the second half of the twentieth century, scandals were often relegated to the realm of manageable inconveniences, not career-altering revelations. Networks of powerful men (and the occasional woman) strategized to defend fallen ministers' reputations, while their faithful followers chose to forgive them—as long as the repentant pastors' confessions served to reassert orthodoxy in their sexual politics. That sexual purity has been impossible to achieve for many of these leaders has not slowed down their efforts to impose this ideal on their followers—and on the rest of the nation.[8]

Even as Protestant sex scandals have continued to reveal the contradictions between conservative sexual theologies and unrestrained secret practices of their propagators, vast numbers of contemporary Protestant groups have refused to grapple with the implications of their ministers' missteps. Perhaps the most egregious example of this was the scandal within the Southern Baptist Convention (SBC). In 2019, the *Houston Chronicle* and the *San Antonio Express-News* revealed that hundreds of SBC ministers, employees, and volunteers had been credibly accused of sexually inappropriate behavior or sexual assault, often against minors.[9] At least thirty-five of the accused remained employed by religious organizations with the full knowledge of SBC leaders, who often worked to silence victims (of whom there were over seven hundred) and dismiss their complaints. In 2022, an independent third-party investigation revealed that for more than twenty years, SBC leaders systematically silenced and intimidated survivors of sexual assault at the hands of predatory ministers.[10]

This culture of silencing has emerged out of a widely shared commitment to protecting institutional reputations—often at the cost of discarding the victims as troublemakers unwilling to sacrifice themselves for the greater good of the church. White evangelicals, with their emphasis on masculine authority and female submission, have been especially unwilling to introduce meaningful reforms in response to allegations against powerful men in their communities.[11] As a result, the epidemic of sexual abuse has infected all kinds of Protestant institutions: from the editorial offices of *Christianity Today* to the campuses of Moody Bible Institute and Liberty University.[12]

White evangelicals are not the only religious group suffering from a refusal to honestly grapple with this reality. Charismatic religious leaders representing all manner of denominations have managed to avoid the consequences of their sexual misconduct. In 1997, Henry Lyons, then president of the National Baptist Convention (the largest historically Black Christian denomination), was accused of adultery and indicted on a long list of financial mishandling charges.[13] After serving four years in prison for misappropriating the denomination's funds, Lyons returned to ministry—pastoring a church and even winning an election for the presidency of the Florida General Baptist Convention. In 2009, Lyons ran to be reinstated as president of the National Baptist Convention, from which he had stolen millions of dollars.[14] He lost the bid, but his persistence and the support of his followers sustained the disgraced minister for decades after his crimes became public.

In 2010, Bishop Eddie Long, the anti-gay Black pastor of an Atlanta megachurch, faced five separate accusations of sexual abuse by young men who said the abuse happened when they were children.[15] Long denied all accusations, cried persecution, and portrayed himself as a victim of slander. Church attendance briefly waned after the three young men filed civil lawsuits against the pastor, but Long managed to retain his position and regain popularity after settling the case for an undisclosed sum in 2011.[16]

Religious hypocrisy does not discriminate with regard to race or creed. A 2004 John Jay College of Criminal Justice study of sexual abuse of minors by Catholic clergy found allegations against 4,392 priests between 1950 and 2002.[17] In 2009, sex and relationship advice columnist Dan Savage started a regular column he called "Youth Pastor Watch," which documented news stories of Christian youth ministers abusing the children and young adults in their care. A 2018 study of child sexual abuse in Protestant congregations analyzed 326 cases that led to the arrests of purported offenders between 1999 and 2014—a small fraction of the total sample of 2,240 allegations of abuse in Protestant congregations made between 1982 and 2014.[18]

The fact that the sexual abuse of children has become a subject of public conversation about religion since the 2002 *Boston Globe* investigation revealed its epidemic proportions in the Catholic Church is not an indication of the phenomenon's novelty. This trend is much older than new disclosures would make it appear. A large number of nineteenth-century eloping ministers, for example, groomed and then ran away with much younger parishioners—many of them underage by contemporary standards, but not under the consent laws of their time. These stories are not new.

Collective moral outrage, however, has rarely translated into decisive action or meaningful restructuring of the institutions that enable this kind of abuse.[19] Only with the advent of the #MeToo movement, as well as its cousin #ChurchToo, has the broader public begun to have frank conversations about the fraught nature of unchecked pastoral power.[20] Yet this project remains especially fragile in Protestant communities due to the decentralized nature of authority in many denominations as well as a widespread reluctance to have frank conversations about human sexuality beyond listing prohibitions and denouncing taboos.[21] Billy Graham's grandson Basyle "Boz" Tchividjian believes that much of what Protestant churches teach (or refuse to mention) about sexuality enables abuse. "It's sort of a perfect storm," he said in 2017. "You have an ignorance about anything concerning sex, you have a view that men are in charge and have a higher degree of value, and you have a leadership structure that gives authority often to one person."[22] Tchividjian founded his organization Godly Response to Abuse in the Christian Environment in 2004 to address the problem within Protestant denominations. Other organizations, like the FaithTrust Institute, have been doing this kind of work since the late 1970s, but their admirable efforts have yet to reach the Protestant leaders who seem to need them most.[23] Tchividjian's younger brother Tullian, who is also a minister, was involved in an adultery scandal of his own in 2015. Four years later, claiming rehabilitation and divine forgiveness, the younger Tchividjian was back in the pulpit.[24]

Scandal has ceased to matter in the sense that disgraced ministers have time and again been restored to their positions with seemingly few consequences for their actions or adjustments to their theologies. As long as Christians put reputations above principles and institutions above people, the historical patterns will persist. But perhaps the fundamental creative function of scandal is not punitive, but rather generative: it allows societies to name the things which are deemed unspeakable, unprintable, and otherwise taboo. Scandal may not result in grand or sudden social change, but it does sanction more honest conversations about the dangers and excesses of power—religious or otherwise.

Or perhaps this reading is too optimistic. Only three moments in the long history of Protestant sex scandal coverage stand out as revolutionary: the 1830s, the 1870s, and, however fleetingly, the 1970s and 1980s. In two of these instances, the press dared to name the things that had been considered unprintable and, in all three, it pleaded with the public to keep erring leaders accountable. All three eras also forced religious institutions to adjust in response to scandal. Sometimes these groups tried to eliminate sexually hypocritical pastors from their ranks, but more often, the explosion of scandal only led to more effective ways of protecting the groups' reputations. Still, scandal enabled a public reckoning with the sexual and theological issues that transgressive behavior laid bare.

Since the 1970s, the sheer volume of sex scandals has desensitized the public. Few are shocked to discover new revelations of ministers' transgressive private passions—or even harmful abuses. As religious studies scholar Megan Goodwin reminds us, "Abuse happens because we let it."[25] When there are too many things to be outraged about, the singularity of a particular scandal loses its potency. The work that lies ahead for contemporary consumers of scandal is to relearn outrage in the face of disgrace.

Notes

Introduction

1. Jeff Sharlet, "Soldiers of Christ," *Harper's Magazine*, May 2005, 42.
2. National Association of Evangelicals, "Homosexuality 2004," quoted in Cylor Spaulding, "Evangelical Christian Crisis Responses to Same-Sex Sex Scandals," *Journal of Media and Religion* 17, no. 1 (2018): 29.
3. "Evangelical Leader Quits, Denies Male Escort's Allegations," *CNN*, Nov. 2, 2006, http://www.cnn.com/2006/US/11/02/haggard.allegations/; Josh Levs, "Pastor at Haggard's Church: 'We Stand with Him,'" *CNN*, Nov. 3, 2006, http://www.cnn.com/2006/US/11/03/church.reaction/; "Evangelical Confesses to 'Sexual Immorality' in Letter," *CNN*, Nov. 6, 2006, http://www.cnn.com/2006/US/11/05/haggard.allegations/index.html; Delia Gallagher and Rose Arce, "Haggard's 'Restoration' Won't Come Easy," *CNN*, Nov. 10, 2006, http://www.cnn.com/2006/US/11/10/haggard.restoration/index.html; "Ted Haggard Talks," *Oprah.com*, June 30, 2009, https://www.oprah.com/oprahshow/ted-haggard-and-his-wife-talk-about-the-gay-sex-scandal; Gayle Haggard with Angela Elwell Hunt, *Why I Stayed: The Choices I Made in My Darkest Hour* (Carol Stream: Tyndale House, 2010).
4. William Lobdell, "Ex-Worker Accusing TBN Pastor Says He Had Sex to Keep His Job," *Los Angeles Times*, Sept. 22, 2004, 16.
5. See, for instance, Dan Savage, "The Code of the Callboy," *New York Times*, Nov. 8, 2006, https://www.nytimes.com/2006/11/08/opinion/the-code-of-the-callboy.html; David Niose, *Nonbeliever Nation: The Rise of Secular Americans* (New York: Palgrave Macmillan, 2012).
6. Leith Anderson, "The Night Ted Haggard Made the News," *National Association of Evangelicals*, June 21, 2021, https://www.nae.net/the-night-ted-haggard-made-the-news/.
7. As historian R. Marie Griffith argues, American Christianity has long propagated the notion, "both overt and unspoken, that Christian morality should provide the basis for our nation's law and politics." R. Marie Griffith, *Moral Combat: How Sex Divided American Christians and Fractured American Politics* (New York: Basic Books, 2017), ix.
8. For a history of interactions between the pulpit and the press during the Gilded Age and Progressive Era, see Ronald R. Rodgers, *The Struggle for the Soul of Journalism: The Pulpit versus the Press, 1833–1923* (Columbia: University of Missouri Press, 2018).
9. Leslie Dorrough Smith, *Compromising Positions: Sex Scandals, Politics, and American Christianity* (New York: Oxford University Press, 2019).
10. On the ritual of public confession developed in the twentieth century, see Susan Wise Bauer, *The Art of the Public Grovel: Sexual Sin and Public Confession in America* (Princeton: Princeton University Press, 2008).
11. The origin of the colloquial expression "I know it when I see it" is most famously attributed to Supreme Court justice Potter Stewart, who used the phrase to explain why the movie *The Lovers* did not constitute hardcore pornography. In his concurrence, Stewart wrote, "I shall not today attempt further to define the kinds of material I understand to be embraced within that shorthand description, and perhaps I could never succeed in intelligibly doing so. But I know it when I see it, and the motion picture involved in this case is not that." See *Jacobellis v. Ohio*, 378 U.S. 184 (1964).
12. See, for instance, James Lull and Stephen Hinerman, "The Search for Scandal," in *Media Scandals: Morality and Desire in the Popular Culture Marketplace*, ed. James Lull and Stephen Hinerman (New York: Columbia University Press, 1997), 7.
13. James Lull and Stephen Hinerman describe scandal as a process in which "private acts that disgrace or offend the idealized, dominant morality of a social community are made public and narrativized by the media, producing a range of effects from ideological and cultural retrenchment to disruption and change." Lull and Hinerman, "The Search for Scandal," 3.

Sociologist John B. Thompson provides a similar definition of scandal as "actions or events involving certain kinds of transgressions which become known to others and are sufficiently serious...to elicit a public response." John B. Thompson, "Scandal and Social Theory," in *Media Scandals: Morality and Desire in the Popular Culture Marketplace*, ed. James Lull and Stephen Hinerman (New York: Columbia University Press, 1997), 38. Sociologist Ari Adut defines scandal simply as "the disruptive publicity of transgression." Ari Adut, "A Theory of Scandal: Victorians, Homosexuality, and the Fall of Oscar Wilde," *American Journal of Sociology* 111, no. 1 (2005): 219.

14. Historian M. J. D. Roberts emphasizes scandal's propensity to cause damage "to the standing of a person (or organization) of existing reputation." M. J. D. Roberts, "Evangelicalism and Scandal in Victorian England: The Case of the Pearsall Smiths," *History* 95, no. 320 (2010): 439. Literary scholar Theodore Ziolkowski argues that "in contrast to such notions as disgrace, shame, dishonor, infamy, and other terms that define personal reputation, 'scandal' suggests *public* disapproval in response to improper acts or conduct and, to this extent, presupposes a shared aesthetic or ethical sense in the general public that condemns the act." Theodore Ziolkowski, *Scandal on Stage: European Theater as Moral Trial* (New York: Cambridge University Press, 2009), 12.

15. In her book on public confession in modern America, historian Susan Wise Bauer argues that a successful confession—that is, one that leads to the rehabilitation of the public figure who has been caught in wrongdoing—requires both the admission of wrongdoing and the re-articulation of the shared moral code. See Bauer, *Public Grovel*, 52.

16. Mark D. Jordan, *Telling Truths in Church: Scandal, Flesh, and Christian Speech* (Boston: Beacon Press, 2003), 34.

17. Here I follow historian Ann Taves's call to "take sexuality as a starting point for rethinking American religious history" and extend it into the realm of the scandalous. See Ann Taves, "Sexuality in American Religious History," in *Retelling U.S. Religious History*, ed. Thomas A. Tweed (Berkeley: University of California Press, 1997), 29.

Chapter 1

1. David Richard Kasserman, *Fall River Outrage: Life, Murder, and Justice in Early Industrial New England* (Philadelphia: University of Pennsylvania Press, 1986), 7.

2. Benjamin Franklin Hallett, *Trial of Rev. Mr. Avery: A Full Report of the Trial of Ephraim K. Avery, Charged with the Murder of Sarah Maria Cornell: Before the Supreme Court of Rhode Island, at a Special Term in Newport, Held in May, 1833* (Boston: Daily Commercial Gazette, 1833), 189–90.

3. Historian Bruce Dorsey points out that the facsimile of the note, produced ten months after Cornell's death, differs from the wording that appeared in newspapers and trial transcripts. Bruce Dorsey, *Murder in a Mill Town: Sex, Faith, and the Crime That Captivated a Nation* (New York: Oxford University Press, 2023), 11. The surviving facsimile reads, "If I should be missing enquire of the Rev Mr Avery of Bristol he will know where I am Dec 20th S M Cornell." David Melvill, *A Fac-Simile of the Letters Produced at the Trial of the Rev. Ephraim K. Avery, on an Indictment for the Murder of Sarah Maria Cornell: Taken with Great Care, by Permission of the Hon. Supreme Judicial Court of Rhode Island from the Original Letters in the Office of the Clerk of Said Court* (Boston: Pendleton's Lithography, 1833), 12.

4. Luke Drury, *A Report of The Examination of Rev. Ephraim K. Avery, Charged with The Murder of Sarah Maria Cornell* (Rhode Island, 1833), 3.

5. Judith Flanders, *The Invention of Murder: How the Victorians Revelled in Death and Detection and Created Modern Crime* (New York: St. Martin's Griffin, 2014).

6. Michael Schudson, *Discovering the News: A Social History of American Newspapers* (New York: Basic Books, 1981), 13, 15.

7. Ammi Rogers, *Memoirs of the Rev. Ammi Rogers, A. M.*, 2nd ed. (Schenectady: G. Ritchie, 1826).

8. New York's *Long-Island Star*, for instance, summarized the case simply as a "crime of [s]eduction, and attempts of the most wicked and corrupt character to cover his villainy." The story included minimal commentary: "We have avoided going into detail at this time," the editors wrote, while also assuring readers that although "the offense which was committed had not been previously made public, the denomination to which [Rogers] belonged declared him unworthy of the clerical character." *Long-Island Star* (Brooklyn, NY), Oct. 18, 1820, 2. Nashville newspaper reported that Rogers was charged "with a high crime and misdemeanor,

'a deed of nameless note.'" The next sentence summarized the "nameless" charges: "The extremes of seduction and child murder, and poisons and violence were shown to be in use to conceal his crime and shelter from disgrace, the object of his cruelty." "Norwich, Conn, Oct. 11," *Clarion and Tennessee State Gazette* (Nashville, TN), Nov. 14, 1820, 2. Legal scholar Lolita Bucker Inniss cites four other contemporary newspaper accounts, which mention seduction and proceed to characterize Rogers as a "clerical monster" and a "degraded priest." See Lolita Buckner Inniss, "Abortion Law as Protection Narrative," *Oregon Law Review* 101, no. 2 (2023): 232.

9. *Report of the Trial of Ammi Rogers, for a High Crime and Misdemeanor, in a Brutal and High Handed Assault on Asenath Caroline Smith, of Griswold, Con. Before the Hon. Asa Chapman of the Supreme Court of Connecticut* (New London: Samuel Green, 1820).

10. *Trial of Ammi Rogers*, iii.

11. Quoted in *Trial of Ammi Rogers*, 49.

12. *The Christian Herald*, quoted in Nathan O. Hatch, *The Democratization of American Christianity* (New Haven: Yale University Press, 1989), 142.

13. William Turner Coggeshall, *The Newspaper Record: Containing a Complete List of Newspapers and Periodicals in the United States, Canada, and Great Britain, Together with a Sketch of the Origin and Progress of Printing, with Some Facts about Newspapers in Europe and America* (Philadelphia: Lay & Brother, 1856), 127.

14. Hatch, *Democratization of American Christianity*.

15. Speeches, pamphlets, and newspaper articles dedicated to discrediting the movement were produced en masse. In 1846, one critic compiled a list of published material dedicated explicitly to the "refutation of Methodism" since the denomination's origin in 1729. The list contained several hundred volumes. See Curtis H. Cavender, *Catalogue of Works in Refutation of Methodism: From Its Origin in 1729, to the Present Time* (Philadelphia: John Peninglon, 1846). Typical charges against the Methodists involved undemocratic clerical practices, despotism, and secrecy. See, for example, John W. Barber, *Thoughts on Some Parts of the Discipline of the Methodist Episcopal Church; with a Statement of Some Transactions and Usages in Said Church* (New York: Baldwin & Treadway, 1829).

16. Nathan O. Hatch, "The Puzzle of American Methodism," *Church History* 63, no. 2 (1994): 178.

17. John H. Wigger, *Taking Heaven by Storm: Methodism and the Rise of Popular Christianity in America* (New York: Oxford University Press, 1998), 3.

18. For more on Cornell's religious background, see Dorsey, *Murder in a Mill Town*, especially 29–36 and 48–56.

19. Sam Haselby, *The Origins of American Religious Nationalism* (New York: Oxford University Press, 2014), 166.

20. Rodney Hessinger, *Smitten: Sex, Gender, and the Contest for Souls in the Second Great Awakening* (Ithaca: Cornell University Press, 2022).

21. Dorsey, *Murder in a Mill Town*, 100.

22. "The Fall River Outrage," *Workingman's Advocate* (New York, NY), Jan. 5, 1833, 2; "Outrage and Murder," *Free Enquirer* (New York, NY), Jan. 12, 1833, 5.

23. The usage appears in several local statutes and is illustrated in this later example from the *Albany Law Journal* (1870): "A man may commit a rape upon a woman, outrage her person and feelings, and bring sorrow and shame upon herself and family for life, and escape with a punishment of five years' imprisonment." See "The Penal Code of New York," *Albany Law Journal* 1 (Jan.–July 1870): 177. See also Shani D'Cruze, *Crimes of Outrage: Sex, Violence, and Victorian Working Women* (DeKalb: Northern Illinois University Press, 1998).

24. Quoted in "The Fall River Outrage," *Workingman's Advocate* (New York, NY), Jan. 5, 1833, 4.

25. Quoted in Drury, *Report of the Examination*, 61.

26. See the *Pawtucket Chronicle* (Pawtucket, RI) issue from Jan. 11, 1833, and the *Rhode-Island Republican* (Newport, RI) issue from Jan. 15, 1833, quoted in Kasserman, *Fall River Outrage*, 118.

27. Peter C. Welsh, "Henry R. Robinson: Printmaker to the Whig Party," *New York History* 53, no. 1 (1972): 25–53.

28. "Arrest of Avery," *Liberator* (Boston, MA), Jan. 26, 1833, 3.

29. "Rev. Mr. Avery," *Trumpet and Universalist Magazine* (Boston, MA), Feb. 16, 1833, 5.

30. The *New York Courier and Enquirer* (New York, NY), quoted in *Trumpet and Universalist Magazine* (Boston, MA), Feb. 16, 1833, 5: "To such an extent was the religious determination to save [Avery] carried, that one of the daily papers in Providence which dared to publish the

particulars of his examination, has been persecuted to an extent that has compelled the editor to give notice that it will be discontinued after the first of February!"

31. Catherine Read Williams, *Fall River: An Authentic Narrative* (Providence: Marshall, Brown, 1834), 49.
32. Kasserman, *Fall River Outrage*, 3.
33. "Methodist Justice," *Christian Intelligencer* (New York, NY), quoted in *Trumpet and Universalist Magazine* (Boston, MA), June 15, 1833, 5.
34. Kristin Boudreau, "The Scarlet Letter and the 1833 Murder Trial of the Reverend Ephraim Avery," *ESQ: A Journal of the American Renaissance* 47, no. 2 (2001): 89–112; Ian C. Pilarczyk, "The Terrible Haystack Murder: The Moral Paradox of Hypocrisy, Prudery and Piety in Antebellum America," *American Journal of Legal History* 41, no. 1 (1997): 25–60. On the ideology of republican motherhood, see Linda Kerber, "The Republican Mother: Women and the Enlightenment—an American Perspective," *American Quarterly* 28, no. 2 (1976): 187–205. On true womanhood, see Barbara Welter, "The Cult of True Womanhood: 1820–1860," *American Quarterly* 18, no. 2 (1966): 151–74.
35. *New Haven Palladium* quoted in "Sarah Maria Cornell," *The Episcopal Watchman* (Hartford, CT), June 22, 1833, 7.
36. "Letter 1," *Christian Advocate and Journal and Zion's Herald* (New York, NY), June 14, 1833, 7.
37. "Acquittal of the Rev. E. K. Avery," *Boston Atlas*, quoted in *Western Luminary* (Lexington, KY), June 26, 1833, 9.
38. M. Clarke, *Sarah Maria Cornell, or The Fall River Murder: A Domestic Drama in Three Acts* (New York: No. 5 Chatham Square, 1833), 47.
39. *Boston Transcript*, quoted in *Workingman's Advocate* (New York, NY), June 22, 1833, 4.
40. *Providence Gazette*, quoted in *Workingman's Advocate* (New York, NY), June 22, 1833, 4.
41. See, for instance, "Another Avery Mob," *Free Enquirer* (New York, NY), Jan. 12, 1834, 1.
42. "E. K. Avery," *Herald of Universal Salvation* (New Haven, CT), Aug. 15, 1833, 4.
43. *Christian Advocate and Journal and Zion's Herald* (New York, NY), June 21, 1833, 7.
44. Erik J. Chaput, *The People's Martyr: Thomas Wilson Dorr and His 1842 Rhode Island Rebellion* (Lawrence: University Press of Kansas, 2013), 29.
45. Aristides, *Strictures on the Case of Ephraim K. Avery: Originally Published in the Republican Herald, Providence, R. I. With Corrections, Revisions and Additions* (Providence: William Simons Jr.—Herald Office, 1833).
46. Aristides, *Strictures of the Case*, 6.
47. Aristides, *Strictures of the Case*, 95.
48. *A Vindication of the Result of the Trial of Rev. Ephraim K. Avery; To Which Is Prefixed His Statement of Facts Relative to the Circumstances by Which He Became Involved in the Prosecution* (Boston: Russell, Odiorne, 1834).
49. Kasserman, *Fall River Outrage*, 245.
50. "The Rev. Ephraim K. Avery: Death of a Methodist Minister Who Was Tried for Murder, and Acquitted, Nearly Forty Years Ago," *Semi-Weekly Wisconsin* (Milwaukee, WI), Nov. 17, 1869.
51. For histories of the Avery trial that emphasize the importance of gender in the case, see William G. McLoughlin, "Untangling the Tiverton Tragedy: The Social Meaning of the Terrible Haystack Murder of 1833," *Journal of American Culture* 7, no. 4 (1984): 75–84; Karin E. Gedge, *Without Benefit of Clergy: Women and the Pastoral Relationship in Nineteenth-Century American Culture* (New York: Oxford University Press, 2003), 23–32.
52. Bruce Dorsey, "'Making Men What They Should Be': Male Same-Sex Intimacy and Evangelical Religion in Early Nineteenth-Century New England," *Journal of the History of Sexuality* 24, no. 3 (2015): 345–77.
53. *Trial of the Rev. John Robert McDowall by the Presbytery of New York, in February, March, and April, 1836, in the Session Room of the Bleeker-Street Presbyterian Church* (New York: n.p., 1836).
54. *Trial of McDowall*, 5.
55. Whitmarsh's tactics eventually landed him in jail on accusations of libel. See *Baltimore Sun*, Nov. 23, 1837, 2. See also Patricia Cline Cohen, Timothy J. Gilfoyle, and Helen Lefkowitz Horowitz, *The Flash Press: Sporting Male Weeklies in 1840s New York* (Chicago: University of Chicago Press, 2008), 26 n. 15.
56. "Rev. Mr. McDowall," *Long-Island Farmer* (New York, NY), Nov. 11, 1835, 3.

57. "Christian Connection," *Encyclopædia Britannica*, 11th ed. (1911).
58. Eleazer Sherman, *The Narrative of Eleazer Sherman, Giving an Account of His Life, Experience, Call to the Ministry of the Gospel, and Travels as Such to the Present Time* (Providence: H.H. Brown, 1832).
59. *Trial of Elder Eleazer Sherman before an Ecclesiastical Council Held at the Meeting-House of the Christian Society in Providence, July 20 and 21, 1835* (Providence: H.H. Brown, 1835), iv.
60. *Trial of Elder Eleazer Sherman*, 11; Rom. 1:27 (KJV).
61. *Trial of Elder Eleazer Sherman*, 9, 8.
62. *Trial of Elder Eleazer Sherman*, 9, iv.
63. *Trial of Elder Eleazer Sherman*, 9.
64. *Trial of Elder Eleazer Sherman*, iii.
65. "Elder Eleazer Sherman," *Christian Journal* (Exeter, NH), Aug. 6, 1835, 38.
66. See, for instance, Christopher Grasso, "Skepticism and American Faith: Infidels, Converts, and Religious Doubt in the Early Nineteenth Century," *Journal of the Early Republic* 22, no. 3 (2002): 465–508.
67. "Clerical Morality," *Boston Investigator*, Nov. 13, 1835, 2.
68. *Trial of Elder Eleazer Sherman*, 8–9.
69. The murder of sex worker Helen Jewett in 1836 would be one of the most sensationalized media stories of the era precisely because one of the protagonists was a known sex worker. See Patricia Cline Cohen, *The Murder of Helen Jewett: The Life and Death of a Prostitute in Nineteenth-Century New York* (New York: Vintage, 1999), 20–21.
70. Gedge, *Without Benefit of Clergy*, 51–52.
71. See Boudreau, "Scarlet Letter."
72. Michael Emery, Edwin Emery, and Nancy L. Roberts, *The Press and America: An Interpretive History of the Mass Media*, 9th ed. (Boston: Pearson, 1997), 102.
73. Philip McFarland, *Hawthorne in Concord* (New York: Grove Press, 2004), 136.
74. *Washington Union*, quoted in Lambert A. Wilmer, *Our Press Gang; or, A Complete Exposition of the Corruptions and Crimes of the American Newspapers* (Philadelphia: J. T. Lloyd, 1859), 64.
75. Henry Ward Beecher, "Scandal Mongering," *Independent* (New York, NY), reprinted in *Frederick Douglass' Paper* (Rochester, NY), Oct. 15, 1852, 1.

Chapter 2

1. Leon Oliver, *The Great Sensation: A Full, Complete and Reliable History of the Beecher-Tilton-Woodhull Scandal, with Biographical Sketches of the Principal Characters…Also a Clear and Concise Statement of the Views of "The Woodhull" Upon Social Reform, Free Love, Etc., Etc.* (Chicago: Beverly Company, 1873), 135–36; Victoria Woodhull, "The Beecher-Tilton Scandal," *Woodhull and Claflin's Weekly*, Nov. 2, 1872, 9–13.
2. Charles F. Marshall, *The True History of the Brooklyn Scandal: Being a Complete Account of the Trial of the Rev. Henry Ward Beecher, of Plymouth Church, Brooklyn, Upon Charges Preferred by Theodore Tilton, Including All the Original Letters, Documents and Private Correspondence, with Biographies of the Leading Actors in the Great Drama. Containing Also the Full Statements of Moulton, Beecher, and Tilton, and Many Additional Facts, Private Letters, Etc., Never Before Published* (Philadelphia: National Publishing Company, 1874), 23.
3. In their textual analysis study of sensational journalism, historians David W. Bulla and Heather R. Haley found that between 1853 and 1873, sensational stories in six major US newspapers grew in terms of number, volume, headline length, and "strength of rhetoric." Gilded Age reporters employed an unprecedented number of modifiers and relied heavily on moralistic commentary and humorous asides as they covered crime, violence, oddities, public drunkenness, local characters, and unexpected deaths. And, as Bulla and Haley show, whereas the trend toward sensationalism continued to grow steadily between 1853 and 1873, the Gilded Age also brought with it a new emphasis in reporting: in the 1870s, the focus shifted from minor local curiosities to scandals of regional and national importance. Scandals allowed the press to probe questions about the nature of authority and the dangers of unmitigated power. See David W. Bulla and Heather R. Haley, "Sensational Journalism in the Mid-19th Century," in *Sensationalism: Murder, Mayhem, Mudslinging, Scandals, and Disasters in 19th-Century Reporting*, ed. David B. Sachsman and David W. Bulla (New Brunswick: Transaction Publishers, 2013), 75–100.

4. For more on the history of graphic news, see Amanda Frisken, *Graphic News: How Sensational Images Transformed Nineteenth-Century Journalism* (Urbana: University of Illinois Press, 2020).

5. "Thomas Nast: A Memorial by Otto Washington Greubel, in the *Western Critic*," *Issues and Events* 7, no. 20 (Nov. 17, 1917): 310.

6. Anne DiFabio, "Thomas Nast Takes Down Tammany: A Cartoonist's Crusade against a Political Boss," *Museum of the City of New York* (blog), Sept. 24, 2013, https://blog.mcny.org/2013/09/24/thomas-nast-takes-down-tammany-a-cartoonists-crusade-against-a-political-boss/.

7. J. Spencer Fluhman, *"A Peculiar People": Anti-Mormonism and the Making of Religion in Nineteenth-Century America* (Chapel Hill: University of North Carolina Press, 2012); John Corrigan and Lynn S. Neal, *Religious Intolerance in America: A Documentary History* (Chapel Hill: University of North Carolina Press, 2010), 73–98.

8. Sarah Barringer Gordon, *The Mormon Question: Polygamy and Constitutional Conflict in Nineteenth-Century America* (Chapel Hill: University of North Carolina Press, 2002).

9. On anti-Catholic preaching, see Katie Oxx, *The Nativist Movement in America: Religious Conflict in the 19th Century* (New York: Routledge, 2013).

10. For an example of nineteenth-century anti-Mormon literature, see Orvilla S. Belisle, *The Prophets: or, Mormonism Unveiled* (Philadelphia: W.W. Smith, 1855). On the history of anti-Mormonism, see Fluhman, *A Peculiar People*.

11. Katrina J. Quinn, "The Making of a 'Scoundrel': Brigham Young and the Sensationalist Press, 1855–1860," in *Sensationalism: Murder, Mayhem, Mudslinging, Scandals, and Disasters in 19th-Century Reporting*, ed. David B. Sachsman and David W. Bulla (New Brunswick: Transaction Publishers, 2013), 293–315.

12. Debby Applegate, *The Most Famous Man in America: The Biography of Henry Ward Beecher* (New York: Doubleday, 2006).

13. "Beecher and Brooklyn: A Real Estate Man's Real Views," *New York Times*, Nov. 29, 1860, 2.

14. Noyes L. Thompson, *The History of Plymouth Church* (New York: G. W. Carleton, 1873), 22.

15. "The Gospel of Love," *New York Times*, May 31, 1875, 4.

16. Beecher preached, "Love is God's nature. Not that no other feeling exists in him; not that justice and abhorrence of evil are not co-ordinated with it; not that these do not take part in the divine administration among men; but that the central and peculiarly divine element is love, in which all other feelings live, within whose bounds they all act, to which they are servants, and for which they are messengers and helpers." Lyman Abbott, ed., *The Sermons of Henry Ward Beecher: In Plymouth Church, Brooklyn*, vol. 1 (New York: Harper & Brothers, 1869), 38.

17. For more on Beecher's "gospel of love," see William G. McLoughlin, *The Meaning of Henry Ward Beecher: An Essay on the Shifting Values of Mid-Victorian America, 1840–1870* (New York: Knopf, 1970), 84–96.

18. Woodhull, "The Beecher-Tilton Scandal," 11.

19. *Rowell's American Newspaper Directory* (New York: Geo. P. Rowell, 1871), 107.

20. *Rowell's American Newspaper Directory* (New York: Geo. P. Rowell, 1872), 124.

21. "By marriage, the husband and wife are one person in law: that is, the very being or legal existence of the woman is suspended during the marriage, or at least is incorporated and consolidated into that of the husband: under whose wing, protection, and cover, she performs every thing; and is therefore called in our law-French a *feme-covert*; is said to be *covert-baron*, or under the protection and influence of her husband, her baron, or lord; and her condition during her marriage is called her coverture." William Blackstone, *Commentaries on the Laws of England, Book 1* (Oxford: Clarendon Press, 1765), 430.

22. Hendrik A. Hartog, "Marital Exits and Marital Expectations in Nineteenth Century America," *Georgetown Law Journal* 80, no. 95 (1991): 95–129.

23. Victoria Woodhull, *"And the Truth Shall Make You Free": A Speech on the Principles of Social Freedom, Delivered in Steinway Hall, Nov. 20, 1871* (New York: Woodhull, Claflin, 1871).

24. Woodhull, "The Beecher-Tilton Scandal," 11.

25. Woodhull wrote, "I condemn him because I know, and have had every opportunity to know, that he entertains, on conviction, substantially the same views which I entertain on the social question: that, under the influence of these convictions, he has lived for many years, perhaps for his whole adult life, in a manner which the religious and moralistic public ostensibly, and to some extent really, condemn; that he has permitted himself, nevertheless, to be over-awed by public opinion, to profess to believe otherwise than as he does believe, to have helped to

maintain for these many years that very social slavery under which he was chaffing, and against which he was secretly revolting both in thought and practice; and that he has, in a word, consented, and still consents to be a hypocrite." Woodhull, "The Beecher-Tilton Scandal," 11.

26. Amanda Frisken, *Victoria Woodhull's Sexual Revolution: Political Theater and the Popular Press in Nineteenth-Century America* (Philadelphia: University of Pennsylvania Press, 2004), 91.

27. "The Claflin Family," *New York Times*, Nov. 3, 1872, 1.

28. See Helen Lefkowitz Horowitz, "Victoria Woodhull, Anthony Comstock, and Conflict over Sex in the United States in the 1870s," *Journal of American History* 87, no. 2 (2000): 403–34.

29. Oliver, *The Great Sensation*, 3.

30. Quoted in "The Beecher-Tilton Scandal: How It Stand at Present—a Forthcoming Card from Tilton," *Atlanta Constitution*, Feb. 21, 1873, 1.

31. Altina Waller, *Reverend Beecher and Mrs. Tilton: Sex and Class in Victorian America* (Amherst: University of Massachusetts Press, 1982), 8–9.

32. "The Result of Slander," *Chicago Daily Tribune*, Nov. 18, 1872, 1.

33. *New York Evening Telegram*, quoted in "Woodhull & Flash Sheet—Its Outrageous Charges Against Henry Ward Beecher—Woodhull Bevels In Congenial Dirt," *Atlanta Constitution*, Nov. 5, 1872, 1.

34. "The Beecher Scandal: 'Contempt and Silence' Commended," *Brooklyn Daily Eagle*, Jan. 17, 1873, 2.

35. *Advance*, quoted in "Shall Beecher Be Investigated?," *Chicago Tribune*, Feb. 2, 1873, 12.

36. "The Tilton Beecher Scandal," *Vermont Christian Messenger* (Montpelier, VT), Mar. 6, 1873, 2.

37. *The Thunderbolt*, May 1873, Newspaper Collection, American Antiquarian Society, Worcester, Massachusetts.

38. Quoted in Robert Shaplen, *Free Love and Heavenly Sinners: The Story of the Great Henry Ward Beecher Scandal* (New York: Knopf, 1954), 177.

39. Henry Ward Beecher, letter to the editor of the *Daily Eagle*, in "The Bowen-Woodhull Combination—Mr. Beecher Speaks," *Brooklyn Daily Eagle*, June 30, 1873, 2.

40. "Beecher's Silence," *Chicago Daily Tribune*, June 28, 1874, 8.

41. See, for instance, "Beecher-Tilton: Comments of the Press," *Chicago Daily Tribune*, June 29, 1874, 2.

42. *New York Tribune*, quoted in "Mr. Tilton and Mr. Beecher," *Elevator* (San Francisco, CA), July 18, 1874, 1.

43. "Mr. Beecher and Mr. Tilton," *New York Evangelist*, July 9, 1874, 4.

44. J. O. Smith to Henry Ward Beecher, Aug. 14, 1874, Beecher Family Papers (MS 71), box 15, Manuscripts and Archives, Yale University Library.

45. *Charleston News and Courier*, c. summer of 1874, quoted in Mark Silk, *Unsecular Media: Making News of Religion in America* (Urbana: University of Illinois Press, 1998), 84.

46. "The Beecher-Tilton Scandal," *Frank Leslie's Illustrated Newspaper* (New York, NY), July 11, 1874, 275.

47. Henry Ward Beecher, quoted in William Drysdale, ed., *Proverbs from Plymouth Pulpit* (New York: D. Appleton, 1887), 79.

48. *Brooklyn Argus*, quoted in J. E. P. Doyle, *Plymouth Church and Its Pastor, or Henry Ward Beecher and His Accusers* (St. Louis: Bryant, Brand, 1875), 286.

49. *Daily Graphic*, Aug. 21, 1874, quoted in Marshall, *True History*, 380.

50. Susan B. Anthony to Isabella Beecher Hooker, Jan. 6, 1873, University of Rochester Special Collections, https://digitalcollections-legacy.lib.rochester.edu/ur/letter-susan-b-anthony-isabella-beecher-hooker-january-6-1873-2.

51. Elizabeth Cady Stanton to Susan Brownell Anthony, July 30, 1874, in *Elizabeth Cady Stanton, as Revealed in Her Letters, Diary and Reminiscences*, vol. 2, ed. Harriot Stanton Blatch and Theodore Stanton (New York: Harper & Brothers Publishers, 1922), 369.

52. "The Woman Suffrage Question," *Detroit Free Press*, Aug. 13, 1874, 2.

53. Elizabeth Cady Stanton to Susan Brownell Anthony, July 30, 1874, in *Elizabeth Cady Stanton*, 146.

54. For a broad overview of the history of American newspapers, see Frank L. Mott, *American Journalism: A History of Newspapers in the United States through 250 Years, 1690–1940* (New York: Macmillan, 1941). On the number of daily newspapers, see Alfred McClung Lee, *The*

Daily Newspaper in America (New York: Macmillan, 1937); Alexander Saxton, "Problems of Class and Race in the Origins of the Mass Circulation Press," *American Quarterly* 36, no. 2 (1984): 211–34.

55. "The Tilton Letters," *Chicago Daily Tribune*, Aug. 13, 1874.
56. "Beecher-Tilton: The Vital Question in the Case," *Chicago Daily Tribune*, July 3, 1874, 8.
57. "The Beecher Scandal: A Stormy Meeting at Plymouth Church," *New York Times*, Aug. 29, 1874, 5.
58. "Mr. Beecher's Friends," *Christian Union* (New York, NY), Sept. 9, 1874, 186.
59. Gregory Eiselein and Anne K. Phillips, *The Louisa May Alcott Encyclopedia* (Westport: Greenwood Publishing Group, 2001), 54.
60. Henry B. Tompkin to Henry Ward Beecher, July 25, 1874; Franklin S. Stebbins to Henry Ward Beecher, Aug. 3, 1874, Beecher Family Papers (MS 71), box 15, Manuscripts and Archives, Yale University Library.
61. Applegate, *Most Famous Man*, 436.
62. One editorial argued facetiously that "the publication of the Plymouth Church Committee can have no more effect on the public morals than the publishing of the Tammany frauds, or of the Credit-Mobilier scandal." "Newspaper Morality," *Galveston Daily News*, Aug. 13, 1874, 1.
63. "The Brooklyn Muss," *Public Ledger* (Memphis, TN), Sept. 2, 1874, 2.
64. "'The Beecher Scandal!' Sung by Dick Brown," broadside, c. 1874, American Antiquarian Society.
65. "The Beecher-Tilton Scandal," *Weekly Louisianian* (New Orleans), Nov. 28, 1974, 3.
66. Blanche Butler Ames to Adelbert Ames, Aug. 1, 1874, in *Chronicles from the Nineteenth Century: Family Letters of Blanche Butler and Adelbert Ames Married July 21st, 1870*, vol. 1 (Clinton: [privately published], 1957), 719.
67. Anthony Trollope to Harriet Knower, Sept. 30, 1874, in *The Letters of Anthony Trollope*, vol. 2, ed. N. John Hall (Stanford: Stanford University Press, 1983), 630.
68. Austin Abbott, *Official Report of the Trial of Henry Ward Beecher* (New York: G.W. Smith, 1875), 1–2.
69. See, for example, the trial transcript produced by a *New York Tribune* reporter: *Theodore Tilton vs. Henry Ward Beecher: Action for Crim. Con. Tried in the City Court of Brooklyn, Chief Justice Joseph Neilson, Presiding* (New York: McDivitt, Campbell, 1875).
70. "Skeletons of the Ideal," *Frank Leslie's Illustrated Newspaper* (New York, NY), Aug. 8, 1874, 339.
71. See, for example, Emily Hawley Gillespie, "Diary of Emily Hawley Gillespie, August, 1874," in *A Secret to Be Buried: The Diary and Life of Emily Hawley Gillespie, 1858–1888*, ed. Judy Nolte Lensink (Iowa City: University of Iowa Press, 1989), 200; Mary Richardson Walker, "Diary of Mary Richardson Walker, 1874," in *Mary Richardson Walker: Her Book*, ed. Ruth K. McKee (Caldwell: Caxton Printers, 1945), 350.
72. George E. Pond, "Kings and Clergy of Journalism," *Galaxy* 19, no. 3 (1875), 408.
73. "The Beecher-Tilton Trial: The Suit to Be Resumed to-Day the Sick Juror Fully Recovered— the Attendance to Be Limited to the Seating Capacity of the Court—Room Mr. Beecher Not Denounced by Dr. Duryea Mr. Ovington Sails for Europe Health of the Litigants the History of Bessie Turner a Denial by Mr. Scott," *New-York Tribune*, Mar. 8, 1875, 2.
74. Shaplen, *Free Love*, 216.
75. "The Beecher Trial and Bouquets," *New York Times*, quoted in *Cincinnati Enquirer*, Jan. 19, 1875, 9.
76. *The Nation* (New York, NY), Feb. 4, 1875, 71.
77. *The Sun* (New York, NY), Apr. 13, 1875, quoted in "Trial Notings," *Chicago Tribune*, Apr. 16, 1875, 3.
78. "The Great Scandal Trial," *Frank Leslie's Illustrated Newspaper* (New York, NY), July 10, 1875, 310.
79. *Chicago Tribune*, Apr. 16, 1875, 4.
80. "Gossip of the Trial: Speculations about the Verdict—Talk of Disagreement—the Brooklyn Support of Beecher Zeal of the Women," *Atlanta Constitution*, June 25, 1875, 2.
81. J. A. Cook to the editor of the *Tribune*, May 19, 1875, Theodore Tilton correspondence and other material, Manuscripts and Archives Division, New York Public Library.
82. "The Jury Disagree: Nine Men Believe Brooklyn's Pastor Innocent," *San Francisco Chronicle*, July 3, 1875, 2.
83. "The Verdict," *Minneapolis Daily Tribune*, July 2, 1875, 1.

84. "Let Us Have No More of It," *Public Ledger* (Memphis, TN), July 3, 1875, 2.
85. As legal historian Richard K. Sherwin puts it, "the deep current of anxiety that gave the Beecher trial its almost unbearable intensity" betrayed a recognition "that the sentimental belief in unitary character (as within, so without) could no longer be maintained." Richard K. Sherwin, *When Law Goes Pop: The Vanishing Line between Law and Popular Culture* (Chicago: University of Chicago Press, 2000), 86.
86. "Out of Suspense: End of the Great Tilton-Beecher Trial," *New York Herald*, July 3, 1875, 3–4.
87. *The Beecher Trial: A Review of the Evidence; Reprinted from the New York Times of July 3, 1875; with Some Revisions and Additions* (New York: Nabu Press, 1875).
88. "Topics of the Day," *Daily Graphic* (New York, NY), July 3, 1875, 18.
89. "End of the Great Trial," *Republican Banner* (Nashville, TN), July 3, 1875, 2.
90. Henry Ward Beecher to the editor of the *New York Times*, Apr. 15, 1878, cited in the *Christian Union* (New York, NY), quoted in *Pacific School and Home Journal* (San Francisco, CA) 2, no. 3 (May 1878): 117.
91. "Mrs. Tilton Buried," *New York Tribune*, Apr. 17, 1897, 7.
92. Quoted in "Out of Suspense: End of the Great Tilton-Beecher Trial," *New York Herald*, July 3, 1875, 3–4.
93. Fox's *Trials of Intimacy* questions the historical certainty of accounts that find Beecher guilty. For examples of biographies and histories that consider Beecher guilty, see Hibben, *Henry Ward Beecher*; Shaplen, *Free Love*; Waller, *Reverend Beecher*; Applegate, *Most Famous Man*.

Chapter 3

1. "The Rev. Alfred Thompson," *Chicago Daily Tribune*, Oct. 19, 1877, 2.
2. M. E. Billings, *Crimes of Preachers in the United States and Canada*, 10th ed. (New York: Truth Seeker, 1914).
3. Although Gilded Age and Progressive Era newspapers frequently used the terms "scandal" and "sensation" interchangeably, the two should not be read synonymously. In the history of journalism, the label "sensationalism" has been applied to a variety of news stories that are meant to evoke a strong emotional response and, as Frank Luther Mott puts it, appeal to "fundamental and primitive human desires." Historian George Juergens provides a helpful definition when he writes that sensational newspapers "expanded the meaning of the human interest story to report what had hitherto been regarded as private, the gossip and scandal about individuals, and discovered a rich source of news in crime and everyday tragedy." Sensationalism, then, can broadly be defined as a genre that is meant to appeal to the emotions and curiosity of readers by exposing the surprising, the shocking, the scandalous, and the grotesque. Scandal is a narrower category. While often revealed through sensational reporting, scandal has to do with public figures' private transgressions that become sensationalized and generate significant public interest. See Frank Luther Mott, *American Journalism: A History of Newspapers in the United States through 250 Years, 1690–1940* (New York: Macmillan, 1941), 119; George Juergens, *Joseph Pulitzer and the New York World* (Princeton: Princeton University Press, 2015), viii–ix; James Lull and Stephen Hinerman, "The Search for Scandal," in *Media Scandals: Morality and Desire in the Popular Culture Marketplace*, eds. James Lull and Stephen Hinerman (New York: Columbia University Press, 1997), 7; John D. Stevens, *Sensationalism and the New York Press* (New York: Columbia University Press, 1991), 3–9.
4. Billings, *Crimes of Preachers*, 41.
5. In addition to the 121 cases found in the *Crimes of Preachers*, digitized newspaper searches (performed through *ProQuest Historical Newspapers*, *Chronicling America*, and *Newspapers. com* databases) supplied an additional 145 instances, for a total of 266 Protestant elopement cases between 1870 and 1914. Although Protestant ministers were not the only denominational group who were reported to have eloped, they were the most representative, with Catholic priests and Jewish rabbis making up a small minority of clerical elopers.
6. M. E. Billings, editor of the *Crimes of Preachers*, provocatively asked whether it might "be possible that the most orthodox are the most criminal, and *vice versa*" and set out to show that such a correlation existed in his sample. A closer look at the numbers in both Billings's larger project and in the elopers cohort in particular shows no such connection. Nineteenth-century church membership and ministerial statistics are notoriously unreliable, but comparing the data found in the 1890 census and the numbers of elopers by denomination shows that the distribution of ministers by denomination was proportional to their numbers as percentage of

American clergy. For example, Methodist elopers represent 33 percent of the sample and account for 33 percent of clergy in the census. The second most represented denomination, the Baptists, make up 21 percent of elopers and 28 percent of clergy overall. The same pattern of close correlation applies to the other represented denominations: Presbyterians represent 6 percent of elopers and 11 percent of the census, Congregationalists 4 percent and 5 percent respectively, etc. See Billings, *Crimes of Preachers*, 58; *Abstract of the Eleventh Census: 1890* (Washington, DC: US Government Printing Office, 1896), 258–63.

7. As historian Lawrence M. Friedman explains, the nineteenth-century United States was "a society quite literally on the move—a society of men (and, to a lesser extent, women) who tore themselves loose from the soils of their birth, or who created their own rootlessness." Lawrence M. Friedman, "Crimes of Mobility," *Stanford Law Review* 43, no. 3 (1991): 638.

8. Americans, Friedman writes, were "busily engaged in climbing, falling, and maneuvering through and about the many levels of social strata." Friedman, "Crimes of Mobility," 638.

9. On confidence men, the possibilities of mobility, and the abuses of power in the Gilded Age, see Edward J. Balleisen, *Fraud: An American History from Barnum to Madoff* (Princeton: Princeton University Press, 2017); Karen Halttunen, *Confidence Men and Painted Women: A Study of Middle-Class Culture in America, 1830–1870* (New Haven: Yale University Press, 1982); Stephen Mihm, *A Nation of Counterfeiters: Capitalists, Con Men, and the Making of the United States* (Cambridge: Harvard University Press, 2007); Scott A. Sandage, *Born Losers: A History of Failure in America* (Cambridge: Harvard University Press, 2005).

10. On the role of the press in exposing Gilded Age corruption scandals, see Daniel Czitrom, *New York Exposed: The Gilded Age Police Scandal That Launched the Progressive Era* (New York: Oxford University Press, 2016); David B. Sachsman and David W. Bulla, eds., *Sensationalism: Murder, Mayhem, Mudslinging, Scandals, and Disasters in 19th-Century Reporting* (New Brunswick: Transaction Publishers, 2013); Michael Schudson, *Discovering the News: A Social History of American Newspapers* (New York: Basic Books, 1981); Stevens, *Sensationalism and the New York Press*.

11. Several historians have explored the kinds of sensational elopements that the Gilded Age and Progressive Era introduced. Carolee Anne Klimchock's research on elite women's elopements with their coachmen documents the fascinating interplay of race and class that is impossible to understand outside of the framework of the scandalous in the Gilded Age. Carolee Anne Klimchock, "Heiress Weds Coachman: Elopement Scandals and the Performance of Coach Driving in the Gilded Age" (PhD diss., Yale University, 2015). Paul Emory Putz's work on ministers who performed on-demand marriage ceremonies for eloping couples reveals how the "marrying parsons" both benefited from and undermined Protestantism's grip on American culture in the Progressive Era. Paul Emory Putz, "Commercializing the Sacred Office: Sexual Revolution and the Scandal of the Modern Marrying Parson, 1895–1930," *Journal of the Gilded Age and Progressive Era* 17 (Jan. 2018): 56–76.

12. The *Washington Union*, quoted in Lambert A. Wilmer, *Our Press Gang; or, A Complete Exposition of the Corruptions and Crimes of the American Newspapers* (Philadelphia: J. T. Lloyd, 1859), 64.

13. See Wilmer, *Our Press Gang*, for sustained criticism of the unprecedented power the press had acquired by the late 1860s.

14. E. L. Godkin, "Opinion-Moulding," The *Nation* (New York, NY), Aug. 12, 1869, 126.

15. The reliability of late nineteenth-century newspaper reporting is difficult to quantify, yet it is telling that even Godkin, a contemporary concerned with good taste in reporting, was not castigating colleagues for falsifying sensational reports, but for engaging with that type of material. Indeed, while several high-profile newspapers (most notably the *New York Sun* and the *New York World*) were discovered to have published false reports on matters not pertaining to pastoral crimes, historians of journalism have found little evidence of falsification of scandal. To be sure, newspapers were known to reprint each other's stories, occasionally embellishing their details and supplying flowery descriptions of sensational subjects not found in the original, but no evidence of outright fabrication exists. While copyright was not a concern, libel suits were common, so newspapers were likely cautious to publish unsubstantiated reports for fear of litigation. With regard to Protestant pastors in particular, many elopement stories can further be confirmed using census records and denominational conference proceedings that list ministers removed from their posts in the preceding years. On journalistic practices and ethics, see Hazel Dicken-Garcia, *Journalistic Standards in Nineteenth-Century*

America (Madison: University of Wisconsin Press, 1989); Heather A. Haveman, *Magazines and the Making of America: Modernization, Community, and Print Culture, 1741–1860* (Princeton: Princeton University Press, 2015), 55–105; Mott, *American Journalism*.

16. US Congress, An Act for the Suppression of Trade in, and Circulation of, Obscene Literature and Articles of Immoral Use, 42nd Cong., 3rd Sess., Mar. 3, 1873, ch. 258, 598–99.

17. On the vulnerability of freethinkers to religious persecution, see Leigh Eric Schmidt, *Village Atheists: How America's Unbelievers Made Their Way in a Godly Nation* (Princeton: Princeton University Press, 2016).

18. These illustrations, Frisken writes, "erased (with a few exceptions) white male rape, denied white female sexuality, ignored violence against Black women, and exaggerated the threat of criminal sexuality perpetrated by men of color." Amanda Frisken, *Graphic News: How Sensational Images Transformed Nineteenth-Century Journalism* (Urbana: University of Illinois Press, 2020), 45–46.

19. Horace Cooke, quoted in "Sensation in New York," *Stark County Democrat* (Canton, OH), Jan. 19, 1870, 2.

20. "The Church Scandal: Further Particulars of the Cooke-Johnston Case," *New York Times*, Jan. 12, 1870, 2.

21. Nicholas L. Syrett, *American Child Bride: A History of Minors and Marriage in the United States* (Chapel Hill: University of North Carolina Press, 2016), 46.

22. Syrett, *American Child Bride*, 98–117.

23. Rachel Hope Cleves, *Unspeakable: A Life beyond Sexual Morality* (Chicago: University of Chicago Press, 2020), 4.

24. As Syrett explains, "Their anxieties were instead about eradicating illicit sex, preventing prostitution, and protecting the good name of marriage." Syrett, *American Child Bride*, 122.

25. Syrett, *American Child Bride*, 168.

26. "The Clerical Eloper," *Pittsburgh Gazette*, Jan. 12, 1870, 1.

27. "The Rev. Mr. Cooke in the *World* Office," *Buffalo Commercial*, Jan. 13, 1870, 3.

28. "Mr. Cooke Interviewed," *Brooklyn Daily Eagle*, Jan. 14, 1870, 4.

29. "A Priestly Scandal," *New York World*, Jan. 11, 1870, 1.

30. For more on the forgery controversy, see George T. McJimsey, *Genteel Partisan: Manton Marble, 1834–1917* (Ames: Iowa State University Press, 1971), 52–55.

31. Manton Marble, *Freedom of the Press Wantonly Violated: Letter of Mr. Marble to President Lincoln, Reappearance of the Journal of Commerce, Opinions of the Press on This Outrage* (New York: Society for the Diffusion of Political Knowledge, 1864).

32. Mary Cortona Phelan, "Manton Marble of the New York *World*" (PhD diss., Catholic University of America, 1957), 9.

33. Manton Marble to Rev. H. C. Graves (n.d.), quoted in Phelan, "Manton Marble," 10.

34. On Marble's agnosticism, see Phelan, "Manton Marble," 9–23.

35. Quoted in the *Bolivar Bulletin* (Bolivar, TN), Feb. 12, 1870, 2.

36. "Editorial Perspective," *The Nation* (New York, NY), Jan. 27, 1870, 55.

37. "A Growing Evil," *Philadelphia Day*, quoted in *Indianapolis News*, Jan. 24, 1870, 2.

38. Hendrik A. Hartog, *Man and Wife in America: A History* (Cambridge: Harvard University Press, 2002), 12.

39. Hartog, *Man and Wife*, 20.

40. Glenda Riley, *Divorce: An American Tradition* (Lincoln: University of Nebraska Press, 1991), 5.

41. "Elopement Eccentricities: Some Recent Notable Instances of Runaway Matches and Curious Family Complications," *New York World*, quoted in *Cincinnati Enquirer*, Feb. 4, 1882, 10.

42. *Chicago Daily Tribune*, Aug. 21, 1881, 10.

43. "The Janesville Sinners," *St. Paul Daily Globe*, Sept. 25, 1887, 4.

44. "A Naughty Parson," *Bismarck Weekly Tribune* (Bismarck, ND), Aug. 12, 1887, 1.

45. *Champaign Daily Gazette* (Champagne, IL), Aug. 11, 1887, 3.

46. *Wichita Beacon*, Oct. 18, 1887, 2.

47. "Sensational Journalism," *Los Angeles Times*, July 14, 1883, 2.

48. *Puck* (New York, NY), June 3, 1885, 1.

49. "How to Cure the Plague," *Christian Union*, Jan. 15, 1885, 3.

50. J. M. Buckley, "The Morality of Ministers," *Forum*, Jan. 1887, 502–14.

51. The authenticity of the letter is impossible to establish. Some of the ideas conveyed in the letter, such as the comment on "civilized nations," as well as the purported spelling and grammar

mistakes, suggest that the letter may not have in fact been written by an immigrant but rather invented by the editors for the purposes of racist moralizing.

52. Anonymous letter to a San Francisco editor, quoted in "Shocked the Japs," *Salt Lake Herald*, Apr. 18, 1895, 1.

53. "Current Opinions," *Boston Investigator*, Aug. 16, 1893, 6.

54. "How He Was Converted," *Kansas City Gazette*, Feb. 23, 1893, 2.

55. "For Men Only," *Daily World* (Pittsburg, KS), Jan. 16, 1893, 4.

56. "A Bad Egg," *Wichita Daily Eagle*, June 23, 1893, 5.

57. "Leigh Vernon Located," *Daily World* (Pittsburg, KS), June 26, 1893, 4.

58. "Claims She Was Hypnotized," *Pittsburgh Press* (Pittsburg, KS), July 11, 1893, 3.

59. "Jumped from Car—Rev. Leigh Vernon Attempts Suicide," *Emporia Gazette* (Emporia, KS), July 17, 1893, 1.

60. "Elopers at Toronto," *Morning News* (Wilmington, DE), June 2, 1904, 1.

61. "Preacher Tells Why He Eloped," *Evening World* (New York, NY), July 13, 1904, 3.

62. "Cordova Leads New Life, Says Wife," *Daily Home News* (New Brunswick, NJ), Nov. 8, 1904, 2.

63. "Divorce Me—Cordova," *Daily Home News* (New Brunswick, NJ), Mar. 9, 1905, 1.

64. "'Rev.' Cordova Will Stand Trial on Two Charges," *Daily Home News* (New Brunswick, NJ), Mar. 8, 1905, 1.

65. Michael Willrich, "Home Slackers: Men, the State, and Welfare in Modern America," *Journal of American History* 87, no. 2 (2000): 460.

66. Riley, *Divorce*, 87.

67. Anna R. Igra, *Wives without Husbands: Marriage, Desertion, and Welfare in New York, 1900–1935* (Chapel Hill: University of North Carolina Press, 2006).

68. On changing ideas about love and marriage, see John D'Emilio and Estelle B. Freedman, *Intimate Matters: A History of Sexuality in America*, 3rd ed. (Chicago: University Of Chicago Press, 2012); Stephanie Coontz, *Marriage, a History: How Love Conquered Marriage* (New York: Penguin Books, 2006).

69. George D. Herron, quoted in "Wages Warfare on Marriage System," *Ness County News* (Ness City, KS), Oct. 21, 1905, 7.

70. Albert Fried, *Socialism in America: From the Shakers to the Third International* (New York: Columbia University Press, 1993), 346.

71. "Cordova Dropped by M. E. Conference," *Philadelphia Inquirer*, Mar. 9, 1905, 2.

72. "Eloping Minister Is Unfrocked Speedily: Even His Clerical Advocate Votes against Cordova," *Saint Paul Globe*, Mar. 9, 1905, 1.

73. "Preacher Sentenced," *East Oregonian* (Pendleton, OR), Mar. 18, 1905, 1.

74. *Morning Astorian* (Astoria, OR), Mar. 19, 1905, 8.

75. "The Old, Old Story," *Blue-grass Blade* (Lexington, KY), Feb. 24, 1907, 3.

76. "Search for a Pastor Who Abandoned Family Dropped for Fear of Scandal," *Cincinnati Enquirer*, Dec. 24, 1909, 1.

77. "The Minister Went Astray," *Independence Daily Reporter* (Independence, KS), Sept. 2, 1910, 8.

78. "Pretty Choir Girl Lured by Minister," *Star Press* (Muncie, IN), Nov. 5, 1912, 3.

79. "Accuse Minister as White Slaver," *Quad-City Times* (Davenport, IA), Jan. 17, 1913, 13.

80. "Pastor Violates Mann Law," *Carroll County Democrat* (Huntington, TN), May 18, 1917, 2.

81. "Erring Preacher and Girl Arrested," *Great Falls Tribune* (Great Falls, MT), Dec. 31, 1907, 1.

82. "Husband's Cowardly Words Turn Wife's Clinging Love to Hate," *Inter Ocean* (Chicago, IL), Jan. 19, 1908, 5.

83. "Cooke's Wife Frees Him for Boys' Sake," *Washington Post*, Apr. 17, 1913, 2.

84. See, for instance, *Wichita Beacon*, May 10, 1913, 8.

85. "Floretta Whaley and Cooke Marry after Six Years," *St. Louis Post-Dispatch*, June 10, 1913, 1.

86. Popular culture, too, by that point seems to have accept the phenomenon as amusing if not altogether moral. Composer Will E. Skidmore and lyricist Marshall Walker (both white) released the song "It Takes a Long Tall Brown-Skin Gal to Make a Preacher Lay His Bible Down" in 1917. The minstrel ballad included a number of racist stereotypes, but, ironically, the story it told more closely mirrored the experience of white clergy, who far outnumbered Black elopers. See Will E. Skidmore, "It Takes a Long Tall Brown-Skin Gal to Make a Preacher Lay His Bible Down," Charles H. Templeton, Sr. sheet music collection. Special Collections, Mississippi State University Libraries, https://scholarsjunction.msstate.edu/cht-sheet-music/3833/.

87. C. M. Dinsmore, "How Preachers Go Wrong," quoted in "Silly Women Aid Fall of Pastors," *Star Press* (Muncie, IN), June 3, 1912, 1.

88. C. M. Dinsmore, quoted in "Pastor Blames Women for Ministers' Downfall," *Inter Ocean* (Chicago, IL), June 24, 1912, 9.

Chapter 4

1. F. E. Hopkins, "Gossip Responsible for Church Scandals," *Holbrook News* (Holbrook, AZ), May 28, 1909, 3.
2. "Fallen Ministers Worth First Page," *Los Angeles Times*, Aug. 21, 1917, 2.
3. Timothy E. W. Gloege, *Guaranteed Pure: The Moody Bible Institute, Business, and the Making of Modern Evangelicalism* (Chapel Hill: University of North Carolina Press, 2015), 36.
4. As historian Timothy E. W. Gloege explains, MBI sought to raise up "an army of Christian workers that would convert the working classes and restore social stability." Gloege, *Guaranteed Pure*, 3.
5. Microfilm collection of student records, Moody Bible Institute Archives, Chicago, IL (hereafter cited as MBI Archives).
6. Microfilm collection of student records, MBI Archives.
7. Microfilm collection of student records, MBI Archives.
8. "Condensed Annual Statement for 1903," *Institute Tie* 4 (Feb. 1904): 185.
9. Thekla Ellen Joiner, *Sin in the City: Chicago and Revivalism, 1880–1920* (Columbia: University of Missouri Press, 2007), 44–62.
10. "Condensed Annual Statement for 1903," *Institute Tie*, 186.
11. As historian Margaret Lamberts Bendroth writes, "By the 1920s, fundamentalists had adopted the belief that it was men, not women, who had the true aptitude for religion." Margaret Lamberts Bendroth, *Fundamentalism & Gender: 1875 to the Present* (New Haven: Yale University Press, 1993), 3.
12. Bendroth, *Fundamentalism & Gender*, 64.
13. Meeting minutes from Sept. 19, 1903, Minutes, Reports, Records, & Plans of MBI, MIS, & BICA, Box 17, Item 42, MBI Archives.
14. "Future Engagements," *Institute Tie* (Apr. 1908): 644.
15. "F. Leroy Enslow," *U.S. City Directories, 1822–1995*, http://ancestry.com.
16. Meeting minutes from Sept. 8, 1903, Minutes, Reports, Records, & Plans of MBI, MIS, & BICA, Box 17, Item 42, MBI Archives.
17. Meeting minutes from Apr. 13, 1905, Minutes, Reports, Records, & Plans of MBI, MIS, & BICA, Box 17, Item 42, MBI Archives.
18. Some of the alumni files from the era, for example, contain letters that accuse former students of backsliding or practicing such unorthodox practices as speaking in tongues. The administration seemed to deem these accusations serious enough to attach them to student records. See microfilm collection of student records, MBI Archives.
19. "Wedding Succeeds Lovers' Quarrel," *Chicago Tribune*, June 12, 1896, 1.
20. "St. Louis Has a Bible Class of 1500 Members," *St. Louis Post-Dispatch*, Oct. 26, 1902, 49.
21. Some of the details of the accusations against Newell and his alleged confessions emerge in R. A. Torrey's letter to A. C. Dixon. In the letter, Torrey mentions the medication addiction and the fact that "the woman who claimed [Newell] had made the improper proposals to her" was in China "as a missionary." See R. A. Torrey to A. C. Dixon and the Committee of Chicago Avenue Church (Sept. 15, 1909), Untitled (Wooden) File Cabinet—Drawer 3, Biographical Collection of the Moody Bible Institute, MBI Archives.
22. "First Methodist Church May Bar Famed Preacher," *Chicago Tribune*, Sept. 6, 1912, 1.
23. R. A. Torrey to A. C. Dixon and the Committee of Chicago Avenue Church (Sept. 15, 1909), Untitled (Wooden) File Cabinet—Drawer 3, Biographical Collection of the Moody Bible Institute, MBI Archives.
24. R. A. Torrey to A. C. Dixon and the Committee of Chicago Avenue Church (Sept. 15, 1909), Untitled (Wooden) File Cabinet—Drawer 3, Biographical Collection of the Moody Bible Institute, MBI Archives.
25. A. P. Fitt to the Executive Committee of MBI (Apr. 8, 1908), AP Fitt (Correspondence), Biographical Collection of the Moody Bible Institute, MBI Archives.
26. Lyman Stewart to A. C. Dixon (Nov. 20, 1909), Fundamental Letters (beginning—June 1, 1911), The Bible Institute of Los Angeles Archives, Los Angeles, CA (henceforth BIOLA Archives).
27. A. C. Dixon to Lyman Stewart (Dec. 17, 1909), Fundamental Letters (beginning—June 1, 1911), BIOLA Archives.

28. "Church Would Bar Naughty Preacher," *Wakefield Republican* (Wakefield, NE), Sept. 12, 1912, 7.
29. "First Methodist Church May Bar Famed Preacher," *Chicago Tribune*, Sept. 6, 1912, 1.
30. "Preacher a Prisoner in Hut," *St. Louis Post-Dispatch*, Sept. 13, 1912, 8.
31. "Newell Ousted by Moody Church," *Chicago Tribune*, Oct. 10, 1912.
32. "Expelled from Chicago Church," *Owensboro Messenger* (Owensboro, KY), Oct. 11, 1912, 3.
33. See, for example, *Chicago Tribune*, May 23, 1914, 12.
34. See "Pacific Garden Mission Installs New President," *Moody Global Ministries*, Sept. 15, 2013, https://www.moodyglobal.org/news/education/2013/pacific-garden-mission-installs-new-president/.
35. Leona Hertel, *Man with a Mission: Mel Trotter and His Legacy for the Rescue Mission Movement* (Grand Rapids: Kregel Publications, 2000), 29–36.
36. "Evangelist 'Mel' Trotter Kissed Her, Widow Says in Divorce Suit Trial," *Pittsburgh Press*, June 27, 1922, 1.
37. "Wife Accuses 'Mel' Trotter, Slum Evangel," *Chicago Tribune*, June 14, 1922, 21; "Saw Evangelist Hug Girl," *Lincoln Journal Star* (Lincoln, NE), June 26, 1922, 11.
38. "Blushing Pillar Tells of Trotter," *Pittsburgh Daily Post*, June 15, 1922, 3.
39. "Says Mrs. Trotter Often Swatted Mel," *Daily Times* (Davenport, IA), June 15, 1922, 15.
40. "His Greatest Fight," *Detroit News*, [n.d.], 1922, Box 2, Folder 15, Papers of Melvin Ernest Trotter (Collection 47), Billy Graham Center Archives, Wheaton College.
41. "Trotter Thinks Wife Plotting Degenerate; Evangelist on Stand," *Greensboro Daily News* (Greensboro, NC), July 6, 1922, 1.
42. Billy Sunday, quoted in "His Greatest Fight: Devil Never So Close to Him as Now, Says Trotter," *Detroit News*, June 24, 1922, [n.p.], Box 2, Folder 15, Papers of Melvin Ernest Trotter (Collection 47), Billy Graham Center Archives, Wheaton College.
43. "Wife Says Preacher Struck Her Several Blows with His Fist," *Greensboro Daily News* (Greensboro, NC), July 8, 1922, 1.
44. "Trotter Is off Speakers List," *Lansing State Journal* (Lansing, MI), July 12, 1922, 1.
45. "Trotter Thinks Wife Plotting Degenerate; Evangelist on Stand," *Greensboro Daily News* (Greensboro, NC), July 6, 1922, 1.
46. "Greensboro Pastor Supports Trotter," *Bee* (Danville, VA), July 6, 1922, 3.
47. "Paragraphics," *Greensboro Daily News* (Greensboro, NC), July 9, 1922, 4.
48. "Trotter's Wife on Stand Tells of Mel's 'Confession,'" *Bee* (Danville, VA), July 18, 1922, 1.
49. "Rev. Trotter Hypnotized Girls, Witness Says," *Eau Claire Leader* (Eau Claire, WI), July 28, 1922, 6.
50. "Trotter Was Hypnotist," *Lincoln Journal Star* (Lincoln, NE), July 27, 1922, 5.
51. "Girl Takes Stand for Evangelist," *Los Angeles Times*, July 29, 1922, 1.
52. "Mel Trotter Given a Divorce Today," *Logansport Pharos-Tribune* (Logansport, IN), Aug. 25, 1922, 2.
53. "Mel Trotter Wins Verdict in Suit," *Herald-Press* (Saint Joseph, MI), Aug. 25, 1922, 1.
54. "Mel Trotter Invited to Hold Revival Campaigns," *St. Louis Star and Times*, Aug. 27, 1922, 7.
55. *Lansing State Journal* (Lansing, MI), Aug. 28, 1922, 4.
56. "Radio Rialto," *Dixon Evening Telegraph* (Dixon, IL), Apr. 15, 1932, 10.
57. For a brief survey of the changing ideas about sexuality in this era, see John D'Emilio and Estelle B. Freedman, *Intimate Matters: A History of Sexuality in America*, 3rd ed. (Chicago: University of Chicago Press, 2012), 222–28.
58. George Chauncey, *Gay New York: Gender, Urban Culture, and the Makings of the Gay Male World, 1890–1940* (New York: Basic Books, 1994).
59. As historian Heather R. White explains, in the first half of the century, the "notorious 'sin of Sodom' (and of those seen to be guilty of committing it) involved capacious kinds of deviance that do not align with the medical ideas and identity categories that became ascendant in the second half of the twentieth century." Heather R. White, *Reforming Sodom: Protestants and the Rise of Gay Rights* (Chapel Hill: University of North Carolina Press, 2015), 6.
60. See a compilation of state-by-state sodomy statutes at midcentury in Donald Webster Cory, *The Homosexual in America: A Subjective Approach* (New York: Greenberg, 1951), Appendix B.
61. "Preacher Convicted of Revolting Acts: Rev. W. E. Golding of Placer County Found Guilty and Dismissed from the Ministry," *San Francisco Chronicle*, July 12, 1898, 4. Nevada's *Daily Appeal* reported on the case by calling Golding's alleged crimes "revolting and unprintable." See *Daily Appeal* (Carson City, NV), July 14, 1898, 3.

62. Heather R. White convincingly argues that homosexuality was not a serious concern for Protestants before the 1940s. Indeed, White calls the scriptural condemnation of homosexuality "an invention of the twentieth century" and demonstrates how religious liberals in particular "un-muddled the confused category of 'sodomical sin' and assigned to it a singular same-sex meaning." See White, *Reforming Sodom*, 3–4.

63. "Suicide to Hide Shame, Then Ruin: Self-Destruction of the Rev. George H. Simmons, Banker-Politician, Stirs Peoria," *Chicago Daily Tribune*, Feb. 7, 1906, 1–2.

64. As Mark Jordan argues, "The most effective American rhetoric for condemning civil or religious toleration of homosexuality has repeatedly warned of dangers to the young." See Mark D. Jordan, *Recruiting Young Love: How Christians Talk about Homosexuality* (Chicago: University of Chicago Press, 2011), xiii. This trend, as Jordan's work demonstrates, began in the early twentieth century and intensified from the 1970s on, as public religious figures like Anita Bryant explicitly linked homosexuality with child abuse and child recruitment. Few made this connection in the earlier decades of the twentieth century. The 2011 John Jay College of Criminal Justice report on the sexual abuse of minors by Catholic priests concluded that, despite speculations about a correlation between same-sex attraction, acts, and identities with the sexual abuse of minors, the data "do not support a finding that homosexual identity and/or pre-ordination same-sex behavior are significant risk factors for the sexual abuse of minors." See Karen J. Terry et al., *The Causes and Context of Sexual Abuse of Minors by Catholic Priests in the United States, 1950–2010* (Washington, DC: United States Conference of Catholic Bishops, 2011), 64, https://www.usccb.org/sites/default/files/issues-and-action/child-and-youth-protection/upload/The-Causes-and-Context-of-Sexual-Abuse-of-Minors-by-Catholic-Priests-in-the-United-States-1950-2010.pdf.

65. "He Flees in Disgrace: Dr. Simmons Takes His Own Life," *Los Angeles Times*, Feb. 7, 1906, 1.

66. For more on the medicalization of homosexuality in the twentieth century, see Katie Batza, "Sickness and Wellness," in *The Routledge History of Queer America*, ed. Don Romesburg (New York: Routledge, 2018), 287–99.

67. As historian Mark Jordan notes, "By a remarkable coincidence, which is no coincidence at all, the homosexual and the adolescent entered English-speaking science in the same years." Jordan, *Recruiting Young Love*, 1.

68. "Pastor Moral Degenerate," *Tribune* (Seymour, IN), Dec. 26, 1906, 1.

69. Walter J. Hollenweger and Iain MacRobert, *The Black Roots and White Racism of Early Pentecostalism in the USA* (London: Palgrave Macmillan, 1988), xii.

70. Daniel Silliman, "The 1st Pentecostal Scandal" (blog), May 18, 2012, http://danielsilliman.blogspot.com/2012/05/1st-pentecostal-scandal.html (accessed July 1, 2018).

71. Andrea S. Johnson, "All Manner of Evil Spoken Falsely: Acts of Sodomy, the Pentecostal Presses, and the Narrative of Charles Fox Parham," *Pneuma* 41, no. 1 (2019): 31–49.

72. Johnson, "All Manner of Evil," 33–36.

73. James R. Goff Jr., *Fields White unto Harvest: Charles F. Parham and the Missionary Origins of Pentecostalism* (Fayetteville: University of Arkansas Press, 1988), 137–41.

74. Alan F. Bearman and Jennifer L. Mills, "Charles M. Sheldon and Charles F. Parham: Adapting Christianity to the Challenges of the American West," *Kansas History: A Journal of the Central Plains* 32 (Summer 2009): 116. See also Goff, *Fields White unto Harvest*, 138, 142; Tony Cauchi, "Charles Fox Parham (1873–1929)," *The Revival Library*, 2004, https://revival-library.org/heroes/charles-parham/.

75. "Choir Boys Accuse Rector," *Des Moines Tribune*, July 11, 1908, 2.

76. "Charged by Boys, Rector Disappears," *Scranton Truth* (Scranton, PA), July 11, 1908, 11; "Chicago Rector Doubly Charged," *Des Moines Tribune*, July 13, 1908, 1.

77. "Rector Kemp Out; Charge Dropped," *Chicago Tribune*, July 14, 1908, 5.

78. "Dr. Griffin Is Back; Ready for Trial," *Chicago Tribune*, Sept. 13, 1908, 3.

79. "Minister's Friends Deny Boys' Charges," *Inter Ocean* (Chicago, IL), Aug. 14, 1908, 12.

80. "Commissions Meets in Secret to Consider Rector's Case," *Chicago Tribune*, Oct. 31, 1908, 11.

81. "Services Reveal Split on Griffin," *Chicago Tribune*, Sept. 14, 1908, 3.

82. "Rector Cleared of Charge," *Chicago Tribune*, Oct. 15, 1908, 1.

83. "Griffin Trouble Ends in Rejoicing," *Chicago Tribune*, Oct. 19, 1908, 3.

84. "Kemp's Exoneration Is Seen When Choirmaster Resigns," *Chicago Tribune*, Nov. 13, 1908, 2; "The Rev. R. M. Kemp Found Not Guilty, One Vote Dissents," *Inter Ocean* (Chicago, IL), Dec. 2, 1908, 1.

85. "Rev. R. M. Kemp Found Not Guilty, One Vote Dissents," 5.
86. "Canonical Trial Denied Kemp," *Chicago Tribune*, Dec. 3, 1908, 5.
87. "Kemp Arraigned; Released on Bond," *Chicago Tribune*, Dec. 25, 1908, 3.
88. "Kemp as Witness Roused to Anger," *Chicago Tribune*, Jan. 17, 1909, 3.
89. "Episcopal Rectors Faithful to Kemp," *Inter Ocean* (Chicago, IL), Jan. 30, 1908, 3.
90. "Clergyman Indicted," *Cincinnati Enquirer*, Feb. 3, 1909, 1.
91. "Indictment against Kemp," *Chicago Tribune*, May 2, 1909, 6.
92. "Criminal Cases Postponed," *Inter Ocean* (Chicago, IL), June 24, 1909, 5; "Rev. Kemp May Never Be Tried," *Muscatine News-Tribune* (Muscatine, IA), July 11, 1909, 1.
93. "Ex-curate in Police Clutches," *Times Union* (Brooklyn, NY), July 16, 1909, 1.
94. "Kemp Acquitted; Still under Fire on Other Charges," *Inter Ocean* (Chicago, IL), Mar. 23, 1910, 1.
95. "Kemp Will Testify Today in Effort to Prove Alibi," *Chicago Tribune*, June 9, 1910, 7.
96. "Kemp Acquitted by Jury; Other Charges Wiped Off," *Chicago Tribune*, June 12, 1910, 7.
97. "Rev. Robert M. Kemp, Dies; Brother of Bath Woman," *Democrat and Chronicle* (Rochester, NY), July 19, 1930, 36.
98. "To Keep Minister's Secret: Dr. Mortimer, It Is Said, Will Be Unfrocked and Return to England," *New York Times*, Dec. 29, 1912, 5.
99. "Rector of Exclusive Church Resigns—Scandal?," *Day Book* (Chicago, IL), Dec. 27, 1912, 29.
100. "Sailing of Rev. Alfred Mortimer Is Hastened When an Irate Husband Hints at Intention to Interview Unfrocked Minister," *Cincinnati Enquirer*, Jan. 4, 1913, 1.
101. Mortimer's reference to degeneracy was not the only evidence of his queerness. Historian John Loughery has argued that the reason behind Mortimer's dismissal was indeed his proclivity toward homosexuality. Loughery has written about rumors of a homosexual ring at Mortimer's church, and the historian cites the fact that Mortimer's curates were also dismissed as evidence of the men's queerness. On Loughery's reading, Mortimer's case illustrates how the Episcopal Church responded to "a moral and public relations debacle" that "threatened to tar the whole profession." And even though the evidence in Mortimer's particular case is frustratingly thin, Loughery is justified in asserting that Protestant denominations had become quick to disassociate themselves from potentially deviant ministers in this era. John Loughery, *The Other Side of Silence: Men's Lives & Gay Identities—a Twentieth-Century History* (New York: Henry Holt, 1998), 14.
102. See, for instance, Max Carocci, "Sodomy, Ambiguity, and Feminization," in *Indigenous Bodies: Reviewing, Relocating, Reclaiming*, ed. Jacqueline Fear-Segal and Rebecca Tillett (Albany: SUNY Press, 2013), 73.
103. Katie M. Hemphill, "'Pastor Was Trapped': Queer Scandal and Contestations over Christian Anti-vice Reform," *Journal of the Gilded Age and Progressive Era* 21, no. 4 (2022): 1–16.
104. Hemphill, "'Pastor Was Trapped,'" 5.
105. Hemphill, "'Pastor Was Trapped,'" 2.
106. Kathryn Lofton, "Queering Fundamentalism: John Balcom Shaw and the Sexuality of a Protestant Orthodoxy," *Journal of the History of Sexuality* 17, no. 3 (2008): 439–68.
107. Lofton, "Queering Fundamentalism," 464.
108. George Chauncey, "Christian Brotherhood or Sexual Perversion? Homosexual Identities and the Construction of Sexual Boundaries in the World War One Era," *Journal of Social History* 19, no. 2 (1985): 200.
109. *Alleged Immoral Conditions at Newport (R.I.) Naval Training Station: Report of the Committee on Naval Affairs, United States Senate, Sixty-Seventh Congress, First Session Relative to Alleged Immoral Conditions and Practices at the Naval Training Station, Newport, R.I.* (Washington: Government Printing Office, 1921), 3.
110. *Alleged Immoral Conditions at Newport*, 4.
111. *Alleged Immoral Conditions at Newport*, 5.
112. Quoted in Lawrence Murphy, *Perverts by Official Order: The Campaign against Homosexuals by the United States Navy* (New York: Routledge, 2014), 103.
113. *Journal of the One Hundred and Twenty-Ninth Annual Session of the Rhode Island Episcopal Convention* (Providence: The Providence Press, Snow & Farnham, 1919), 89.
114. Chauncey, "Christian Brotherhood," 200.
115. By 1923, As of 1923, Kent was working for Swarthmore College in a non-chaplain capacity. Still, his gravestone at the Pine Grove Cemetery reads, "Samuel Neal Kent, 1873–1943, A Priest of the Church." See Loughery, *Other Side of Silence*, 13; Ernest Gamble, "How

Swarthmore Does It," *Luceum Magazine* 33, no. 2 (1923): 20; FindAGrave.com, "Samuel Neal Kent," https://www.findagrave.com/memorial/43898642/samuel-neal-kent.

116. For an overview of church publicity efforts between 1900 and 1930, see John P. Ferré, "Protestant Press Relations in the United States, 1900–1930," *Church History* 62, no. 4 (1993): 514–27.

117. Herbert Heebner Smith, *Publicity and Progress: Twentieth Century Methods in Religious, Educational and Social Activities* (New York: George H. Doran, 1915), 17.

118. For more on the Men and Religion Forward Movement, see Gail Bederman, "'The Women Have Had Charge of the Church Work Long Enough': The Men and Religion Forward Movement of 1911–1912 and the Masculinization of Middle-Class Protestantism," *American Quarterly* 41, no. 3 (1989): 432–65.

119. *Messages of the Men and Religion Movement*, vol. 7 (New York: Association Press, 1912), 8–9, 13, 39.

120. Christian F. Reisner, *Church Publicity: The Modern Way to Compel Them to Come In* (New York: Methodist Book of Concern, 1913).

121. Smith, *Publicity and Progress.*

122. See, for instance, "Ad Men's Convention Takes on Church Publicity Department; Church Advertising Is Popular," *Greensboro Daily News* (Greensboro, NC), July 9, 1916, 10.

123. Audrey Farley, "Lovers under an Apple Tree," *Contingent Magazine*, Mar. 8, 2020, https://contingentmagazine.org/2020/03/08/lovers-under-an-apple-tree/.

124. "Most Important Conference in Church Publicity in History of Christian Church," *Chicago Commerce* 18, no. 2 (Nov. 4, 1922): 14.

125. "Churches Urged to Aid Journals Clean up Cities," *Oakland Tribune* (Oakland, CA), Oct. 27, 1924, 17.

126. American Society of Newspaper Editors, *Problems of Journalism: Proceedings of the Convention, American Society of Newspaper Editors* (Milwaukee, 1923), 8.

127. For more on how the press negotiated its relationship with the pulpit and with its role in shaping American morality writ large between 1833 and 1923, see Ronald R. Rodgers, *The Struggle for the Soul of Journalism: The Pulpit versus the Press, 1833–1923* (Columbia: University of Missouri Press, 2018).

128. Gay Talese, *The Kingdom and the Power: Behind the Scenes at the New York Times* (New York: Random House, 2013), 61.

129. Ralph Valentine Gilbert, *The Church and Printer's Ink* (New York: Fleming H. Revell, 1925), 81.

Chapter 5

1. Thomas A. Robinson and Lanette D. Ruff, *Out of the Mouths of Babes: Girl Evangelists in the Flapper Era* (New York: Oxford University Press, 2011), 157.

2. Aimee Semple McPherson, *This Is That: Personal Experiences, Sermons and Writings of Aimee Semple McPherson, Evangelist* (Los Angeles: Bridal Call Publishing House, 1919), 103, 102.

3. For an excellent account of female preachers in earlier generations, see Catherine A. Brekus, *Strangers and Pilgrims: Female Preaching in America, 1740–1845* (Chapel Hill: University of North Carolina Press, 1998). For a broad overview of women's religious leadership in US churches, see Susan Hill Lindley, *You Have Stept Out of Your Place: A History of Women and Religion in America* (Louisville: Westminster John Knox Press, 1996).

4. "'Undo Eve's Sin, Women's Duty,' Says Only Feminine Evangelist," *Sheboygan Press* (Sheboygan, WI), Feb. 8, 1919, 2.

5. Edith L. Blumhofer, *Aimee Semple McPherson: Everybody's Sister* (Grand Rapids: William B. Eerdmans, 1993), 3; "Both Knees, Not One Knee," *Tampa Times*, Apr. 17, 1919, 4; "'Female Billy Sunday' Who Is 'Redeeming Sinful San Francisco,'" *Buffalo Enquirer*, Mar. 27, 1919, 9.

6. As historian Matthew Avery Sutton puts it, McPherson was "the first religious celebrity of the mass media era." Matthew Avery Sutton, *Aimee Semple McPherson and the Resurrection of Christian America* (Cambridge: Harvard University Press, 2007), 3.

7. See, for example, Stanley Coben, *Rebellion against Victorianism: The Impetus for Cultural Change in 1920s America* (New York: Oxford University Press, 1991); Lynn Dumenil, *The Modern Temper: American Culture and Society in the 1920s* (New York: Hill and Wang, 1995); Niall Palmer, *The Twenties in America: Politics and History* (Edinburgh: Edinburgh

University Press, 2006); Charles J. Shindo, *1927 and the Rise of Modern America* (Lawrence: University Press of Kansas, 2010).

8. According to the US census designation, urban (or non-rural) places are areas with more than twenty-five hundred inhabitants.

9. Nancy F. Cott, "Passionlessness: An Interpretation of Victorian Sexual Ideology, 1790–1850," *Signs* 4, no. 2 (1978): 219–36.

10. Frederick Lewis Allen, *Only Yesterday: An Informal History of the Nineteen Twenties* (New York: Harper & Row, 1931), 89.

11. G. W. Butts to Henry Allen, July 10, 1919, quoted in Gerald R. Butters, *Banned in Kansas: Motion Picture Censorship, 1915–1966* (Columbia: University of Missouri Press, 2007), 141.

12. On sexuality and censorship in the film industry, see Richard S. Randall, *Censorship of the Movies: The Social and Political Control of a Mass Medium* (Madison: University of Wisconsin Press, 1968); Butters, *Banned in Kansas.*

13. Alma Whitaker, "Reveals Intimate Charm of Angelus Temple Head," *Los Angeles Times*, Mar. 23, 1924, 21.

14. "Aimee Semple McPherson," *Wichita Eagle*, May 5, 2022, 2.

15. Roberta Semple Salter, cited in Sutton, *Aimee Semple McPherson*, 14.

16. Darren Dochuk, *Anointed with Oil: How Christianity and Crude Made Modern America* (New York: Basic, 2019), 215; Fred W. Viehe, "Black Gold Suburbs: The Influence of the Extractive Industry on the Suburbanization of Los Angeles, 1890–1930," *Journal of Urban History* 8, no. 1 (1981): 3–26.

17. Jules Tygiel, "Metropolis in the Making: Los Angeles in the 1920s," in *Metropolis in the Making: Los Angeles in the 1920s*, ed. Tom Sitton (Berkeley: University of California Press, 2001), 2.

18. Robert S. Lynd and Helen Merrell Lynd, *Middletown: A Study in Contemporary American Culture* (New York: Harcourt, Brace, 1929), 341, 343.

19. Lynd and Lynd, *Middletown*, 341, 343.

20. Lynd and Lynd, *Middletown*, 380.

21. Both groups, it should be noted, operated on the terms modernity afforded them. In contrast to the binary representations the groups have sometimes received, both fundamentalists and modernists were products of their "modern" age. For more on this, see Kathryn Lofton, "Commonly Modern: Rethinking the Modernist-Fundamentalist Controversies," *Church History* 83, no. 1 (2014): 137–44; Matthew Avery Sutton, "New Trends in the Historiography of American Fundamentalism," *Journal of American Studies* 51, no. 1 (2017): 235–41.

22. For more on US fundamentalists' responses to modernity, see Margaret Lamberts Bendroth, *Fundamentalism and Gender, 1875 to the Present* (New Haven: Yale University Press, 1996); Joel A. Carpenter, *Revive Us Again: The Reawakening of American Fundamentalism* (New York: Oxford University Press, 1997); George M. Marsden, *Fundamentalism and American Culture*, 2nd ed. (New York: Oxford University Press, 2006); Simon A. Wood and David Harrington Watt, eds., *Fundamentalism: Perspectives on a Contested History* (Columbia: University of South Carolina Press, 2014).

23. Marsden, *Fundamentalism and American Culture*, 3.

24. Tennessee House Bill no. 185 (1925).

25. For more on the Scopes trial and its cultural significance, see Edward J. Larson, *Summer for the Gods: The Scopes Trial and America's Continuing Debate over Science and Religion* (New York: Basic Books, 2008); Michael Lienesch, *In the Beginning: Fundamentalism, the Scopes Trial, and the Making of the Antievolution Movement* (Chapel Hill: University of North Carolina Press, 2007).

26. Sutton, "New Trends"; Michael Hochgeschwender, "The Scopes Trial in the Context of Competing Modernity Discourses," in *Fractured Modernity: America Confronts Modern Times, 1890s to 1940s*, ed. Alan Lessoff and Thomas Welskopp (Berlin: de Gruyter, 2016), 213–33.

27. *New York World Telegram & Sun*, July 9, 1956, 19.

28. H. L. Mencken, "Trial as a Religious Orgy," *Baltimore Evening Sun*, July 11, 1925, 2; H. L. Mencken, "Yearning Mountaineers' Souls Need Reconversion Nightly," *Baltimore Evening Sun*, July 13, 1925, 1; H. L. Mencken, "Darrow's Eloquent Appeal Wasted on Ears That Heed Only Bryan," *Baltimore Evening Sun*, July 14, 1925, 1; H. L. Mencken, "Mencken Declares Strictly Fair Trial Is beyond Ken of Tennessee Fundamentalists," *Baltimore Evening Sun*, July 16, 1925, 1.

29. H. L. Mencken, "Bryan," *Baltimore Evening Sun*, July 27, 1925, 15.
30. Although Mencken and others used the trial to disparage fundamentalists, previous scholars have overemphasized the damage that the trial had done to the movement as a whole. As Darren Dochuk and Matthew Avery Sutton have shown, the trial would ultimately lead fundamentalists to mobilize and reorganize under the "evangelical" umbrella and exert significant cultural influence in the second half of the twentieth century. See Darren Dochuk, *From Bible Belt to Sunbelt: Plain-Folk Religion, Grassroots Politics, and the Rise of Evangelical Conservatism* (New York: W.W. Norton, 2011); Matthew Avery Sutton, *American Apocalypse: A History of Modern Evangelicalism* (Cambridge: Belknap Press of Harvard University Press, 2014).
31. For a brief account of—and an intervention in—the historiography of pentecostalism's relationship to fundamentalism and evangelicalism, see Matthew A. Sutton, "'Between the Refrigerator and the Wildfire': Aimee Semple McPherson, Pentecostalism, and the Fundamentalist-Modernist Controversy," *Church History* 72, no. 1 (2003): 159–88.
32. Arlene M. Sánchez Walsh, *Pentecostals in America* (New York: Columbia University Press, 2018).
33. For more on early pentecostalism and race, see Blaine Charles Hamilton, "The Spirit in Black and White: Early Twentieth-Century Pentecostals and Race Relations, 1905–1945" (PhD diss., Rice University, 2013); Gastón Espinosa, *William J. Seymour and the Origins of Global Pentecostalism: A Biography and Documentary History* (Durham: Duke University Press, 2014).
34. See Susan Wise Bauer, *The Art of the Public Grovel: Sexual Sin and Public Confession in America* (Princeton: Princeton University Press, 2008), 51.
35. Grant Wacker, *Heaven Below: Early Pentecostals and American Culture* (Cambridge: Harvard University Press, 2003), 160.
36. By 1918, women occupied half of all assistant minister positions among Assemblies of God churches but made up only 5 percent of sole pastors. See Charles H. Barfoot and Gerald T. Sheppard, "Prophetic vs. Priestly Religion: The Changing Role of Women Clergy in Classical Pentecostal Churches," *Review of Religious Research* 22, no. 1 (1980): 2–17.
37. Wacker, *Heaven Below*, 160.
38. Leah Payne, *Gender and Pentecostal Revivalism: Making a Female Ministry in the Early Twentieth Century* (New York: Palgrave Macmillan, 2015), 2.
39. Payne, *Gender and Pentecostal Revivalism*, 109–20.
40. Betty A. DeBerg, *Ungodly Women: Gender and the First Wave of American Fundamentalism* (Macon: Mercer University Press, 2000), 141, 144.
41. Daniel Mark Epstein, *Sister Aimee: The Life of Aimee Semple McPherson* (New York: Harcourt, 1994), 134.
42. On the gendered nature of McPherson's ministry, see Kristy Maddux, "The Feminized Gospel: Aimee Semple McPherson and the Gendered Performance of Christianity," *Women's Studies in Communication* 35, no. 1 (2012): 42–67.
43. See Robert Pierce Shuler, *McPhersonism: A Study of Healing Cults and Modern Day "Tongues" Movements Containing Summary of Facts as to Disappearance and Re-appearance of Aimee Semple McPherson* (Los Angeles: Bob Shuler, 1924).
44. Gail Bederman, "'The Women Have Had Charge of the Church Work Long Enough': The Men and Religion Forward Movement of 1911–1912 and the Masculinization of Middle-Class Protestantism," *American Quarterly* 41, no. 3 (1989): 432–65.
45. Quoted in Epstein, *Sister Aimee*, 259.
46. Whitaker, "Reveals Intimate Charm," 21.
47. Epstein, *Sister Aimee*, 289.
48. Raymond L. Cox, *The Verdict Is In* (Los Angeles: Heritage Foundation, 1983), 36.
49. Quoted in Blumhofer, *Aimee Semple McPherson*, 285.
50. "Our Beloved Leader," *Bridal Call Foursquare* 10, no. 1 (1926): 4.
51. Upton Sinclair, "An Evangelist Drowns," *New Republic*, June 30, 1926, 171.
52. See, for example, this article from the *Chicago Tribune* that, just eleven days after the disappearance, implicated Ormiston, spoke of a sighting in San Francisco, and mentioned a ransom note McPherson's mother was supposed to have received: "Cast Doubt on Evangelist's Death in Sea," *Chicago Daily Tribune*, May 29, 1926, 1.
53. See, for instance, "Missing Woman Is Not Yet Located," *Nebraska State Journal* (Lincoln, NE), June 1, 1926, 1.
54. "Hailed as One Risen from the Dead," *Oakland Tribune* (Oakland, CA), June 28, 1926, 2.

55. See, for instance, the take of a Douglas, Arizona, resident L. R. Budron in "Quite Possible for Kidnapers [sic] to Hold Aimee," *Santa Ana Register* (Santa Ana, CA), June 25, 1926, 3. While he refused to speculate on the validity of McPherson's entire account, he "thought that it was strange that her clothing, particularly the hose and shoes, did not show traces of having come into conflict with the mesquite and catspaw of the desert. He also ventured to remark that a 20-mile hike over the desert in the heat of the sun would have left the walker considerably sunburned."

56. Aimee Semple McPherson, "Kidnapped!," *Bridal Call Foursquare* 10, no. 3 (1926): 11.

57. Telegram from John J. Kershner to the Department of Justice (June 25, 1926), obtained from the FBI through a Freedom of Information Act request.

58. Blumhofer, *Aimee Semple McPherson*, 285.

59. Blumhofer, *Aimee Semple McPherson*, 295.

60. "Aimee Identified as Woman in Car with Ormiston in Salinas," *Modesto News-Herald* (Modesto, CA), July 16, 1926, 1.

61. "Foundation for Story Not Thought Sound," *Santa Cruz Evening News* (Santa Cruz, CA), July 26, 1926, 1.

62. "Says McPherson Was Not in Carmel," *Santa Cruz Evening News* (Santa Cruz, CA), July 26, 1926. 8.

63. "Refuse Finger Prints to Make Comparison with Those in House," *Santa Cruz Evening News* (Santa Cruz, CA), July 27, 1926, 1.

64. "Shack Notes Identified as Aimee's," *Oakland Tribune* (Oakland, CA), July 31, 1926, 1.

65. "This and That," *Oakland Tribune* (Oakland, CA), Aug. 5, 1926, 18.

66. "Busy Now," *Santa Ana Register* (Santa Ana, CA), Aug. 7, 1926, 18.

67. Lyrics to "The Ballad of Aimee McPherson" (year unknown).

68. Louis Adamic, "Aimee Semple McPherson's Fight with Satan," *Haldeman-Julius Monthly*, Sept. 1926, in Louis Adamic, ed., *The Truth about Aimee Semple McPherson: A Symposium* (Girard: Haldeman-Julius, 1926), 45–46.

69. Sinclair Lewis, *Elmer Gantry* (London: Jonathan Cape, 1930), 211.

70. Quoted in Epstein, *Sister Aimee*, 301.

71. "Trunk, Famed in McPherson Case, Arrives," *Santa Ana Register* (Santa Ana, CA), Nov. 1, 1926, 1.

72. Willis W. Blossom to Calvin Coolidge (Nov. 2, 1926), obtained from the FBI through a Freedom of Information Act request.

73. Quoted in Epstein, *Sister Aimee*, 356.

74. Aimee Semple McPherson, "Christ, Our Spiritual Gibraltar," *Bridal Call Foursquare* 10, no. 4 (1926): 4.

75. H. L. Mencken, "Sister Aimee," *Baltimore Evening Sun*, Dec. 13, 1926, quoted in H. L. Mencken, *A Mencken Chrestomathy* (reprint, New York: Knopf, 1949), 292. Although Mencken appreciated McPherson's savvy for properly exploiting the new media age, he was still predictably critical of her religion. When explaining her popularity in the same article, for example, Mencken wrote that "she was a roaring success" in Los Angeles "for the plain reason that there were more morons collected in Los Angeles than in any other town on earth—because it was a pasture foreordained for evangelists, and she was the first comer to give it anything low enough for its taste and comprehension."

76. "Shot during Argument," *Los Angeles Times*, Nov. 15, 1926, 24. Also see footnote 31 in chapter 4 in Sutton, *Sister Aimee*.

77. Quoted in "The Public Forum: The McPherson Case," *Santa Ana Daily Register* (Santa Ana, CA), Nov. 22, 1926, 9.

78. Theodore Peterson, *Magazines in the Twentieth Century* (Urbana: University of Illinois Press, 1956), 50.

79. Peterson, *Magazines*, 376.

80. Quoted in Peterson, *Magazines*, 377.

81. Harold Ross, prospectus to the *New Yorker*, http://xroads.virginia.edu/~ug02/newyorker/prospectus.html.

82. Mencken, "Sister Aimee," *Baltimore Evening Sun*, Dec. 13, 1926, quoted in Mencken, *A Mencken Chrestomathy*, 291.

83. Mencken, "Sister Aimee," *Baltimore Evening Sun*, Dec. 13, 1926, quoted in Mencken, *A Mencken Chrestomathy*, 292.

84. H. L. Mencken, "Two Enterprising Ladies," *American Mercury*, Apr. 1928, 506–7.

85. Mencken, "Sister Aimee," *Baltimore Evening Sun*, Dec. 13, 1926, quoted in Mencken, *A Mencken Chrestomathy*, 292.

86. Louis Adamic, "Was Aimee McPherson's 'Shack' in the Grove of Aphrodite?," in Adamic, *Truth about Aimee Semple McPherson*, 59, 61.

87. Paxton Hibben, "Aimee and Tex," *New Yorker*, Mar. 5, 1927, 65.

88. Paxton Hibben, *Henry Ward Beecher: An American Portrait* (New York: George H. Doran, 1927), 250–51.

89. Sarah Comstock, "Aimee Semple McPherson: Prima Donna of Revivalism," *Harper's Magazine*, Dec. 1927, 16–19.

90. Dorothy Parker, "Our Lady of the Loud-Speaker," *New Yorker*, Feb. 25, 1928, 79–81.

91. Sutton, *Aimee Semple McPherson*, 94.

92. Mencken, "Two Enterprising Ladies," 506–7.

93. Aimee Semple McPherson interview on WJR radio in Detroit, Oct. 28, 1933.

94. Sutton, *Aimee Semple McPherson*, 138.

95. Quoted in Cox, *The Verdict Is In*, preface.

96. Cox, *The Verdict Is In*, 2–3.

97. Original Broadway Cast & Male Ensemble, "Hollywood Aimee," *Scandalous, the Musical*, Shout! Broadway (2013), MP3.

98. David Ng and Mike Boehm, "Broadway Flop 'Scandalous' a Costly Investment for Foursquare Church," *Los Angeles Times*, Feb. 14, 2013, https://www.latimes.com/entertainment/la-xpm-2013-feb-14-la-et-scandalous-20130215-story.html.

Chapter 6

1. One important exception to this trend was the embrace of scintillating topics including sex, divorce, and scandal by the Black press in the interwar period. See Kim Gallon, "Silences Kept: The Absence of Gender and Sexuality in Black Press Historiography," *History Compass* 10, no. 2 (2012): 207–18; Kim Gallon, *Pleasure in the News: African American Readership and Sexuality in the Black Press* (Urbana: University of Illinois Press, 2020).

2. Joseph Medill Patterson, quoted in Frank Luther Mott, *American Journalism: A History of Newspapers in the United States through 250 Years, 1690–1940* (New York: Macmillan, 1941), 669.

3. Mott, *American Journalism*, 675.

4. The radio was not always in direct competition—newspaper managers sometimes bought radio stations to broadcast the news and stimulate newspaper sales—but the rise of the radio still interfered with the monopoly of print media on news coverage.

5. Joseph Clark, *News Parade: The American Newsreel and the World as Spectacle* (Minneapolis: University of Minnesota Press, 2020), 2.

6. Mott, *American Journalism*, 710.

7. Historian Adam Laats found a record of the case—as well as evidence of the tactics used to manage the scandal—in the archives of Wheaton College. See Adam Laats, *Fundamentalist U: Keeping the Faith in American Higher Education* (New York: Oxford University Press, 2018).

8. Janet M. Black, *Colorado Christian University: The First 100 Years* (Lakewood: Colorado Christian University, 2014), 10.

9. Quoted in Laats, *Fundamentalist U*, 61–62.

10. Will H. Houghton to J. Oliver Buswell, Aug. 31, 1936, quoted in Laats, *Fundamentalist U*, 62.

11. Laats, *Fundamentalist U*, 64.

12. Black, *Colorado Christian University*, 31.

13. "Says Billy Graham Was a Swinger," *Freeport Journal-Standard* (Freeport, IL), Mar. 10, 1973, 8.

14. Billy Graham, *Just as I Am: The Autobiography of Billy Graham* (Grand Rapids: Zondervan, 2007), 59.

15. *The Beacon* (Tampa: Bickers Printing Company, 1939), http://library.trinitycollege.edu/ld.php?content_id=28730956; *The Beacon* (Tampa: Florida Bible Institute, 1940), http://library.trinitycollege.edu/ld.php?content_id=28731086.

16. Graham, *Just as I Am*, 59.

17. Graham, *Just as I Am*, 128.

18. Thomas A. Robinson and Lanette D. Ruff, *Out of the Mouths of Babes: Girl Evangelists in the Flapper Era* (New York: Oxford University Press, 2011).

19. Deb Nicklay, "Salvation and Scandal," *Globe Gazette* (Mason City, IA), Jan. 28, 2007.

20. Barbara Selig, "Kathryn Johanna Kuhlman (May 9, 1907–February 20, 1976)," *German Life; La Vale* 21, no. 4 (2014): 56; Amy Collier Artman, *The Miracle Lady: Kathryn Kuhlman and the Transformation of Charismatic Christianity* (Grand Rapids: William B. Eerdmans, 2019), 40.

21. Historian Amy Collier Artman suggests that the quick dissolution of the relationship was due, in part, to Kuhlman's regrets about the affair and its negative effects on her ministry. See Artman, *The Miracle Lady*, 43.

22. Burroughs A. Waltrip, quoted in Artman, *The Miracle Lady*, 41–42.

23. Artman, *The Miracle Lady*, 49; Jamie Buckingham, *Daughter of Destiny: Kathryn Kuhlman, Her Story* (New York: Pocket Books, 1978), 94.

24. "Hunt Missing Minister and Choir Singer, 20: Brother Fears They Left Together," *Chicago Daily Tribune*, Jan. 31, 1928, 40; John Steele, "Rector Admits Kisses, but 'Had No Lust in Heart'! Insists He Avoided One Made 'Offensively,'" *Chicago Daily Tribune*, May 22, 1932, 9; "Pastor Bailed Out; Faithful Sing Praises," *Chicago Daily Tribune*, May 29, 1936, 1.

25. This was not the first instance of libel lawsuits brought by religious figures against newspaper publishers, but it was among the first successful and highly publicized instances of the phenomenon. In 1931, the Methodist bishop James Cannon Jr. sued the publishing mogul William Randolph Heart twice to the tune of several million dollars in damages for libel on account of Hearst newspapers reprinting rumors of the questionable morality behind Cannon's marriage to his second wife, which took place in secret shortly after the death of his first wife. Cannon also sued several dozen other newspapers for defamation. In the 1933 decision in *Cannon v. Bee News Publishing Company* (against the *Omaha Bee-News*), the court concluded "that the plaintiff is supersensitive, and in this he may be excused do to the 'pitiless publicity' to which his prominence subjects him." Cannon needed to realize, however, the judgment went all "that it is the price which he must pay for being in the limelight.... It may be irksome, but the law gives no redress for such publicity." The two Cannon-Hearst suits were dismissed in 1934 by a federal judge "for lack of prosecution." See *Cannon v. Bee News Pub. Co. et al*, 2747 (D NE 1933); "Libel Suites Dismissed," *Salt Lake Telegram*, Nov. 13, 1934, 2.

26. Wallace Best, "Lessons from the Rev. Eddie Long Scandal: Some Historical Context," *Huffington Post*, Oct. 2, 2010, https://www.huffingtonpost.com/wallace-best-phd/eddie-long-lessons-from-a_b_747517.html.

27. Wallace D. Best, *Passionately Human, No Less Divine: Religion and Culture in Black Chicago, 1915–1952* (Princeton: Princeton University Press, 2005), 189.

28. For a brief survey of the changing ideas about sexuality in this era, see John D'Emilio and Estelle B. Freedman, *Intimate Matters: A History of Sexuality in America*, 3rd ed. (Chicago: University of Chicago Press, 2012), 222–28. For a survey of the history of heterosexuality, see Rebecca L. Davis and Michele Mitchell, eds., *Heterosexual Histories* (New York: New York University Press, 2021).

29. Heather R. White, *Reforming Sodom: Protestants and the Rise of Gay Rights* (Chapel Hill: University of North Carolina Press, 2015), 3–4.

30. Terrance Dean, "Saved 'Out,' Sanctified 'Out,' and Souled 'Out': A Critical Analysis of Disgust and the Prophetic Immanence of James Baldwin's Gender Sexual Politics" (PhD diss., Vanderbilt University, 2019), 65.

31. "Dr. Powell's Crusade against Abnormal Vice Is Approved," *New York Age*, Nov. 23, 1929, 1.

32. A. Clayton Powell Sr., *Against the Tide: An Autobiography* (New York: Richard R. Smith, 1938), 215–16.

33. Best, *Passionately Human*, 188.

34. "State's Attorney Probes Scandal on Rev. Cobb [sic]," *Chicago Defender*, Nov. 25, 1939, 1.

35. "Radio Pastor Sues *Defender* for $250,000: Says 'Virtue and integrity Were Injured,'" *Chicago Defender*, Dec. 9, 1939, 9.

36. *Cobbs v. Chicago Defender, Inc.*, 31 N.E.2nd 323 (Ill. App. Ct. 1941).

37. Quoted in St Sukie de la Croix, *Chicago Whispers: A History of LGBT Chicago before Stonewall* (Madison: University of Wisconsin Press, 2012), 157.

38. David Randall Davies, *The Postwar Decline of American Newspapers, 1945–1965* (Westport: Praeger, 2006).

39. Mott, *American Journalism*, 635.

40. Debra L. Mason, "Religion News Coverage between 1930 and 1960," in *The Oxford Handbook of Religion and the American News Media*, ed. Diane H. Winston (New York: Oxford University Press, 2012), 65.

41. Michael Emery, Edwin Emery, and Nancy L. Roberts, *The Press and America: An Interpretive History of the Mass Media*, 9th ed. (Boston: Pearson, 1997), 242.

42. Margot Canaday, *The Straight State: Sexuality and Citizenship in Twentieth-Century America* (Princeton: Princeton University Press, 2009); Douglas M. Charles, *The FBI's Obscene File: J. Edgar Hoover and the Bureau's Crusade against Smut* (Lawrence: University Press of Kansas, 2012); Douglas M. Charles, *Hoover's War on Gays: Exposing the FBI's "Sex Deviates" Program* (Lawrence: University Press of Kansas, 2015); David K. Johnson, *The Lavender Scare: The Cold War Persecution of Gays and Lesbians in the Federal Government* (Chicago: University of Chicago Press, 2004).

43. For more on Adrienne Rich's notion of "compulsory heterosexuality," see Adrienne Rich, "Compulsory Heterosexuality and Lesbian Existence," *Signs* 5, no. 4 (1980): 631–60.

44. For more on religio-racial communities in this period, see Judith Weisenfeld, *New World A-Coming: Black Religion and Racial Identity during the Great Migration* (New York: New York University Press, 2017).

45. Jill Watts, *God, Harlem, U.S.A.: The Father Divine Story* (Berkeley: University of California Press, 1995).

46. Weisenfeld, *New World A-Coming*, 185–97.

47. Watts, *God, Harlem, U.S.A.*, 153–54.

48. K. K. K. to Father Divine, Feb. 5, 1937, Federal Bureau of Investigation, "Father Divine Part 01 of 01" file.

49. Watts, *God, Harlem, U.S.A.*, 149–56.

50. Lerone A. Martin, *The Gospel of J. Edgar Hoover: How the FBI Aided and Abetted the Rise of White Christian Nationalism* (Princeton: Princeton University Press, 2023).

51. Watts, *God, Harlem, U.S.A.*, 165.

52. Watts, *God, Harlem, U.S.A.*, 170.

53. William N. Eskridge, *Dishonorable Passions: Sodomy Laws in America, 1861–2003* (New York: Viking, 2008), 63.

54. Historian Heather R. White tells the complicated history of the construction and condemnation of the category of homosexuality in this period in her book *Reforming Sodom*. Importantly, White demonstrates that homosexuality was not a serious concern for Protestants before the 1940s, but was formulated in later decades. See White, *Reforming Sodom*.

55. Felix B. Wold, "'Prophet' Jones Is a Predicter and His Flock Is Awed by What He Says," *Owensboro Messenger*, Jul. 2, 1944, 3.

56. "Prophet Jones," *Life*, Nov. 27, 1944, 57–63.

57. Tim Retzloff, "'Seer or Queer?' Postwar Fascination with Detroit's Prophet Jones," *GLQ: A Journal of Lesbian and Gay Studies* 8, no. 3 (2002): 271–96.

58. "Clear Prophet of Sex Charge," *New York Age*, Jul. 21, 1956, 2.

59. Adam Clayton Powell Sr. and Adam Clayton Powell Jr. both wrote disparagingly about Jones's ministry. Though they never publicly named Jones in their diatribes against the growing problem of homosexuality among Black religious leaders, their contemporaries would have little trouble in identifying Jones as the target of their attacks. See Powell, *Against the Tide*, 215–16; Adam Clayton Powell Jr., "Sex in the Church," *Ebony*, Nov. 1951, 27–34.

60. Darren Dochuk, "Religion in Post-1945 America," *Oxford Research Encyclopedia of American History*, Aug. 31, 2016, https://doi.org/10.1093/acrefore/9780199329175.013.37.

61. Kevin M. Schultz, *Tri-faith America: How Catholics and Jews Held Postwar America to Its Protestant Promise* (New York: Oxford University Press, 2011), 10.

62. The definitional debates about what precisely constitutes an "evangelical" or a "fundamentalist" are rich and ongoing. David W. Bebbington's 1989 definition, known as "the Bebbington quadrilateral," has informed much of this scholarship. For Bebbington, the four features that define "evangelicalism" are biblicism (often expressed through biblical inerrancy or, at the very least, a particular regard for the Bible as a central source of religious authority), crucicentrism (a focus on the atoning work of Christ), conversionism (an emphasis on personal conversion and individual salvation), and activism (or evangelism). See David W. Bebbington, *Evangelicalism in Modern Britain: A History from the 1730s to the 1980s* (London: Routledge, 1989). Recently, Daniel Silliman has challenged this definition and proposed that evangelicalism is best understood "as a discourse community which is structured by its communication networks." See Daniel Silliman, "An Evangelical Is Anyone Who Likes Billy Graham: Defining Evangelicalism with Carl Henry and Networks of Trust," *Church History* 90, no. 3 (2021): 621–43.

Historian Kate Bowler has offered this definition of post-Scopes American evangelicalism: "Evangelicals are known for their emphasis on scripture, conversion, revivalism, and, later, a subculture that defines their place over and against the wider American culture." Kate Bowler, *The Preacher's Wife: The Precarious Power of Evangelical Women* (Princeton: Princeton University Press, 2019), xv. The most widely accepted definition of "fundamentalism" comes from George M. Marsden, who defines it as a militant anti-modernist "subspecies of evangelicalism" that came into its own during the culture wars of the 1920s and which emphasizes the impending apocalypse and attendant urgent tasks of growing the church and winning souls for Jesus. See George M. Marsden, "Evangelical and Fundamental Christianity," in *The Encyclopedia of Religion*, ed. Mircea Eliade (New York: Macmillan, 1993); George M. Marsden, *Fundamentalism and American Culture* (New York: Oxford University Press, 2006).

63. Grant Wacker, *America's Pastor: Billy Graham and the Shaping of a Nation* (Cambridge: Belknap Press of Harvard University Press, 2014).

64. Darren Dochuk, *From Bible Belt to Sunbelt: Plain-Folk Religion, Grassroots Politics, and the Rise of Evangelical Conservatism* (New York: W.W. Norton, 2012).

65. See Table 7.2, "Market Shares of Religious Denominations per 1,000 Church Members, 1940–2000," in Roger Finke and Rodney Stark, *The Churching of America, 1776–2005: Winners and Losers in Our Religious Economy*, rev. ed. (New Brunswick: Rutgers University Press, 2005), 246. The denominations Finke and Stark include in their "mainline" classification are United Methodists, Presbyterian Church (USA), Episcopal, Christian (Disciples), United Church of Christ (Congregationalists). The "evangelicals" considered in this particular table include Southern Baptists, Church of God in Christ, Assemblies of God, Pentecostal Assemblies of the World, Church of God (Cleveland, TN), and Church of the Nazarene. Finke and Stark note that the membership of LDS and Jehovah's Witnesses denominations likewise saw substantial gains in this period.

66. *Yearbook of American Churches* (New York: National Council of the Churches of Christ in the United States of America, 1959).

67. Bertram Crocker, "Pastoral Aid for the Abnormal," *Crozer Quarterly* 22 (1945): 242.

68. Crocker, "Pastoral Aid," 243.

69. *The People of the State of New York, Respondent, against Bertram Crocker, Appellant*, 272 N.Y.S. 1087 (N.Y. App. Div. 1947).

70. "Former Pastor Furnishes Bail for Grand Jury," *Ogdensburg Journal* (Ogdensburg, NY), Aug. 24, 1946, 8.

71. *The People v. Crocker*, 272 N.Y.S. 1087 at 74–75.

72. *People v. Crocker*, 439–50.

73. *People v. Crocker*, 667.

74. John M. Nichols to Howard Stone Anderson, Dec. 14, 1946, Rockingham Association of Congregational Christian Churches and Ministers, MS052, Box 2, Folder 4, Portsmouth Athenaeum Research Library, Portsmouth, NH (hereafter Rockingham Association, Portsmouth Library).

75. Frederick W. Alden to Oliver C. Northcott, Dec. 18, 1946, MS052, Box 2, Folder 4, Rockingham Association, Portsmouth Library; Kenneth Clinton to the Registrar of the Rockingham Association of Congregational Churches, May 27, 1949, MS052, Box 2, Folder 4, Rockingham Association, Portsmouth Library.

76. "Conviction of Massena Pastor on Morals Charges Reversed, New County Court Trial Ordered," *Ogdensburg Journal* (Ogdensburg, NY), Dec. 24, 1947, 5.

77. "Conviction of Massena Pastor on Morals Charges Reversed, New County Court Trial Ordered," *Ogdensburg Journal* (Ogdensburg, NY), Dec. 24, 1947, 5.

78. Frederick W. Alden to Kenneth Clinton, July 19, 1949, MS052, Box 2, Folder 4, Rockingham Association, Portsmouth Library.

79. "16, Instead of 15, Youth Faces Prison Sentence," *Plattsburgh Press-Republican* (Plattsburgh, NY), Jan. 8, 1948, 3.

80. "State Police Trace Jail Trusty Found in Massena," *Plattsburgh Press-Republican* (Plattsburgh, NY), Feb. 20, 1948, 5; "May, Two Youths, Plead Guilty to Felony Charges," *Plattsburgh Press-Republican* (Plattsburgh, NY), Apr. 29, 1948, 5.

81. "Francis Breyette Rites Will Be Held Tomorrow," *Plattsburgh Press-Republican* (Plattsburgh, NY), Apr. 22, 1952, 5.

82. Kenneth Clinton to the Registrar of the Rockingham Association of Congregational Churches, May 27, 1949, MS052, Box 2, Folder 4, Rockingham Association, Portsmouth Library.
83. Bertram Crocker to Floyd Kinsley, June 9, 1949, MS052, Box 2, Folder 4, Rockingham Association, Portsmouth Library.
84. Bertram Crocker to Floyd Kinsley, June 9, 1949, MS052, Box 2, Folder 4, Rockingham Association, Portsmouth Library.
85. H. George Robertson to Everett A. Babcock, Feb. 15, 1950, MS052, Box 2, Folder 4, Rockingham Association, Portsmouth Library.
86. Bertram Crocker to Floyd Kinsley, Feb. 28, 1951, MS052, Box 2, Folder 4, Rockingham Association, Portsmouth Library.
87. Frederick W. Alden to Floyd Kinsley, Mar. 6, 1951, MS052, Box 2, Folder 4, Rockingham Association, Portsmouth Library.
88. Rockingham Association resolution, n.d., MS052, Box 2, Folder 4, Rockingham Association, Portsmouth Library.
89. "Meeting of Radnor Bethel Congregational Church," Oct. 5, 1951, MS052, Box 2, Folder 4, Rockingham Association, Portsmouth Library.
90. Everett A. Babcock to Floyd Kinsley, Oct. 26, 1951, MS052, Box 2, Folder 4, .
91. "Higher Degrees in Sociology, 1952," *American Journal of Sociology* 59, no. 1 (July 1953): 62.
92. "Membership," *AAUP Bulletin* 44, no. 2 (1958): 533; *Oberlin Alumni Magazine* (Oberlin College, 1959), 23.
93. *Oberlin Alumni Magazine* (Oberlin College, 1959), 23.
94. "PTA Speaker," *Daily Register* (Red Bank, NJ), Mar. 20, 1962, 3.
95. "First Methodist," *Daily Record* (Long Beach, NJ), Sept. 16, 1967, 4.
96. Edgar C. Bundy, *Collectivism in the Churches: A Documented Account of the Political Activities of the Federal, National, and World Council of Churches* (Wheaton: Church League of America, 1958).
97. Edgar C. Bundy to J. Edgar Hoover, Oct. 27, 1958, Federal Bureau of Investigation, "FOIA: Bundy, Edgar C.-Church League of America-HQ-1" file.
98. See, for one of many examples, memo from William C. Sullivan to A. H. Belmont, Mar. 14, 1961, Federal Bureau of Investigation, "FOIA: Bundy, Edgar C.-Church League of America-HQ-1" file.
99. R. W. Smith to William C. Sullivan, May 6, 1963, Federal Bureau of Investigation, "FOIA: Bundy, Edgar C.-Church League of America-HQ-3" file.
100. [Redacted] at Evangelical Covenant Church to [Redacted] in San Diego, California, n.d., Federal Bureau of Investigation, "FOIA: Bundy, Edgar C.-Church League of America-HQ-3" file.
101. Markku Ruotsila, *Fighting Fundamentalist: Carl McIntire and the Politicization of American Fundamentalism* (New York: Oxford University Press, 2016), 127–28, 135.
102. The American Council of Christian Churches and the International Council of Christian Churches were formed in the 1940s to counter the liberal World Council of Churches.
103. Edgar Bundy to [Redacted], June 21, 1954, Federal Bureau of Investigation, "FOIA: Bundy, Edgar C.-Church League of America-HQ-3" file.
104. Edgar C. Bundy to George A. Smathers, May 18, 1964, Federal Bureau of Investigation, "FOIA: Bundy, Edgar C.-Church League of America-HQ-3" file.
105. Note to a letter from J. Edgar Hoover to [Redacted], Sept. 1, 1964, Federal Bureau of Investigation, "FOIA: Bundy, Edgar C.-Church League of America-HQ-3" file.
106. Lerone Martin, "Bureau Clergyman: How the FBI Colluded with an African American Televangelist to Destroy Dr. Martin Luther King, Jr.," *Religion and American Culture* 28, no. 1 (2018): 1–51.
107. Allan J. Lichtman, *White Protestant Nation: The Rise of the American Conservative Movement* (New York: Grove Press, 2008), 198.
108. Ruotsila, *Fighting Fundamentalist*, 280.
109. "Edgar C. Bundy," ReCollections: Retelling Stories from Buswell Library Special Collections, Wheaton College, https://recollections.wheaton.edu/2011/12/edgar-c-bundy/.
110. Sean McCloud, *Making the American Religious Fringe: Exotics, Subversives, and Journalists, 1955–1993* (Chapel Hill: University of North Carolina Press, 2004), 26.
111. As religious studies scholar Megan Goodwin explains, "Allegations of sex abuse facilitate the minoritization of religious outsiders.... These stories relegate domestic and sexual abuse to

the nation's religious margins and manufacture consent for the demonization of American religious and sexual difference." Megan Goodwin, *Abusing Religion: Literary Persecution, Sex Scandals, and American Minority Religions* (New Brunswick: Rutgers University Press, 2020), 14, 15.

112. Kevin M. Lerner, *Provoking the Press: (MORE)Rocking Magazine and the Crisis of Confidence in American Journalism* (Columbia: University of Missouri Press, 2019), 46.

113. For more on the broader phenomenon of the re-emergence of investigative reporting in this area, see James L. Aucoin, "The Re-emergence of American Investigative Journalism 1960–1975," *Journalism History* 21, no. 1 (1995): 3–15.

114. McCloud, *Making the American Religious Fringe*, 136.

115. Herbert J. Gans, *Deciding What's News: A Study of CBS Evening News, NBC Nightly News, Newsweek, and Time*, 2nd ed. (Evanston: Northwestern University Press, 2005), 12, quoted in McCloud, *Making the American Religious Fringe*, 137.

116. Patricia Moy and Michael Pfau, *With Malice toward All? The Media and Public Confidence in Democratic Institutions* (Westport: Praeger, 2000), xiii; Lerner, *Provoking the Press*, 34.

117. Richard Nixon, quoted in "The Nixon Years: Down from the Highest Mountaintop," *Time*, Aug. 19, 1974, 40–51.

118. Katharine Graham, *Personal History* (New York: Vintage, 1998), 508.

119. "Covering Watergate: Success and Backlash," *Time*, July 8, 1974, 68–73.

120. Jimmy Carter, "Energy and National Goals" (speech, July 15, 1979), *The American Presidency Project*, https://www.presidency.ucsb.edu/node/249458.

121. David E. Rosenbaum, "Public Trust in Institutions Found to Decline," *New York Times*, Dec. 3, 1973, 34.

122. For more on the "age of evangelicalism," see Steven Patrick Miller, *The Age of Evangelicalism: America's Born-Again Years* (New York: Oxford University Press, 2014).

Chapter 7

1. Susan Wise Bauer, *The Art of the Public Grovel: Sexual Sin and Public Confession in America* (Princeton: Princeton University Press, 2008).

2. Kenneth L. Woodward and Patricia King, "When a Pastor Turns Seducer (Sexual Misconduct by Clergy)," *Newsweek*, Aug. 28, 1989, 48–49.

3. On the emergence of evangelical networks at the midcentury, see Daniel Silliman, "An Evangelical Is Anyone Who Likes Billy Graham: Defining Evangelicalism with Carl Henry and Networks of Trust," *Church History* 90, no. 3 (2021): 621–43.

4. For an analysis of the role of Focus on the Family's media empire and political influence, see Susan B. Ridgely, "Conservative Christianity and the Creation of Alternative News: An Analysis of Focus on the Family's Multimedia Empire," *Religion and American Culture* 30, no. 1 (2020): 1–25. See also Hilde Løvdal Stephens, *Family Matters: James Dobson and Focus on the Family's Crusade for the Christian Home* (Tuscaloosa: University of Alabama Press, 2019).

5. *Christian Echoes National Ministry, Inc., Plaintiff-appellee, v. United States of America, Defendant-appellant*, 470 F.2d 849 (10th Cir. 1973).

6. Historian R. Laurence Moore has argued that self-proclaimed religious outsiders have been a constant force in American history. "Those who play the role of outsiders," Moore writes, "can wield enormous public influence that the alleged insiders and powerless to block. They can also determine in crucial ways the outlook and behavior of the insiders." R. Laurence Moore, *Religious Outsiders and the Making of Americans* (New York: Oxford University Press, 1986), xiii.

7. Billy James Hargis, *My Great Mistake* (Berryville: New Leaf Press, 1985), 41.

8. For more on sex education wars of the 1960s and 1970s and Hargis's role in them, see R. Marie Griffith, *Moral Combat: How Sex Divided American Christians and Fractured American Politics* (New York: Basic Books, 2017), 155–200.

9. For more on fundamentalist higher education in the twentieth century, see Adam Laats, *Fundamentalist U: Keeping the Faith in American Higher Education* (New York: Oxford University Press, 2018).

10. Hargis, *My Great Mistake*, 80.

11. Hargis, *My Great Mistake*, 88.

12. "The Sins of Billy James," *Time*, Feb. 16, 1976, 68.

13. Billy James Hargis, quoted in "Sins of Billy James," 68.

14. As historian Emily Suzanne Johnson explains, "Bryant popularized many of the religious right's most tenacious arguments against homosexuality including the ideas that gay men 'recruit' children through molestation, that homosexuality is incompatible with family life, and that homosexuality is not a legitimate minority status in part because it is allegedly a preference that can be 'cured.'" Emily Suzanne Johnson, *This Is Our Message: Women's Leadership in the New Christian Right* (New York: Oxford University Press, 2019), 152.

15. Mike Royko, "Minister Knows Wedding Couple," *Chicago Daily News*, reprinted in the *Manhattan Mercury* (Manhattan, KS), Feb. 13, 1976, 4.

16. "Evangelist Blames 'Genes' for His Homosexual Acts," *Daily Leader* (Pontiac, IL), Feb. 11, 1976, 4.

17. "Sins of Billy James," 68. Curiously, the first studies that suggested that there might be a link between homosexuality and genetics would not be conducted until the early 1990s, which makes Hargis's defense of his behavior as biologically predetermined especially surprising for the mid-1970s. See, for example, J. M. Bailey and R. Pillard, "A Genetic Study of Male Homosexual Orientation," *Archives of General Psychiatry* 48 (1991): 1089–96; Dean Hamer and Peter Copeland, *The Science of Desire: The Search for the Gay Gene and the Biology of Behavior* (New York: Simon and Schuster, 1994).

18. For an in-depth study of *Time*'s religion coverage, see Julius (Rex) Gurney, "Religion in the American Century: 'Time' Magazine and the Reporting of Christianity in the United States, 1950–1975" (PhD diss., Presbyterian School of Christian Education, 1999).

19. "Heavyweight Champ," *Time*, Aug. 17, 1962, 71.

20. One study found that sexual morality was the leading issue in religion media coverage between 1969 and 1998. See S. Robert Lichter, Linda S. Lichter, and Daniel R. Amundsen, *Media Coverage of Religion in America, 1969–1998* (Washington, DC: Center for Media and Public Affairs, 2000), 39. Another example of how magazines dealt with religion and sex in this period comes from the coverage of Hargis's fellow fundamentalist Marble Morgan and her bestselling Christian sex advice manual *The Total Woman* (1973). The same year *Time* broke Hargis's scandal, the *Christian Century* featured a review of Morgan's book titled "Fundies and the Fetishes," in which historian Martin Marty quipped that Morgan's typical reader "expects an imminent and literal Second Coming." See Martin E. Marty, "Fundies and the Fetishes," *Christian Century*, Dec. 8, 1976, 1111, quoted in Amy DeRogatis, "What Would Jesus Do? Sexuality and Salvation in Protestant Evangelical Sex Manuals, 1950s to the Present," *Church History* 74, no. 1 (2005): 97–137.

21. Gurney, "Religion in the American Century," 200–212.

22. Henry Grunwald, "An Editorial: The President Should Resign," *Time*, Nov. 12, 1973, 20–21.

23. Henry Grunwald, "Don't Love the Press, but Understand It," *Time*, July 8, 1974, 74–75.

24. Billy James Hargis, quoted in Carol Mason, *Oklahomo: Lessons in Unqueering America* (Albany: SUNY Press, 2015), 106.

25. Hargis, *My Great Mistake*, 89.

26. Hargis, *My Great Mistake*, 108–9.

27. Kirk Johnson, "Church Tries to Cope after Minister's Dismissal," *New York Times*, Nov. 6, 2006, https://www.nytimes.com/2006/11/06/us/06minister.html.

28. *Tomorrow with Tom Snyder*, "Billy James Hargis," National Broadcasting Company, Dec. 27, 1977.

29. For more on these and other organizations, see Amy DeRogatis, *Saving Sex: Sexuality and Salvation in American Evangelicalism* (New York: Oxford University Press, 2014); Johnson, *This Is Our Message*; Sara Moslener, *Virgin Nation: Sexual Purity and American Adolescence* (New York: Oxford University Press, 2015); Stephens, *Family Matters*.

30. Johnson, *This Is Our Message*, 1–2, 147.

31. Kate Bowler, *The Preacher's Wife: The Precarious Power of Evangelical Women Celebrities* (Princeton: Princeton University Press, 2019), 86.

32. Bauer, *Public Grovel*.

33. The most recent book-length account of Jim and Tammy Faye Bakkers' careers and scandals is John Wigger's *PTL: The Rise and Fall of Jim and Tammy Faye Bakker's Evangelical Empire* (New York: Oxford University Press, 2017). For more on Tammy Faye, see Johnson, *This Is Our Message*, 93–120.

34. Wigger, *PTL*, 46–51.

35. For more on the rise of televangelism, see Stewart M. Hoover, *Mass Media Religion: The Social Sources of the Electronic Church* (Newbury Park: Sage, 1988).

36. Although it remains unclear whether actual adultery occurred between Tammy Faye and musician Gary S. Paxton, they developed an intimate relationship over the course of two years. Tammy's counselors would decide that she "had committed adultery in her heart with Paxton and needed to repent." See Wigger, *PTL*, 117–19.

37. See Wigger, *PTL*, 121–24.

38. Tim Funk, "Jessica Hahn, Woman at Center of Televangelist's Fall 30 Years Ago, Confronts Her Past," *Charlotte Observer*, Dec. 17, 2017, a1.

39. "Preacher Claims Plot on Ministry," *Chicago Tribune*, Mar. 24, 1987, 5.

40. Wigger, *PTL*, 261.

41. Jim Bakker, quoted in Wayne King, "Bakker, Evangelist, Resigns His Ministry over Sexual Incident," *New York Times*, Mar. 21, 1987, 1.

42. Emily Suzanne Johnson, "A Theme Park, a Scandal, and the Faded Ruins of a Televangelism Empire," *Religion & Politics*, Oct. 28, 2014, https://religionandpolitics.org/2014/10/28/a-theme-park-a-scandal-and-the-faded-ruins-of-a-televangelism-empire/.

43. Wigger, *PTL*, 274.

44. Art Harris and Michael Isikoff, "The Good Life at PTL: A Litany of Excess," *Washington Post*, May 22, 1987, a1.

45. Assemblies of God, quoted in William E. Schmidt, "For Jim and Tammy Faye Bakker, Excess Wiped Out a Rapid Climb to Success," *New York Times*, May 16, 1987, 8.

46. *Minutes of the Forty-third General Assembly of the Church of God* (Cleveland: Church of God Publishing House, 1950), 231.

47. *Nightline*, American Broadcasting Company, May 27, 1987.

48. Jerry Falwell, "Letter from Jerry Falwell on keeping Old Time Gospel Hour on Air," Aug. 13, 1981, Portal to Texas History, https://texashistory.unt.edu/ark:/67531/metadc177440/.

49. "Tapes Cite 3 Homosexual Acts by Bakker: Falwell Says Church Leaders Received Testimony on Encounters," *Los Angeles Times*, May 28, 1987, 2.

50. "Letters: Bakker Scandal and TV Ministries," *Los Angeles Times*, Mar. 28, 1987, 39.

51. "Jim Bakker's Startling Sentence," *New York Times*, Oct. 29, 1989, 22.

52. Ann Rowe Seaman, *Swaggart: An Unauthorized Biography of an American Evangelist* (New York: Continuum, 1999), 21.

53. Seaman, *Swaggart*, 12.

54. Seaman, *Swaggart*, 329–37.

55. "Religious Broadcasters Adopt Stiffer Ethics Code," *New York Times*, Feb. 4, 1988, 25.

56. Jimmy Swaggart, sermon delivered at the Family Worship Center (Baton Rouge, LA) on Feb. 21, 1988, quoted in Michael J. Giuliano, *Thrice-Born: The Rhetorical Comeback of Jimmy Swaggart* (Macon: Mercer University Press, 1999), 119–23.

57. Swaggart, quoted in Giuliano, *Thrice-Born*, 119–23.

58. Swaggart, quoted in Giuliano, *Thrice-Born*, 119–23.

59. Royal Brightbill, "Swaggart Punished for 'Moral Failure,'" United Press International, Feb. 23, 1988, https://www.upi.com/Archives/1988/02/23/Swaggart-punished-for-moral-failure/1943572590800/.

60. "The Human Comedy," *Los Angeles Times*, Feb. 23, 1988, 29.

61. Judy Mann, "Soap in the Bible Belt," *Washington Post*, Feb. 24, 1988, b3.

62. Steven Hunt, quoted in Michael Granberry, "Ministers Grieve, Worry over Swaggart Scandal," *Los Angeles Times*, Feb. 24, 1988, 42.

63. Daniel Paul Matthews, quoted in Laura Landro, "As Evangelists Fade on Cable TV, Mainline Churches Claim the Air," *Wall Street Journal*, Mar. 9, 1988, 32.

64. Falwell's son, Jerry Falwell Jr., would inherit his father's evangelical empire—and the presidency of the fundamentalist Liberty University—only to be forced to resign after a scandal of his own in 2020. See, for example, Gabriel Sherman, "Inside Jerry Falwell Jr.'s Unlikely Rise and Precipitous Fall at Liberty University," *Vanity Fair*, Jan. 24, 2022, https://www.vanityfair.com/news/2022/01/inside-jerry-falwell-jr-unlikely-rise-and-precipitous-fall.

65. "Preacher Scandals Strengthen TV Evangelism, Falwell Says," *Washington Post*, Mar. 19, 1988, https://www.washingtonpost.com/archive/local/1988/03/19/preacher-scandals-strengthen-tv-evangelism-falwell-says/6230c3d5-8c43-4f20-a447-b5bacd32198b/.

66. Jimmy Swaggart, quoted in "Swaggart Defrocked, Resigns from Church," *Chicago Tribune*, Apr. 9, 1988, 1.

67. Jimmy Swaggart, "Comeback Sermon," quoted in Giuliano, *Thrice-Born*, 124–35.

68. "Televangelist Stopped for Erratic Driving in Indio," United Press International, Oct. 11, 1991.
69. "Swaggart Claims Visit by God in Wake of a 2nd Sex Scandal," *Chicago Tribune*, Oct. 18, 1991, 4.
70. Kevin Spacey, who portrayed the disgraced Jim Bakker, would face a scandal of his own in 2017. Actor Anthony Rapp accused Spacey of making sexual advances toward him when Rapp was still a teenager. Presumably in an attempt to redeem his reputation, Spacey, who had been suspected of being gay, came out on the same day as Rapp's charges became public. In May 2022, Spacey was criminally charged with four counts of sexual assault against three different men in the UK.
71. Judy Mann, "But Disgrace Does Pay," *Washington Post*, Feb. 26, 1988, https://www.washingtonpost.com/archive/local/1988/02/26/but-disgrace-does-pay/db8e2edc-19dc-4705-8f36-a18d6d99d810/.
72. "Jim Bakker's Startling Sentence," *New York Times*, Oct. 29, 1989, 22.
73. "The Flap over PTL: A Necessary Evil for Televangelism," *San Bernardino County Sun*, July 12, 1987, 45.
74. David P. Fan, Robert O. Wyatt, and Kathy Keltner, "The Suicidal Messenger: How Press Reporting Affects Public Confidence in the Press, the Military, and Organized Religion," *Communication Research* 28, no. 6 (2001): 826–52.
75. Leslie Dorrough Smith makes a similar argument about modern political sex scandals and the public's willingness to forgive their leaders as long as Americans values get reaffirmed in the process of discovery, forgiveness, and reconciliation. See Leslie Dorrough Smith, *Compromising Positions: Sex Scandals, Politics, and American Christianity* (New York: Oxford University Press, 2019).
76. Jim Bakker, *I Was Wrong* (Nashville: Thomas Nelson, 1996), 461.
77. Mann, "But Disgrace Does Pay."

Epilogue

1. "Haggard Says He Is 'Completely Heterosexual,'" *Denver Post*, Feb. 5, 2007, https://www.denverpost.com/2007/02/05/haggard-says-he-is-completely-heterosexual/.
2. Roy Zimmerman, "Ted Haggard Is Completely Heterosexual," YouTube, Apr. 6, 2007, https://youtu.be/HZmHC75FDqQ.
3. "Ted and Gayle Haggard," *The Oprah Winfrey Show*, Jan. 28, 2009, YouTube, https://www.youtube.com/watch?v=aWrrNttIMq4.
4. Kevin Roose, "The Last Temptation of Ted," *GQ*, Jan. 26, 2011, https://www.gq.com/story/pastor-ted-haggard.
5. Ted Haggard, "Crisis Facts," tedhaggard.com, https://web.archive.org/web/20230325081920/https://tedhaggard.com/crisis-facts/.
6. Debbie Kelley, "Powerhouse Preacher Ted Haggard Faces New Allegations of Illicit Behavior," *Denver Gazette*, July 24, 2022, https://denvergazette.com/premium/powerhouse-preacher-ted-haggard-faces-new-allegations-of-illicit-behavior/article_dfdd394b-185c-5345-8f4e-b5ae80aa3d36.html.
7. Ted Haggard, quoted in Debbie Kelley, "Powerhouse Preacher."
8. As historian Sara Moslener demonstrates, Protestants have long used the rhetoric of sexual purity to assert their political power as they "employed theories of rise and decline in order to position sexual purity and its purveyor, Protestant evangelicalism, as the salvation of civilization." Sara Moslener, *Virgin Nation: Sexual Purity and American Adolescence* (New York: Oxford University Press, 2015), 5.
9. Robert Downen, Lise Olsen, and John Tedesco, "Abuse of Faith," *Houston Chronicle*, Feb. 10, 2019, https://www.houstonchronicle.com/news/investigations/article/Southern-Baptist-sexual-abuse-spreads-as-leaders-13588038.php.
10. Guidepost Solutions, "Report of the Independent Investigation: The Southern Baptist Convention Executive Committee's Response to Sexual Abuse Allegations and an Audit of the Procedures and Actions of the Credentials Committee," May 15, 2022, https://www.documentcloud.org/documents/22028383-guidepost-investigation-of-the-southern-baptist-convention.
11. White evangelicals," writes historian Kristin Kobes Du Mez, "are significantly more authoritarian than other religious groups, and they express confidence in their religious leaders at much higher rates than do members of other faiths." Kristin Kobes Du Mez, *Jesus and John Wayne: How White Evangelicals Corrupted a Faith and Fractured a Nation* (New York: Liveright, 2020), 4.

12. Daniel Silliman, "Sexual Harassment Went Unchecked at Christianity Today," *Christianity Today*, Mar. 15, 2022, https://www.christianitytoday.com/news/2022/march/sexual-harassment-ct-guidepost-assessment-galli-olawoye.html; Becca Andrews, "They Went to Bible College to Deepen Their Faith. Then They Were Assaulted—and Blamed for It," *Mother Jones*, Sept. 30, 2021, https://www.motherjones.com/politics/2021/09/moody-bible-institute-purity-culture-evangelicalism-sexual-assault-title-ix-mbi-survivors-group/?src=longreads; Hannah Dreyfus, "'The Liberty Way': How Liberty University Discourages and Dismisses Students' Reports of Sexual Assaults," *ProPublica*, Oct. 24, 2021, https://www.propublica.org/article/the-liberty-way-how-liberty-university-discourages-and-dismisses-students-reports-of-sexual-assaults.

13. "New Reports of Misspending by Baptist Leader," *New York Times*, Aug. 28, 1997, 25.

14. "Ousted Baptist Leader Loses Bid," *New York Times*, Sept. 11, 2009, https://www.nytimes.com/2009/09/11/us/11brfs-OUSTEDBAPTIS_BRF.html.

15. Steve Osunsami and Sarah Netter, "Bishop Eddie Long Accused of Sex Abuse by 4th Alleged Victim," *ABC News*, Sept. 22, 2010, https://abcnews.go.com/US/bishop-eddie-long-accused-sex-abuse-fourth-alleged/story?id=11721548.

16. Kim Severson and Robbie Brown, "Charismatic Church Leader, Dogged by Scandal, to Stop Preaching for Now," *New York Times*, Dec. 4, 2011, https://www.nytimes.com/2011/12/05/us/eddie-long-beleaguered-church-leader-to-stop-preaching.html.

17. John Jay College of Criminal Justice, *The Nature and Scope of Sexual Abuse of Minors by Catholic Priests and Deacons in the United States, 1950–2002* (New York: John Jay College of Criminal Justice, 2004), https://www.usccb.org/sites/default/files/issues-and-action/child-and-youth-protection/upload/The-Nature-and-Scope-of-Sexual-Abuse-of-Minors-by-Catholic-Priests-and-Deacons-in-the-United-States-1950-2002.pdf.

18. Andrew S. Denney, Kent R. Kerley, and Nickolas G. Gross, "Child Sexual Abuse in Protestant Christian Congregations: A Descriptive Analysis of Offense and Offender Characteristics," *Religions* 9, no. 1 (2018): 1–13.

19. Megan Goodwin, *Abusing Religion: Literary Persecution, Sex Scandals, and American Minority Religions* (New Brunswick: Rutgers University Press, 2020).

20. Eliza Griswold, "Silence Is Not Spiritual: The Evangelical #MeToo Movement," *New Yorker*, June 15, 2018, https://www.newyorker.com/news/on-religion/silence-is-not-spiritual-the-evangelical-metoo-movement; Emily Joy Allison, *#ChurchToo: How Purity Culture Upholds Abuse and How to Find Healing* (Minneapolis: Broadleaf Books, 2021).

21. As Kaya Oakes explains, "Unlike the Catholic Church, where abuse cases must at least theoretically be reported to central bodies like diocesan offices, evangelical churches have no center of power akin to Rome and there is often no one like a bishop supervising the behavior of pastors." Kaya Oakes, "*Christianity Today*'s Sexual Misconduct Problem and the Complications with Forgiving Institutions," *The Revealer*, May 10, 2022, https://therevealer.org/christianity-todays-sexual-misconduct-problem-and-the-complications-with-forgiving-institutions/.

22. Josiah Hesse, "Billy Graham's Grandson Says Protestants Abuse Kids Just Like Catholics," *Vice*, Aug. 24, 2017, https://www.vice.com/en_us/article/xwwd3w/billy-grahams-grandson-says-protestants-abuse-kids-just-like-catholics.

23. FaithTrust Institute, "About," https://www.faithtrustinstitute.org/about-us.

24. Yonat Shimron, "Tullian Tchividjian Is Back after Sex Scandal, but Should He Be?," *Religion News Service*, Sept. 4, 2019, https://religionnews.com/2019/09/04/tullian-tchividjian-is-back-after-sex-scandal-but-should-he-be/.

25. Megan Goodwin, "Abuse Happens Because We Let It," *Sojourners*, Jul. 7, 2020, https://sojo.net/articles/abuse-happens-because-let-it-Menlo-Park-John-Ortberg-Lavery.

Bibliography

Primary Sources

Manuscript Sources

American Antiquarian Society
  Bowen Family Papers 1847–1934
  "'The Beecher Scandal!' Sung by Dick Brown." Broadside.
  The Thunderbolt
Bible Institute of Los Angeles Archives
  Fundamental Letters (beginning—June 1, 1911)
Billy Graham Center Archives
  Papers of Melvin Ernest Trotter (Collection 47)
Brooklyn Historical Society
  New York City Congregational Church Association ecclesiastical council minutes
  Plymouth Church of the Pilgrims and Henry Ward Beecher collection, 1819–1980
Foursquare Heritage Archives
  Aimee Semple McPherson interview on WJR radio in Detroit, Oct. 28, 1933
  Foursquare Crusader
Mississippi State University Libraries
  Charles H. Templeton, Sr. sheet music collection
Moody Bible Institute
  Biographical Collection of the Moody Bible Institute
  Microfilm collection of student records
  Minutes, Reports, Records, & Plans of MBI, MIS, & BICA
New-York Historical Society
  Brooklyn, NY, newspaper cuttings, 1877–86: scrapbook, 1858–87
  Frey Family Papers
  Henry Ward Beecher Papers, 1854–87
New York Public Library
  Papers relating to the trial, Tilton vs. Beecher
  Theodore Tilton correspondence and misc.
Portsmouth Athenaeum Research Library
  Rockingham Association of Congregational Christian Churches and Ministers
University of Rochester Special Collections
  Isabella Beecher Hooker
Yale University Library Manuscripts and Archives
  Bacon Family Papers
  Beecher Family Papers

Newspapers and Magazines

ABC News
Albany Democrat
Alton Evening Telegraph
American Mercury
Atlanta Constitution
Baltimore Evening Sun

Bayard News
The Bee
Bismarck Weekly Tribune
Blue-grass Blade
Bolivar Bulletin
Boston Globe
Boston Investigator
Bridal Call Foursquare
Brooklyn Daily Eagle
Buffalo Commercial
Buffalo Enquirer
Carroll County Democrat
Central New Jersey Home News
Charlotte Observer
Chicago Commerce
Chicago Daily Tribune
Chicago Defender
Chicago Tribune
Christian Advocate and Journal and Zion's Herald
Christian Century
Christian Intelligencer
Christian Journal
Christian Union
Christianity Today
Cincinnati Enquirer
Clarion and Tennessee State Gazette
Columbus Daily Enquirer
The Congregationalist
Daily Graphic
Daily Times
Daily World
Day Book
Denver Gazette
Detroit Free Press
Detroit News
Dixon Evening Telegraph
East Oregonian
Eau Claire Leader
Ebony
Emporia Gazette
Episcopal Watchman
Evening World
Forum
Frank Leslie's Illustrated Newspaper
Frederick Douglass' Paper
Free Enquirer
Galaxy
Galveston Daily News
Globe Gazette
The Graphic
Great Falls Tribune
Greensboro Daily News
GQ

Haldeman-Julius Monthly
Harper's Magazine
Herald of Universal Salvation
Herald-Palladium
Holbrook News
Houston Chronicle
Independence Daily Reporter
The Independent
Indianapolis News
Institute Tie
Inter Ocean
Issues and Events
Kansas City Gazette
Lansing State Journal
The Liberator
Lincoln Journal Star
Logansport Pharos-Tribune
Long-Island Farmer
Long-Island Star
Los Angeles Times
Manhattan Mercury
Minneapolis Daily Tribune
Modesto News-Herald
Morning Astorian
Morning News
Mother Jones
Munsey's Magazine
The Nation
Nebraska State Journal
Ness County News
New York Courier and Enquirer
New York Evangelist
New York Herald
New Republic
Newsweek
New York Sun
New York Times
New York World
New York World Telegram & Sun
New Yorker
New-York Tribune
Oakland Tribune
The Outlook
Owensboro Messenger
Pawtucket Chronicle
Philadelphia Day
Philadelphia Inquirer
Pittsburgh Daily Post
Pittsburgh Gazette
Pittsburgh Press
ProPublica
Providence Journal
Public Ledger

Quad-City Times
Religion News Service
Republican Banner
The Revealer
Rhode Island American
Rhode Island Republican
Saint Paul Globe
Salt Lake Herald
San Bernardino County Sun
San Francisco Chronicle
Santa Ana Register
Santa Cruz Evening News
Sedalia Weekly Democrat
Semi-Weekly Wisconsin
The Sheboygan Press
Sojourners
St. Louis Post-Dispatch
St. Louis Star and Times
St. Paul Daily Globe
Star Press
Stark County Democrat
The Thunderbolt
Time
The Tribune
Trumpet and Universalist Magazine
Universalist Watchman, Repository and Chronicle
Vanity Fair
Vermont Christian Messenger
Vice
Wall Street Journal
Washington Post
Washington Union
Western Luminary
Wichita Beacon
Wichita Daily Eagle
Woodhull and Claflin's Weekly
Workingman's Advocate

Other Primary Sources

Allison, Emily Joy. #ChurchToo: How Purity Culture Upholds Abuse and How to Find Healing. Minneapolis: Broadleaf Books, 2021.

A Vindication of the Result of the Trial of Rev. Ephraim K. Avery; To Which Is Prefixed His Statement of Facts Relative to the Circumstances by Which He Became Involved in the Prosecution. Boston: Russell, Odiorne, 1834.

Abbott, Austin. Official Report of the Trial of Henry Ward Beecher. New York: G.W. Smith, 1875.

Abbott, Lyman, ed. The Sermons of Henry Ward Beecher: In Plymouth Church, Brooklyn, vol. 1. New York: Harper & Brothers, 1869.

Abstract of the Eleventh Census: 1890. Washington, DC: Government Printing Office, 1896.

Adamic, Louis, ed. The Truth about Aimee Semple McPherson: A Symposium. Girard: Haldeman-Julius, 1926.

Alleged Immoral Conditions at Newport (R.I.) Naval Training Station: Report of the Committee on Naval Affairs, United States Senate, Sixty-Seventh Congress, First Session Relative to Alleged Immoral Conditions and Practices at the Naval Training Station, Newport, R.I. Washington, DC: Government Printing Office, 1921.

The American Almanac and Repository of Useful Knowledge for the Year 1835. Boston: Charles Bowen, 1835.

Anderson, Leith. "The Night Ted Haggard Made the News." National Association of Evangelicals. June 21, 2021.

Aristides. *Strictures on the Case of Ephraim K. Avery: Originally Published in the Republican Herald, Providence, R. I. With Corrections, Revisions and Additions.* Providence: William Simons Jr.—Herald Office, 1833.

Bailey, J. M., and R. Pillard. "A Genetic Study of Male Homosexual Orientation." *Archives of General Psychiatry* 48 (1991): 1089–96.

Bakker, Jim, and Ken Abraham. *I Was Wrong: The Untold Story of the Shocking Journey from PTL Power to Prison and Beyond.* Nashville: Thomas Nelson, 1996.

The Beecher Trial: A Review of the Evidence; Reprinted from the New York Times of July 3, 1875; with Some Revisions and Additions. New York: Nabu Press, 1875.

Billings, M. E. *The Crimes of Preachers in the United States and Canada.* 10th ed. New York: Truth Seeker, 1914.

Black, Janet M. *Colorado Christian University: The First 100 Years.* Lakewood: Colorado Christian University, 2014.

Blackstone, William. *Commentaries on the Laws of England, Book 1.* Oxford: Clarendon Press, 1765, 430.

Blatch, Harriot Stanton, and Theodore Stanton, eds. *Elizabeth Cady Stanton, as Revealed in Her Letters, Diary and Reminiscences.* New York: Harper & Brothers, 1922.

Bundy, Edgar C. *Collectivism in the Churches: A Documented Account of the Political Activities of the Federal, National, and World Council of Churches.* Wheaton: Church League of America, 1958.

Carter, Jimmy. "Energy and National Goals." July 15, 1979, *The American Presidency Project.* https://www.presidency.ucsb.edu/node/249458.

Cavender, Curtis H. *Catalogue of Works in Refutation of Methodism: From Its Origin in 1729, to the Present Time.* Philadelphia: John Penington, 1846.

Chronicles from the Nineteenth Century: Family Letters of Blanche Butler and Adelbert Ames Married July 21st, 1870. Clinton: [privately published], 1957.

Clarke, M. *Sarah Maria Cornell, or The Fall River Murder, a Domestic Drama in Three Acts.* New York: No. 5 Chatham Square, 1833.

Cox, Raymond L. *The Verdict Is In.* Los Angeles: Heritage Foundation, 1983.

Doyle, J. E. P. *Plymouth Church and Its Pastor, or Henry Ward Beecher and His Accusers.* St. Louis: Bryant, Brand, 1875.

Drury, Luke. *A Report of The Examination of Rev. Ephraim K. Avery, Charged with the Murder of Sarah Maria Cornell.* Rhode Island, 1833.

Drysdale, William, ed. *Proverbs from Plymouth Pulpit.* New York: D. Appleton, 1887.

Gillespie, Emily Hawley. *A Secret to Be Buried: The Diary and Life of Emily Hawley Gillespie, 1858–1888.* Iowa City: University of Iowa Press, 1989.

Graham, Billy. *Just As I Am: The Autobiography of Billy Graham.* Grand Rapids: Zondervan, 2007.

Graham, Katharine. *Personal History.* New York: Vintage, 1998.

Guidepost Solutions. "Report of the Independent Investigation: The Southern Baptist Convention Executive Committee's Response to Sexual Abuse Allegations and an Audit of the Procedures and Actions of the Credentials Committee." May 15, 2022.

Haggard, Gayle, and Angela Elwell Hunt. *Why I Stayed: The Choices I Made in My Darkest Hour.* Carol Stream: Tyndale House, 2010.

Hallett, Benjamin Franklin. *Trial of Rev. Mr. Avery: A Full Report of the Trial of Ephraim K. Avery, Charged with the Murder of Sarah Maria Cornell: Before the Supreme Court of Rhode Island, at a Special Term in Newport, Held in May, 1833.* Boston: Daily Commercial Gazette, 1833.

Hargis, Billy James. *My Great Mistake.* Berryville: New Leaf Press, 1985.

John Jay College of Criminal Justice. *The Nature and Scope of Sexual Abuse of Minors by Catholic Priests and Deacons in the United States, 1950–2002.* New York: John Jay College of Criminal Justice, 2004.

Journal of the One Hundred and Twenty-Ninth Annual Session of the Rhode Island Episcopal Convention. Providence: Providence Press, Snow & Farnham, 1919.

Lewis, Sinclair. *Elmer Gantry.* London: Jonathan Cape, 1930.

Lynd, Robert Staughton, and Helen Merrell Lynd. *Middletown: A Study in Contemporary American Culture.* New York: Harcourt, Brace, 1929.

Marble, Manton. *Freedom of the Press Wantonly Violated: Letter of Mr. Marble to President Lincoln, Reappearance of the Journal of Commerce, Opinions of the Press on This Outrage.* New York: Society for the Diffusion of Political Knowledge, 1864.

Marshall, Charles F. *The True History of the Brooklyn Scandal: Being a Complete Account of the Trial of the Rev. Henry Ward Beecher, of Plymouth Church, Brooklyn, Upon Charges Preferred by Theodore Tilton, Including All the Original Letters, Documents and Private Correspondence, with Biographies of the Leading Actors in the Great Drama. Containing Also the Full Statements of Moulton, Beecher, and Tilton, and Many Additional Facts, Private Letters, Etc., Never Before Published.* Philadelphia: National Publishing Company, 1874.

McKee, Ruth K., ed. *Mary Richardson Walker: Her Book.* Caldwell: Caxton Printers, 1945.

McPherson, Aimee Semple. *This Is That: Personal Experiences, Sermons and Writings of Aimee Semple McPherson, Evangelist.* Los Angeles: Bridal Call Publishing House, 1919.

Melvill, David. *A Fac-Simile of the Letters Produced at the Trial of the Rev. Ephraim K. Avery, on an Indictment for the Murder of Sarah Maria Cornell: Taken with Great Care, by Permission of the Hon. Supreme Judicial Court of Rhode Island from the Original Letters in the Office of the Clerk of Said Court.* Boston: Pendleton's Lithography, 1833.

Messages of the Men and Religion Movement. New York: Association Press, 1912.

Minutes of the Forty-Third General Assembly of the Church of God. Cleveland: Church of God Publishing House, 1950.

Nightline. American Broadcasting Company. May 27, 1987.

Nolte Lensink, Judy, ed. *A Secret to Be Buried: The Diary and Life of Emily Hawley Gillespie, 1858–1888.* Iowa City: University of Iowa Press, 1989.

Oliver, Leon. *The Great Sensation: A Full, Complete and Reliable History of the Beecher-Tilton-Woodhull Scandal, with Biographical Sketches of the Principal Characters . . . Also a Clear and Concise Statement of the Views of "The Woodhull" Upon Social Reform, Free Love, Etc., Etc.* Chicago: Beverly Company, 1873.

Original Broadway Cast & Male Ensemble. "Hollywood Aimee." *Scandalous, the Musical.* Shout! Broadway (2013), MP3.

"The Penal Code of New York." *Albany Law Journal* 1 (Jan.–July 1870): 177.

Powell, A. Clayton, Sr. *Against the Tide: An Autobiography.* New York: Richard R. Smith, 1938.

Reisner, Christian F. *Church Publicity: The Modern Way to Compel Them to Come In.* New York: Methodist Book Concern, 1913.

Report of the Trial of Ammi Rogers, for a High Crime and Misdemeanor, in a Brutal and High Handed Assault on Asenath Caroline Smith, of Griswold, Con. Before the Hon. Asa Chapman of the Supreme Court of Connecticut. New London: Samuel Green, 1820.

Rogers, Ammi. *Memoirs of the Rev. Ammi Rogers, A. M.* 2nd ed. Schenectady: G. Ritchie, 1826.

Sherman, Eleazer. *The Narrative of Eleazer Sherman, Giving an Account of His Life, Experience, Call to the Ministry of the Gospel, and Travels as Such to the Present Time.* Providence: H.H. Brown, 1832.

Shuler, Robert Pierce. *McPhersonism: A Study of Healing Cults and Modern Day "Tongues" Movements Containing Summary of Facts as to Disappearance and Re-appearance of Aimee Semple McPherson.* Los Angeles: Bob Shuler, 1924.

Smith, Herbert Heebner. *Publicity and Progress: Twentieth Century Methods in Religious, Educational and Social Activities.* New York: George H. Doran, 1915.

Stanton Blatch, Harriot and Theodore Stanton, eds. *Elizabeth Cady Stanton, as Revealed in Her Letters, Diary and Reminiscences.* Vol. 2. New York: Harper & Brothers, 1922.

Theodore Tilton vs. Henry Ward Beecher: Action for Crim. Con. Tried in the City Court of Brooklyn, Chief Justice Joseph Neilson, Presiding. New York: McDivitt, Campbell, 1875.

Thompson, Noyes L. *The History of Plymouth Church.* New York: G. W. Carleton, 1873.

Tomorrow Coast to Coast. "Billy James Hargis." National Broadcasting Company. Dec. 27, 1977.

Trial of Elder Eleazer Sherman before an Ecclesiastical Council Held at the Meeting-House of the Christian Society in Providence, July 20 and 21, 1835. Providence: H.H. Brown, 1835.

Trial of the Rev. John Robert McDowall by the Presbytery of New York, in February, March, and April, 1836, in the Session Room of the Bleeker-Street Presbyterian Church. New York, 1836.

Trollope, Anthony. *The Letters of Anthony Trollope.* Edited by N. John Hall. Stanford: Stanford University Press, 1983.

Walker, Mary Richardson. *Mary Richardson Walker: Her Book.* Caldwell: Caxton Printers, 1945.

Williams, Catherine Read. *Fall River: An Authentic Narrative.* Providence: Marshall, Brown, 1834.

Williamson, Francis P. *Beecher and His Accusers: A Complete History of the Great Controversy.* Philadelphia: Flint, 1874.

Wilmer, Lambert A. *Our Press Gang; or, A Complete Exposition of the Corruptions and Crimes of the American Newspapers.* Philadelphia: J.T. Lloyd, 1859.

Woodhull, Victoria. *"And the Truth Shall Make You Free": A Speech on the Principles of Social Freedom, Delivered in Steinway Hall, Nov. 20, 1871.* New York: Woodhull, Claflin, 1871.

Yearbook of American Churches. New York: National Council of the Churches of Christ in the United States of America, 1959.

Secondary Sources

Articles

Adut, Ari. "A Theory of Scandal: Victorians, Homosexuality, and the Fall of Oscar Wilde." *American Journal of Sociology* 111, no. 1 (2005): 213–48.

Aucoin, James L. "The Re-emergence of American Investigative Journalism 1960–1975." *Journalism History* 21, no. 1 (1995): 3–15.

Barfoot, Charles H., and Gerald T. Sheppard. "Prophetic vs. Priestly Religion: The Changing Role of Women Clergy in Classical Pentecostal Churches." *Review of Religious Research* 22, no. 1 (1980): 2–17.

Bederman, Gail. "'The Women Have Had Charge of the Church Work Long Enough': The Men and Religion Forward Movement of 1911–1912 and the Masculinization of Middle-Class Protestantism." *American Quarterly* 41, no. 3 (1989): 432–65.

Best, Wallace. "Lessons from the Rev. Eddie Long Scandal: Some Historical Context." *Huffington Post*, Oct. 2, 2010.

Boudreau, Kristin. "The Scarlet Letter and the 1833 Murder Trial of the Reverend Ephraim Avery." *ESQ: A Journal of the American Renaissance* 47, no. 2 (2001): 89–112.

Buckner Inniss, Lolita. "Abortion Law as Protection Narrative." *Oregon Law Review* 101, no. 2 (2023): 213–55.

Carlson, A. Cheree. "The Role of Character in Public Moral Argument: Henry Ward Beecher and the Brooklyn Scandal." *Quarterly Journal of Speech* 77, no. 1 (1991): 38–52.

Chauncey, George. "Christian Brotherhood or Sexual Perversion? Homosexual Identities and the Construction of Sexual Boundaries in the World War One Era." *Journal of Social History* 19, no. 2 (1985): 189–211.

Cott, Nancy F. "Passionlessness: An Interpretation of Victorian Sexual Ideology, 1790–1850." *Signs* 4, no. 2 (1978): 219–36.

Denney, Andrew S., Kent R. Kerley, and Nickolas G. Gross. "Child Sexual Abuse in Protestant Christian Congregations: A Descriptive Analysis of Offense and Offender Characteristics." *Religions* 9, no. 1 (2018): 1–13.

DeRogatis, Amy. "What Would Jesus Do? Sexuality and Salvation in Protestant Evangelical Sex Manuals, 1950s to the Present." *Church History* 74, no. 1 (2005): 97–137.

DiFabio, Anne. "Thomas Nast Takes Down Tammany: A Cartoonist's Crusade against a Political Boss." *Museum of the City of New York* (blog), Sept. 24, 2013.

Dorsey, Bruce. "'Making Men What They Should Be': Male Same-Sex Intimacy and Evangelical Religion in Early Nineteenth-Century New England." *Journal of the History of Sexuality* 24, no. 3 (2015): 345–77.

Fan, David P., Robert O. Wyatt, and Kathy Keltner. "The Suicidal Messenger: How Press Reporting Affects Public Confidence in the Press, the Military, and Organized Religion." *Communication Research* 28, no. 6 (2001): 826–52.

Ferré, John P. "Protestant Press Relations in the United States, 1900–1930." *Church History* 62, no. 4 (1993): 514–27.

Francke, Warren. "Sensationalism and the Development of 19th-Century Reporting: The Broom Sweeps Sensory Details." *Journalism History* 12, no. 3 (1985): 80–85.

Friedman, Lawrence M. "Crimes of Mobility." *Stanford Law Review* 43, no. 3 (1991): 637–58.

Gallon, Kim. "Silences Kept: The Absence of Gender and Sexuality in Black Press Historiography." *History Compass* 10, no. 2 (2012): 207–18.

Gamson, Joshua. "Normal Sins: Sex Scandal Narratives as Institutional Morality Tales." *Social Problems* 48, no. 2 (2001): 185–205.

Grasso, Christopher. "Skepticism and American Faith: Infidels, Converts, and Religious Doubt in the Early Nineteenth Century." *Journal of the Early Republic* 22, no. 3 (2002): 465–508.

Hartog, Hendrik A. "Marital Exits and Marital Expectations in Nineteenth Century America." *Georgetown Law Journal* 80, no. 95 (1991): 95–129.

Hatch, Nathan O. "The Puzzle of American Methodism." *Church History* 63, no. 2 (1994): 175–89.

Hemphill, Katie M. "'Pastor Was Trapped': Queer Scandal and Contestations over Christian Anti-vice Reform." *Journal of the Gilded Age and Progressive Era* 21, no. 4 (2022): 1–16.

Horowitz, Helen Lefkowitz. "Victoria Woodhull, Anthony Comstock, and Conflict over Sex in the United States in the 1870s." *Journal of American History* 87, no. 2 (2000): 403–34.

Johnson, Emily Suzanne. "A Theme Park, a Scandal, and the Faded Ruins of a Televangelism Empire." *Religion & Politics* (blog), October 28, 2014.

Kerber, Linda. "The Republican Mother: Women and the Enlightenment—an American Perspective." *American Quarterly* 28, no. 2 (1976): 187–205.

Korobkin, Laura Hanft. "The Maintenance of Mutual Confidence: Sentimental Strategies at the Adultery Trial of Henry Ward Beecher." *Yale Journal of Law & the Humanities* 7, no. 1 (1995): 1–48.

Lofton, Kathryn. "Commonly Modern: Rethinking the Modernist-Fundamentalist Controversies." *Church History* 83, no. 1 (2014): 137–44.

Lofton, Kathryn. "Queering Fundamentalism: John Balcom Shaw and the Sexuality of a Protestant Orthodoxy." *Journal of the History of Sexuality* 17, no. 3 (2008): 439–68.

Maddux, Kristy. "The Feminized Gospel: Aimee Semple McPherson and the Gendered Performance of Christianity." *Women's Studies in Communication* 35, no. 1 (2012): 42–67.

Martin, Lerone. "Bureau Clergyman: How the FBI Colluded with an African American Televangelist to Destroy Dr. Martin Luther King, Jr." *Religion and American Culture* 28, no. 1 (2018): 1–51.

McLoughlin, William G. "Untangling the Tiverton Tragedy: The Social Meaning of the Terrible Haystack Murder of 1833." *Journal of American Culture* 7, no. 4 (1984): 75–84.

Mills, Jennifer L. "Charles M. Sheldon and Charles F. Parham: Adapting Christianity to the Challenges of the American West." *Kansas History: A Journal of the Central Plains* 32, no. 2 (2009): 106–23.

Pilarczyk, Ian C. "The Terrible Haystack Murder: The Moral Paradox of Hypocrisy, Prudery and Piety in Antebellum America." *American Journal of Legal History* 41, no. 1 (1997): 25–60.

Putz, Paul Emory. "Commercializing the Sacred Office: Sexual Revolution and the Scandal of the Modern Marrying Parson, 1895–1930." *Journal of the Gilded Age and Progressive Era* 17, no. 1 (2018): 56–76.

Retzloff, Tim. "'Seer or Queer?' Postwar Fascination with Detroit's Prophet Jones." *GLQ: A Journal of Lesbian and Gay Studies* 8, no. 3 (2002): 271–96.

Rich, Adrienne. "Compulsory Heterosexuality and Lesbian Existence." *Signs* 5, no. 4 (1980): 631–60.

Ridgely, Susan B. "Conservative Christianity and the Creation of Alternative News: An Analysis of Focus on the Family's Multimedia Empire." *Religion and American Culture* 30, no. 1 (2020): 1–25.

Roberts, M. J. D. "Evangelicalism and Scandal in Victorian England: The Case of the Pearsall Smiths." *History* 95, no. 320 (2010): 437–57.

Saxton, Alexander. "Problems of Class and Race in the Origins of the Mass Circulation Press." *American Quarterly* 36, no. 2 (1984): 211–34.

Selig, Barbara. "Kathryn Johanna Kuhlman (May 9, 1907–February 20, 1976)." *German Life; La Vale* 21, no. 4 (2014): 56.

Silliman, Daniel. "An Evangelical Is Anyone Who Likes Billy Graham: Defining Evangelicalism with Carl Henry and Networks of Trust." *Church History* 90, no. 3 (2021): 621–43.

Smith, Tom W. "Poll Trends: Religious Beliefs and Behaviors and the Televangelist Scandals of 1987–1988." *Public Opinion Quarterly* 56, no. 3 (1992): 360–80.

Soderlund, Gretchen. "Evangelical Christian Crisis Responses to Same-Sex Sex Scandals." *Journal of Media and Religion* 17, no. 1 (2018): 28–40.

Spaulding, Cylor. "Evangelical Christian Crisis Responses to Same-Sex Sex Scandals." *Journal of Media and Religion* 17, no. 1 (2018): 28–40.

Sutton, Matthew A. "'Between the Refrigerator and the Wildfire': Aimee Semple McPherson, Pentecostalism, and the Fundamentalist-Modernist Controversy." *Church History* 72, no. 1 (2003): 159–88.

Sutton, Matthew A. "New Trends in the Historiography of American Fundamentalism." *Journal of American Studies* 51, no. 1 (2017): 235–41.

Welsh, Peter C. "Henry R. Robinson: Printmaker to the Whig Party." *New York History* 53, no. 1 (1972): 25–53.

Welter, Barbara. "The Cult of True Womanhood: 1820–1860." *American Quarterly* 18, no. 2 (1966): 151–74.

Willrich, Michael. "Home Slackers: Men, the State, and Welfare in Modern America." *Journal of American History* 87, no. 2 (2000): 460–89.

Books and Chapters

Allen, Frederick Lewis. *Only Yesterday: An Informal History of the Nineteen Twenties*. New York: Harper & Row, 1931.

Applegate, Debby. *The Most Famous Man in America: The Biography of Henry Ward Beecher*. New York: Doubleday, 2006.

Artman, Amy Collier. *The Miracle Lady: Kathryn Kuhlman and the Transformation of Charismatic Christianity*. Grand Rapids: William B. Eerdmans, 2019.

Balleisen, Edward J. *Fraud: An American History from Barnum to Madoff*. Princeton: Princeton University Press, 2017.

Barringer Gordon, Sarah. *The Mormon Question: Polygamy and Constitutional Conflict in Nineteenth-Century America*. Chapel Hill: University of North Carolina Press, 2002.

Batza, Katie. "Sickness and Wellness." In *The Routledge History of Queer America*, edited by Don Romesburg, 287–99. New York: Routledge, 2018.

Bauer, Susan Wise. *The Art of the Public Grovel: Sexual Sin and Public Confession in America*. Princeton: Princeton University Press, 2008.

Bebbington, David W. *Evangelicalism in Modern Britain: A History from the 1730s to the 1980s*. London: Routledge, 1989.

Bendroth, Margaret Lamberts. *Fundamentalism and Gender, 1875 to the Present.* New Haven: Yale University Press, 1996.

Best, Wallace D. *Passionately Human, No Less Divine: Religion and Culture in Black Chicago, 1915–1952.* Princeton: Princeton University Press, 2005.

Blumhofer, Edith L. *Aimee Semple McPherson: Everybody's Sister.* Grand Rapids: William B. Eerdmans, 1993.

Bowler, Kate. *Blessed: A History of the American Prosperity Gospel.* New York: Oxford University Press, 2013.

Bowler, Kate. *The Preacher's Wife: The Precarious Power of Evangelical Women Celebrities.* Princeton: Princeton University Press, 2019.

Brekus, Catherine A. *Strangers and Pilgrims: Female Preaching in America, 1740–1845.* Chapel Hill: University of North Carolina Press, 1998.

Buckingham, Jamie. *Daughter of Destiny: Kathryn Kuhlman, Her Story.* New York: Pocket Books, 1978.

Butters, Gerald R. *Banned in Kansas: Motion Picture Censorship, 1915–1966.* Columbia: University of Missouri Press, 2007.

Canaday, Margot. *The Straight State: Sexuality and Citizenship in Twentieth-Century America.* Princeton: Princeton University Press, 2009.

Carocci, Max. "Sodomy, Ambiguity, and Feminization." In *Indigenous Bodies: Reviewing, Relocating, Reclaiming,* edited by Jacqueline Fear-Segal and Rebecca Tillett, 69–84. Albany: SUNY Press, 2013.

Carpenter, Joel A. *Revive Us Again: The Reawakening of American Fundamentalism.* New York: Oxford University Press, 1997.

Chaput, Erik J. *The People's Martyr: Thomas Wilson Dorr and His 1842 Rhode Island Rebellion.* Lawrence: University Press of Kansas, 2013.

Charles, Douglas M. *The FBI's Obscene File: J. Edgar Hoover and the Bureau's Crusade against Smut.* Lawrence: University Press of Kansas, 2012.

Charles, Douglas M. *Hoover's War on Gays: Exposing the FBI's "Sex Deviates" Program.* Lawrence: University Press of Kansas, 2015.

Chauncey, George. *Gay New York: Gender, Urban Culture, and the Makings of the Gay Male World, 1890–1940.* New York: Basic Books, 1994.

Clark, Joseph. *News Parade: The American Newsreel and the World as Spectacle.* Minneapolis: University of Minnesota Press, 2020.

Cleves, Rachel Hope. *Unspeakable: A Life beyond Sexual Morality.* Chicago: University of Chicago Press, 2020.

Coben, Stanley. *Rebellion against Victorianism: The Impetus for Cultural Change in 1920s America.* New York: Oxford University Press, 1991.

Coggeshall, William Turner. *The Newspaper Record: Containing a Complete List of Newspapers and Periodicals in the United States, Canadas, and Great Britain, Together with a Sketch of the Origin and Progress of Printing, with Some Facts about Newspapers in Europe and America.* Philadelphia: Lay & Brother, 1856.

Cohen, Patricia Cline. *The Murder of Helen Jewett: The Life and Death of a Prostitute in Nineteenth-Century New York.* New York: Vintage, 1999.

Cohen, Patricia Cline, Timothy J. Gilfoyle, and Helen Lefkowitz Horowitz. *The Flash Press: Sporting Male Weeklies in 1840s New York.* Chicago: University of Chicago Press, 2008.

Coontz, Stephanie. *Marriage, a History: How Love Conquered Marriage.* New York: Penguin Books, 2006.

Corrigan, John and Lynn S. Neal, *Religious Intolerance in America: A Documentary History.* Chapel Hill: University of North Carolina Press, 2010.

Croix, St Sukie de la. *Chicago Whispers: A History of LGBT Chicago before Stonewall.* Madison: University of Wisconsin Press, 2012.

Cushion, Stephen. *News and Politics: The Rise of Live and Interpretive Journalism.* New York: Routledge, 2015.

Czitrom, Daniel. *New York Exposed: The Gilded Age Police Scandal That Launched the Progressive Era*. New York: Oxford University Press, 2016.

Davies, David Randall. *The Postwar Decline of American Newspapers, 1945–1965*. Westport: Praeger, 2006.

D'Cruze, Shani. *Crimes of Outrage: Sex, Violence, and Victorian Working Women*. DeKalb: Northern Illinois University Press, 1998.

DeBerg, Betty A. *Ungodly Women: Gender and the First Wave of American Fundamentalism*. Macon: Mercer University Press, 2000.

D'Emilio, John, and Estelle B. Freedman. *Intimate Matters: A History of Sexuality in America*. 3rd ed. Chicago: University of Chicago Press, 2012.

DeRogatis, Amy. *Saving Sex: Sexuality and Salvation in American Evangelicalism*. New York: Oxford University Press, 2014.

Dicken-Garcia, Hazel. *Journalistic Standards in Nineteenth-Century America*. Madison: University of Wisconsin Press, 1989.

Dochuk, Darren. *From Bible Belt to Sunbelt: Plain-Folk Religion, Grassroots Politics, and the Rise of Evangelical Conservatism*. New York: W.W. Norton, 2012.

Dochuk, Darren. "Religion in Post-1945 America." In *Oxford Research Encyclopedia of American History*, August 31, 2016. Oxford: Oxford University Press. Online.

Dorrough Smith, Leslie. *Compromising Positions: Sex Scandals, Politics, and American Christianity*. New York: Oxford University Press, 2019.

Dorsey, Bruce. *Murder in a Mill Town: Sex, Faith, and the Crime That Captivated a Nation*. New York: Oxford University Press, 2023.

Dumenil, Lynn. *The Modern Temper: American Culture and Society in the 1920s*. New York: Hill and Wang, 1995.

Du Mez, Kristin Kobes. *Jesus and John Wayne: How White Evangelicals Corrupted a Faith and Fractured a Nation*. New York: Liveright, 2020.

Eiselein, Gregory, and Anne K. Phillips. *The Louisa May Alcott Encyclopedia*. Westport: Greenwood Publishing Group, 2001.

Emery, Michael, Edwin Emery, and Nancy L. Roberts. *The Press and America: An Interpretive History of the Mass Media*. 9th ed. Boston: Pearson, 1997.

Epstein, Daniel Mark. *Sister Aimee: The Life of Aimee Semple McPherson*. New York: Harcourt, 1994.

Eskridge, William N. *Dishonorable Passions: Sodomy Laws in America, 1861–2003*. New York: Viking, 2008.

Espinosa, Gastón. *William J. Seymour and the Origins of Global Pentecostalism: A Biography and Documentary History*. Durham: Duke University Press Books, 2014.

Finke, Roger, and Rodney Stark. *The Churching of America, 1776–2005: Winners and Losers in Our Religious Economy*. New Brunswick: Rutgers University Press, 2005.

Flanders, Judith. *The Invention of Murder: How the Victorians Revelled in Death and Detection and Created Modern Crime*. New York: St. Martin's Griffin, 2014.

Fluhman, J. Spencer. *"A Peculiar People": Anti-Mormonism and the Making of Religion in Nineteenth-Century America*. Chapel Hill: University of North Carolina Press, 2012.

Fox, Richard Wightman. *Trials of Intimacy: Love and Loss in the Beecher-Tilton Scandal*. Chicago: University of Chicago Press, 1999.

Fried, Albert. *Socialism in America: From the Shakers to the Third International*. New York: Columbia University Press, 1993.

Frisken, Amanda. *Victoria Woodhull's Sexual Revolution: Political Theater and the Popular Press in Nineteenth-Century America*. Philadelphia: University of Pennsylvania Press, 2004.

Frisken, Amanda. *Graphic News: How Sensational Images Transformed Nineteenth-Century Journalism*. Urbana: University of Illinois Press, 2020.

Gallon, Kim. *Pleasure in the News: African American Readership and Sexuality in the Black Press*. Urbana: University of Illinois Press, 2020.

Gans, Herbert J. *Deciding What's News: A Study of CBS Evening News, NBC Nightly News, Newsweek, and Time*. 2nd ed. Evanston: Northwestern University Press, 2005.

Gedge, Karin E. *Without Benefit of Clergy: Women and the Pastoral Relationship in Nineteenth-Century American Culture*. New York: Oxford University Press, 2003.

Gilbert, Ralph Valentine. *The Church and Printer's Ink*. New York: Fleming H. Revell, 1925.

Giuliano, Michael James. *Thrice-Born: The Rhetorical Comeback of Jimmy Swaggart*. Macon: Mercer University Press, 1999.

Gloege, Timothy E. W. *Guaranteed Pure: The Moody Bible Institute, Business, and the Making of Modern Evangelicalism*. Chapel Hill: University of North Carolina Press, 2015.

Goodwin, Megan. *Abusing Religion: Literary Persecution, Sex Scandals, and American Minority Religions*. New Brunswick: Rutgers University Press, 2020.

Griffith, R. Marie. *Moral Combat: How Sex Divided American Christians and Fractured American Politics*. New York: Basic Books, 2017.

Halttunen, Karen. *Confidence Men and Painted Women: A Study of Middle-Class Culture in America, 1830–1870*. New Haven: Yale University Press, 1982.

Hamer, Dean, and Peter Copeland. *The Science of Desire: The Search for the Gay Gene and the Biology of Behavior*. New York: Simon and Schuster, 1994.

Hartog, Hendrik A. *Man and Wife in America: A History*. Cambridge: Harvard University Press, 2002.

Haselby, Sam. *The Origins of American Religious Nationalism*. New York: Oxford University Press, 2014.

Hatch, Nathan O. *The Democratization of American Christianity*. New Haven: Yale University Press, 1989.

Haveman, Heather A. *Magazines and the Making of America: Modernization, Community, and Print Culture, 1741–1860*. Princeton: Princeton University Press, 2015.

Hertel, Leona. *Man with a Mission: Mel Trotter and His Legacy for the Rescue Mission Movement*. Grand Rapids: Kregel Publications, 2000.

Hessinger, Rodney. *Smitten: Sex, Gender, and the Contest for Souls in the Second Great Awakening*. Ithaca: Cornell University Press, 2022.

Hibben, Paxton. *Henry Ward Beecher: An American Portrait*. New York: George H. Doran, 1927.

Hochgeschwender, Michael. "The Scopes Trial in the Context of Competing Modernity Discourses." In *Fractured Modernity: America Confronts Modern Times, 1890s to 1940s*, edited by Alan Lessoff and Thomas Welskopp, 213–33. Berlin: de Gruyter, 2016.

Hoover, Stewart M. *Mass Media Religion: The Social Sources of the Electronic Church*. Newbury Park: Sage, 1988.

Hudson, Frederic. *Journalism in the United States, from 1690 to 1872*. New York: Harper & Brothers, 1873.

Igra, Anna R. *Wives without Husbands: Marriage, Desertion, and Welfare in New York, 1900–1935*. Chapel Hill: University of North Carolina Press, 2006.

Johnson, David K. *The Lavender Scare: The Cold War Persecution of Gays and Lesbians in the Federal Government*. Chicago: University of Chicago Press, 2004.

Johnson, Emily Suzanne. *This Is Our Message: Women's Leadership in the New Christian Right*. New York: Oxford University Press, 2019.

Jordan, Mark. *Telling Truths in Church: Scandal, Flesh, and Christian Speech*. Boston: Beacon Press, 2003.

Juergens, George. *Joseph Pulitzer and the New York World*. Princeton: Princeton University Press, 2015.

Kasserman, David Richard. *Fall River Outrage: Life, Murder, and Justice in Early Industrial New England*. Philadelphia: University of Pennsylvania Press, 1986.

Laats, Adam. *Fundamentalist U: Keeping the Faith in American Higher Education*. New York: Oxford University Press, 2018.

Larson, Edward J. *Summer for the Gods: The Scopes Trial and America's Continuing Debate over Science and Religion*. New York: Basic Books, 2008.

Lee, Alfred McClung. *The Daily Newspaper in America: The Evolution of a Social Instrument.* New York: Macmillan, 1937.

Leon, Charles Leonard Ponce de. *Self-Exposure: Human-Interest Journalism and the Emergence of Celebrity in America, 1890–1940.* Chapel Hill: University of North Carolina Press, 2002.

Lerner, Kevin M. *Provoking the Press: (MORE) Magazine and the Crisis of Confidence in American Journalism.* Columbia: University of Missouri Press, 2019.

Lichter, S. Robert, Linda S. Lichter, and Daniel R. Amundsen. *Media Coverage of Religion in America 1969–1998.* Washington, DC: Center for Media and Public Affairs, 2000.

Lichtman, Allan J. *White Protestant Nation: The Rise of the American Conservative Movement.* New York: Grove Press, 2008.

Lienesch, Michael. *In the Beginning: Fundamentalism, the Scopes Trial, and the Making of the Antievolution Movement.* Chapel Hill: University of North Carolina Press, 2007.

Lindley, Susan Hill. *You Have Stept out of Your Place: A History of Women and Religion in America.* Louisville: Westminster John Knox Press, 1996.

Loughery, John. *The Other Side of Silence: Men's Lives & Gay Identities—a Twentieth-Century History.* New York: Henry Holt, 1998.

Løvdal Stephens, Hilde. *Family Matters: James Dobson and Focus on the Family's Crusade for the Christian Home.* Tuscaloosa: University Alabama Press, 2019.

Lull, James, and Stephen Hinerman, eds. *Media Scandals: Morality and Desire in the Popular Culture Marketplace.* New York: Columbia University Press, 1997.

Marsden, George M. "Evangelical and Fundamental Christianity." In *The Encyclopedia of Religion,* edited by Mircea Eliade. New York: Macmillan, 1993.

Marsden, George M. *Fundamentalism and American Culture.* 2nd ed. New York: Oxford University Press, 2006.

Martin, Lerone A. *The Gospel of J. Edgar Hoover: How the FBI Aided and Abetted the Rise of White Christian Nationalism.* Princeton: Princeton University Press, 2023.

Mason, Carol. *Oklahomo: Lessons in Unqueering America.* Albany: SUNY Press, 2015.

Mason, Debra L. "Religion News Coverage between 1930 and 1960." In *The Oxford Handbook of Religion and the American News Media,* edited by Diane H. Winston, 65. New York: Oxford University Press 2012.

McCloud, Sean. *Making the American Religious Fringe: Exotics, Subversives, and Journalists, 1955–1993.* Chapel Hill: University of North Carolina Press, 2004.

McClung Lee, Alfred. *The Daily Newspaper in America.* New York: Macmillan, 1937.

McFarland, Philip. *Hawthorne in Concord.* New York: Grove Press, 2004.

McJimsey, George T. *Genteel Partisan: Manton Marble, 1834–1917.* Ames: Iowa State University Press, 1971.

McLoughlin, William G. *The Meaning of Henry Ward Beecher: An Essay on the Shifting Values of Mid-Victorian America, 1840–1870.* New York: Knopf, 1970.

Mihm, Stephen. *A Nation of Counterfeiters: Capitalists, Con Men, and the Making of the United States.* Cambridge: Harvard University Press, 2007.

Miller, Steven Patrick. *The Age of Evangelicalism: America's Born-Again Years.* New York: Oxford University Press, 2014.

Moore, R. Laurence. *Religious Outsiders and the Making of Americans.* New York: Oxford University Press, 1986.

Moslener, Sara. *Virgin Nation: Sexual Purity and American Adolescence.* New York: Oxford University Press, 2015.

Mott, Frank Luther. *American Journalism: A History of Newspapers in the United States Through 250 Years, 1690–1940.* New York: Macmillan, 1941.

Moy, Patricia, and Michael Pfau. *With Malice toward All? The Media and Public Confidence in Democratic Institutions.* Westport: Praeger, 2000.

Murphy, Lawrence. *Perverts by Official Order: The Campaign against Homosexuals by the United States Navy.* New York: Routledge, 2014.

Niose, David. *Nonbeliever Nation: The Rise of Secular Americans*. New York: Palgrave Macmillan, 2012.

Oxx, Katie. *The Nativist Movement in America: Religious Conflict in the 19th Century*. New York: Routledge, 2013.

Palmer, Niall. *The Twenties in America: Politics and History*. Edinburgh: Edinburgh University Press, 2006.

Payne, Leah. *Gender and Pentecostal Revivalism: Making a Female Ministry in the Early Twentieth Century*. New York: Palgrave Macmillan, 2015.

Peterson, Theodore. *Magazines in the Twentieth Century*. Urbana: University of Illinois Press, 1956.

Randall, Richard S. *Censorship of the Movies: The Social and Political Control of a Mass Medium*. Madison: University of Wisconsin Press, 1968.

Riley, Glenda. *Divorce: An American Tradition*. Lincoln: University of Nebraska Press, 1991.

Robinson, Thomas A., and Lanette D. Ruff. *Out of the Mouths of Babes: Girl Evangelists in the Flapper Era*. New York: Oxford University Press, 2011.

Rodgers, Ronald R. *The Struggle for the Soul of Journalism: The Pulpit versus the Press, 1833–1923*. Columbia: University of Missouri Press, 2018.

Ruotsila, Markku. *Fighting Fundamentalist: Carl McIntire and the Politicization of American Fundamentalism*. New York: Oxford University Press, 2016.

Sachsman, David B., and David W. Bulla, eds. *Sensationalism: Murder, Mayhem, Mudslinging, Scandals, and Disasters in 19th-Century Reporting*. New Brunswick: Transaction Publishers, 2013.

Sánchez-Walsh, Arlene M. *Pentecostals in America*. New York: Columbia University Press, 2018.

Sandage, Scott A. *Born Losers: A History of Failure in America*. Cambridge: Harvard University Press, 2005.

Schmidt, Leigh Eric. *Village Atheists: How America's Unbelievers Made Their Way in a Godly Nation*. Princeton: Princeton University Press, 2016.

Schudson, Michael. *Discovering the News: A Social History of American Newspapers*. New York: Basic Books, 1981.

Schultz, Kevin M. *Tri-faith America: How Catholics and Jews Held Postwar America to Its Protestant Promise*. New York: Oxford University Press, 2011.

Seaman, Ann Rowe. *Swaggart: An Unauthorized Biography of an American Evangelist*. New York: Continuum, 1999.

Shaplen, Robert. *Free Love and Heavenly Sinners: The Story of the Great Henry Ward Beecher Scandal*. New York: Knopf, 1954.

Sherwin, Richard K. *When Law Goes Pop: The Vanishing Line between Law and Popular Culture*. Chicago: University of Chicago Press, 2000.

Shindo, Charles J. *1927 and the Rise of Modern America*. Lawrence: University Press of Kansas, 2010.

Silk, Mark. *Unsecular Media: Making News of Religion in America*. Champaign: University of Illinois Press, 1998.

Sitton, Tom. *Metropolis in the Making: Los Angeles in the 1920s*. Berkeley: University of California Press, 2001.

Soderlund, Gretchen. *Sex Trafficking, Scandal, and the Transformation of Journalism, 1885–1917*. Chicago: University of Chicago Press, 2013.

Stevens, John D. *Sensationalism and the New York Press*. New York: Columbia University Press, 1991.

Sutton, Matthew Avery. *Aimee Semple McPherson and the Resurrection of Christian America*. Cambridge: Harvard University Press, 2007.

Sutton, Matthew Avery. *American Apocalypse: A History of Modern Evangelicalism*. Cambridge: Belknap Press of Harvard University Press, 2014.

Syrett, Nicholas L. *American Child Bride: A History of Minors and Marriage in the United States*. Chapel Hill: University of North Carolina Press, 2016.

Talese, Gay. *The Kingdom and the Power: Behind the Scenes at the* New York Times. New York: Random House, 2013.

Taves, Ann. "Sexuality in American Religious History." In *Retelling U.S. Religious History*, edited by Thomas A. Tweed, 27–56. Berkeley: University of California Press, 1997.

Tucher, Andie. *Froth and Scum: Truth, Beauty, Goodness, and the Ax Murder in America's First Mass Medium*. Chapel Hill: University of North Carolina Press, 1994.

Wacker, Grant. *Heaven Below: Early Pentecostals and American Culture*. Cambridge: Harvard University Press, 2003.

Wacker, Grant. *America's Pastor: Billy Graham and the Shaping of a Nation*. Cambridge: Belknap Press, 2014.

Walkowitz, Judith R. *City of Dreadful Delight: Narratives of Sexual Danger in Late-Victorian London*. Chicago: University of Chicago Press, 1992.

Waller, Altina. *Reverend Beecher and Mrs. Tilton: Sex and Class in Victorian America*. Amherst: University of Massachusetts Press, 1982.

Watts, Jill. *God, Harlem, U.S.A.: The Father Divine Story*. Berkeley: University of California Press, 1995.

Weisenfeld, Judith. *New World A-Coming: Black Religion and Racial Identity during the Great Migration*. New York: New York University Press, 2017.

White, Heather R. *Reforming Sodom: Protestants and the Rise of Gay Rights*. Chapel Hill: University of North Carolina Press, 2015.

Wigger, John H. *Taking Heaven by Storm: Methodism and the Rise of Popular Christianity in America*. New York: Oxford University Press, 1998.

Wigger, John H. *PTL: The Rise and Fall of Jim and Tammy Faye Bakker's Evangelical Empire*. New York: Oxford University Press, 2017.

Wood, Simon A., and David Harrington Watt, eds. *Fundamentalism: Perspectives on a Contested History*. Columbia: University of South Carolina Press, 2014.

Wuthnow, Robert. *The Restructuring of American Religion: Society and Faith since World War II*. Princeton: Princeton University Press, 1988.

Ziolkowski, Theodore. *Scandal on Stage: European Theater as Moral Trial*. New York: Cambridge University Press, 2009.

Dissertations

Dean, Terrance. "Saved 'Out,' Sanctified 'Out,' and Souled 'Out': A Critical Analysis of Disgust and the Prophetic Immanence of James Baldwin's Gender Sexual Politics." PhD diss., Vanderbilt University, 2019.

Gurney, Julius (Rex). "Religion in the American Century: 'Time' Magazine and the Reporting of Christianity in the United States, 1950–1975." PhD diss., Presbyterian School of Christian Education, 1999.

Hamilton, Blaine Charles. "The Spirit in Black and White: Early Twentieth-Century Pentecostals and Race Relations, 1905–1945." PhD diss., Rice University, 2013.

Klimchock, Carolee Anne. "Heiress Weds Coachman: Elopement Scandals and the Performance of Coach Driving in the Gilded Age." PhD diss., Yale University, 2015.

Phelan, Mary Cortona. "Manton Marble of the New York World." PhD diss., Catholic University of America, 1957.

Index